DYNAMIC EQUIVALENCE

"In a higher world
it is otherwise,
But here below
to live is to change,
And to be perfect
is to have changed
often."

John Henry Cardinal Newman
An Essay on the Development of Christian Doctrine

(Chapter 1, Section I/7)
(Doubleday, 1960, 63: Garden City, N.Y.)

The ENGLISH is coming!

A cartoon appearing in the U.S. Vernacular Society's journal *Amen*.

Keith F. Pecklers, s.j.

DYNAMIC EQUIVALENCE

*The Living Language
of Christian Worship*

A PUEBLO BOOK

The Liturgical Press Collegeville, Minnesota

www.litpress.org

A Pueblo Book published by The Liturgical Press

Design by Frank Kacmarcik, OBL.S.B.

Library of Congress Cataloging-in-Publication Data

Pecklers, Keith F., 1958–
    Dynamic equivalence : the living language of Christian worship / Keith F.
        Pecklers.
        p. cm.
    Includes bibliographical references (p.) and indexes.
    ISBN 0-8146-6191-2 (alk. paper)
        1. Language question in the church—History. 2. Catholic Church—
    Liturgy— History. 3. Liturgical language—History. 4. Vernacular Society—
    History.   I. Title.

BX1970.P36 2003
264'.02'0014—dc21
                                                                    2002043346

To John R. Page, PH.D.

Friend and Colleague,
Faithful Servant of the Church's Worship

Associate Editor of
the International Commission
on English in the Liturgy (ICEL)
1972–1974

Associate Executive Secretary
1974–1980

Executive Secretary
1980–2002

Contents

CHAPTER 3: PRESSURE FOR THE VERNACULAR
MOUNTS: 1956–1962

Abbreviations

AAS	*Acta Apostolicae Sedis*
BCP	*The Book of Common Prayer*
CJPE	The Joseph P. Evans Collection
CMRH	The Monsignor Reynold Hillenbrand Collection
CVER	The Vernacular Society Collection

Acknowledgments

This book has been several years in the making and would never have seen the light of day were it not for the helpful staff at the University of Notre Dame Archives where most of the research was done. I am particularly grateful to Sharon K. Sumpter and to Kevin Cawley for their invaluable assistance during the three summers which I spent there. My gratitude goes as well to Charlotte Ames, University Librarian at Notre Dame for Catholic Americana, both for her interest in the project and her ongoing support. To Methodist liturgical historian and my former professor James F. White my heartfelt thanks for having first suggested the project to me. I am grateful to Professor Richard P. McBrien, Crowley-Walker Professor of Theology at Notre Dame, both for his friendship and for sponsoring me as a "Visiting Scholar" during my research.

A special word of gratitude goes to Bishop Maurice Taylor of Galloway, Scotland, chair of the International Commission on English in the Liturgy (ICEL) for graciously accepting my invitation to write the foreword to this book.

A key ingredient to keeping a research project alive is the human support that comes from family and friends. I am grateful to them all, in particular to my mother and brother for their loving support, to the Jesuit communities at the University of Notre Dame, Xavier and America House in New York City, and to my Jesuit brothers of the Bellarmino community in Rome for their companionship and humor. A word of gratitude goes as well to the Jesuit communities of *Sagrado Corazón* in Màlaga, Spain, and *S. Ignazio* in Bologna, Italy, where work on the book was completed.

I am grateful to Peter Dwyer, director of The Liturgical Press, to Michael Naughton, O.S.B., who preceded him, and to Mark Twomey, editorial director, for their interest in this project and willingness to publish the work. Special thanks to Aaron Raverty, O.S.B., of The Liturgical Press, for assisting in the publication of the text. They are all much esteemed and I consider it a great privilege to collaborate with them. To Mark R. Francis, C.S.V., friend and colleague, Superior General of the Clerics of St. Viator, my gratitude for the technical assistance he offered with the computer and the helpful comments which he made on the manuscript.

Finally, gratitude goes to my colleagues on the Faculty of the Pontifical Liturgical Institute of Sant' Anselmo in Rome for their professional support and friendship these past six years.

Foreword

Among the entertainments arranged for us when I was in the seminary in the 1940s were occasional debates. One such debate was on the subject of "Latin vs. vernacular for Mass." "Do you think we should have Mass in the vernacular?"

If I remember correctly, we overwhelmingly voted against the motion. "The liturgy would sound ridiculous in English," we decided. "You can follow the Mass anywhere in the world from Alaska to Tasmania if it's in Latin," etc., etc.

We felt comfortable with what we had, Mass had been celebrated in Latin for many centuries (not quite from the very beginning) and, if we were to think the almost unthinkable, there was no knowing what would happen or where it would stop.

How blinkered we were! How lacking in vision! Thank God for the fathers of the Second Vatican Council who were open to the promptings of the Holy Spirit and, even if somewhat tentatively (because it was so radical), began the process of enabling Catholics to celebrate the liturgy in their own language.

Of course, it is alleged that the limited use of the vernacular language which the council authorized was later and wrongfully extended to every liturgical prayer and text. That is an accusation that has to be answered.

Yes, the use of the vernacular is much wider than explicitly envisaged by *Sacrosanctum Concilium* (Vatican II's Constitution on the Liturgy). But that extension has taken place with the approval of the Church which is guided by the Holy Spirit at all times and not only when the Pope or a council makes a solemn pronouncement. And the widespread use of the vernacular has been accepted and welcomed by the great majority of the Church's members—further evidence of the guiding presence of the Holy Spirit.

Change can seem threatening, but experience is a great teacher. I am sure that the overwhelming majority of Catholics now prefer their liturgy in their own language, and even those who do not, would not want to impose Latin on those who do.

However, there is English and English or, more explicitly, good English and not-so-good English. Moreover, since English is a very living language, what is accepted as good English at the beginning of the twenty-first century will, in due course, become not-bad English, but English that could be better.

Of course, that sentence begs a number of questions. What is good English today? How highbrow or popular should it be for the liturgy? Is good English in the United States the same as good English in Britain or Australia? And, most difficult of all, what do we mean by fidelity to the Latin originals: word-for-word correspondence or fidelity to the Latin concepts but expressed in contemporary English style . . . or something in-between?

All of these issues are discussed in this book. They are also issues that concern the Holy See's Congregation for Divine Worship and the Discipline of the Sacraments, the English-speaking Bishops' Conferences, and their International Commission on English in the Liturgy. But above all, they are important issues for those of us who, in our liturgies, use English to worship God and want the English we use to be as good as it can be and should be.

✠ Maurice Taylor, Bishop of Galloway (Scotland)
Chair Emeritus, the International Commission on
English in the Liturgy (ICEL)
May 2002

Introduction

How we pray when we come together for common worship has always been significant, but the issue of liturgical language received unprecedented attention in the twentieth century when Latin Rite Roman Catholic worship was opened to the vernacular at the Second Vatican Council (1962–65). News of the possibility of worshiping in one's own native tongue received wide-ranging attention in journals from *The New York Times* and *The Wall Street Journal* to *Time* and *Look* and everything in between. Even *Sports Illustrated* ran articles on the subject! In fact, in 1964 Catholic journalists voted the topic of English in the Liturgy the "Top Religious Story" of the year.

Forty years later liturgical language continues to be a hot topic as the churches deliberate over what type of vernacular should be employed. For Roman Catholics, there has been significant attention in recent years to the question of how texts are translated from the Latin *editio typica* into the national language of a particular country or region. All the Christian churches, thanks to the ecumenical liturgical cooperation of these past fifty years, share a common concern: how best to shape liturgical texts able to carry the weight of the tradition, and at the same time, speak comprehensibly to the modern world. Texts, after all, are more than words. They plumb the depths and hold up the truth for us about who we are and what we believe as living members of the Body of Christ.

In the 1960s, as the vernacular debate was unfolding at the Second Vatican Council, linguistic studies were moving in new directions. New approaches to teaching language came to be employed emphasizing the social context. These approaches forged new paths toward a greater understanding of how human language functions. More specifically, the emergence of "sociolinguistics" opened our eyes to the relationship between language and society or particular social groupings, recognizing that language is a dynamic reality—anything but static—varied and flexible, ever changing. Professor of linguistics David Crystal puts it this way:

"Sociolinguistics is that branch of linguistics which . . . observes the range of language varieties which exist, and relates these to patterns of social structure and behaviour—such as age, sex, caste, social class, regional origin and formality of setting. No sociolinguist is content simply to identify a pattern of phonology, grammar or lexicon rather, this pattern must be seen in the light of who uses it, when, where and why."[1]

As the council called for culturally adapted and contextualized worship without sacrificing the substantial unity of the Roman Rite (*Sacrosanctum Concilium* 37–40), the change in liturgical language and subsequent revision of liturgical books reflected a desire for poetic speech capable of communicating something of the numinous in a contextualized way. David Crystal writes: "language changes because society changes—not only in the obvious sense that new concepts give rise to new vocabulary, but more fundamentally, in that new social structures generate new linguistic identities."[2]

In the liturgical field two significant books appeared a decade earlier. In 1950, professor of liturgy at the Pontifical Gregorian University, Dutch Jesuit Herman Schmidt, published the seminal work *Liturgie et Langue Vivante: Le problème de la langue liturgique chez les premiers Réformateurs et au Concile de Trente*. Seven years later in 1957, staff member of the Vatican's Congregation for Oriental Churches Cyril Korolevsky published his own important volume *Living Languages in Catholic Worship: An Historical Inquiry.* The Second Vatican Council followed five years later with its monumental decision in favor of vernacular worship. And those of us who are old enough to remember can recall those first attempts at translation, along with the mimeographed song sheets containing texts to be sung to the tune of Bob Dylan's "Blowin' in the Wind" or "Edelweiss" from "The Sound of Music." Happily, we have made great strides since those early days of vernacular worship rediscovered. Forty years after Vatican II, we can be grateful for the renewal of our worship, thanks largely to the bishop members and consultors of the International Commission on English in the Liturgy (ICEL) who have served us faithfully over the years. Our liturgy is still not perfect, of course, but it is infinitely better than what preceded it! Despite great progress, however, the history of that vernacular remains largely unknown or forgotten; thus this volume.

This book traces the history of liturgical language in the Western Christian tradition as a dynamic and living reality. Particular attention is paid to the twentieth-century Vernacular Society within the United States and how the vernacular issue was treated at the Second Vatican Council, especially within an ecumenical context. The first chapter offers a short history of the vernacular from the first century through the twentieth. We hear, for example, of Cyril and Methodius and their ninth-century vernacular promotion among the Slavic peoples. Interventions on the subject at the sixteenth-century Council of Trent are treated in detail followed by subsequent vernacular developments among the newly founded missionary orders and further promotion during the Catholic Enlightenment. We read of the eighteenth-century Synod of Pistoia and John Carroll, the first bishop in the United States and first archbishop of Baltimore, who insisted on vernacular worship in the mission territory of the United States. The chapter concludes with some examples of Roman Catholic experiments with the vernacular in the years prior to the Second Vatican Council.

The second and third chapters contain a significant amount of archival material, much of which has never been published before. These chapters are based largely on material found in the archives of the Vernacular Society and tell the story of a very mixed group of Catholic laity and clergy dedicated to promoting the vernacular during the first half of the twentieth century. Their message was not always well received. Many saw it as tampering with Catholic doctrine or with God's own words. Even liturgical pioneers such as the members of the North American Liturgical Conference kept a certain distance from the vernacularists, fearful that too much agitation for the vernacular would close the door on the entire liturgical movement. Interestingly, those vernacularists counted a significant number of former Episcopalians and Lutherans among their ranks—those who had been steeped in vernacular worship from their youth and recognized the same potential for Roman Catholics.

It is precisely the ecumenical question which is discussed in the fourth chapter. Beginning with a survey of vernacular promotion in the Reformation itself, the issue of vernacular worship as an instrument of ecumenical hospitality is explored relying on archival materials—letters from non-Catholic spouses living in "mixed marriages" and also from Catholics who expressed their discontent at the alienation experienced by Anglican and Protestant guests at funerals and other liturgical events. The chapter concludes with some examples of ecumenical liturgical cooperation in the years immediately preceding the council, not the least of which included the Vatican's own Secretariat for the Promotion of Christian Unity which argued in favor of the vernacular as an ecumenical issue in the meetings of the council's Preparatory Commission.

Beginning with a look at the work of Vatican II's Preparatory Commission, the final chapter treats the vernacular debate at the council with attention to the Vernacular Society's role in helping with the implementation of the vernacular. Different arguments for and against the vernacular presented during the council are considered. Moreover, the significant role played by two of the council's U.S. *periti,* liturgists Frederick McManus of The Catholic University of America, Washington, D.C. (currently retired in Boston), and the recently deceased Godfrey Diekmann, o.s.b., of Saint John's Abbey, Collegeville, Minnesota, is highlighted. These champions of the vernacular were not alone in their efforts. Several key U.S. bishops at the council, such as Archbishop Paul Hallinan of Atlanta, were a moving force in lobbying on behalf of the vernacular among their episcopal colleagues. And we are in their debt.

NOTES FOR INTRODUCTION

[1] David Crystal, "Liturgical Language in a Sociolinguistic Perspective," in David Jasper and R.C.D. Jasper, *Language and the Worship of the Church* (London: The Macmillan Press Ltd., 1990) 121.

[2] Crystal, "Liturgical Language in a Sociolinguistic Perspective," 145.

Chapter 1
A Brief History of the Vernacular

1.1 INTRODUCTION

When the topic of the vernacular or "English in the Liturgy" surfaces, reference is almost immediately made to the Second Vatican Council (1962–65). Those who appreciate the possibility of worshiping in one's own native language rightly refer to the council as the point of departure, while those who lament the loss of Latin or the current liturgical translations into English put the blame on the same council. There is no question that Vatican II did, indeed, revolutionize the language of worship by granting full vernacular privileges—more than any liturgical pioneer or bishop could have imagined—but the vernacular issue does not find its origins at that historic meeting. Indeed, a careful study of liturgical history both in East and West reveals substantial evidence that the topic was discussed and vernacular concessions granted at different points throughout the Church's two-thousand-year history. Since much of that preconciliar story remains largely unknown, a survey of vernacular history within the Church's liturgical tradition will provide the reader with the proper context for appreciating the twentieth-century birth of the Vernacular Society in the United States and its evolution over some twenty years, culminating in vernacular concessions granted at the ecumenical council.

1.2 THE EARLY CHURCH

As Christians received from their Jewish forebears the tradition of responding "Amen" to prayer as a sign of assent—presumably understanding that which was uttered enabling their assent—vernacularists of the twentieth century often used the passage from 1 Corinthians 14:16-19 as a foundation for their efforts:

"If you say a blessing with the spirit, how can anyone in the position of an outsider say the 'Amen' to your thanksgiving, since the outsider does not know what you are saying? For you may give thanks well enough, but the other person is not built up. I thank God that I speak in tongues more than all of you; nevertheless, in church I would rather speak five words with my mind, in order to instruct others also, than ten thousand words in a tongue."[1]

Commenting on this passage, Elisabeth Schüssler Fiorenza notes that the text draws three conclusions for Christian prayer and worship:

"First, prayer should not only be ecstatic but also should be fruitful for mind and reason. Further, the community is forced into the role of 'the outsider' by such ecstatic prayer, because it does not know when to respond and ratify such prayer. Finally, Paul refers again to his own example. Although he speaks more in tongues than any of the Corinthians, he prefers to say five understandable words of instruction rather than thousands of words in tongues no one can understand."[2]

Vernacular promoters adopted this text as their shield since they viewed Latin as one such "ecstatic tongue," except for the educated elite who were able to grasp what was being said. Instead, they called for a prerequisite level of intelligibility in worship so that congregants could understand what they were celebrating and thus contribute to the upbuilding of the Body of Christ. The inability to understand the liturgical texts further perpetuated the division between "outsiders" and "insiders," i.e., those few "insiders" in the assembly who were able to understand and the majority who remained "outsiders," responding "Amen" to that which they failed to understand.

It is believed that when the early Christians gathered together for worship, they did so in Aramaic—the language in which Jesus himself preached. As the Gospel spread through Asia Minor and into other Greek-speaking parts of the Mediterranean world including Rome, liturgical language shifted to the popularized *koiné* Greek spoken in the major urban areas, while local languages continued to be used in the more rural countryside. Even the Jewish community in Rome spoke Greek. So did the Christian community there, both in its daily life and worship. Usage of Greek is believed to have reached as far as southern Gaul.

The Greek language, however, was to be short-lived in the West. Helped largely by the invasion of the barbarians who wrote their first laws in Latin, that language took hold in North Africa and gradually through the West. Consequently, it was only in the late third and early fourth centuries when Roman Christians were no longer able to understand Greek that Church leaders opted for the use of Latin in its worship as a practical means of helping people to pray publicly in a language which they understood. This question of liturgical language offers one of the earliest examples of what we now call "inculturation," i.e., accommodating worship to particular cultural circumstances and needs, producing a liturgy that exhibits and reflects the cultural genius of that particular celebrating people.

From Rome, the diffusion of Latin continued throughout central and western Europe. This shift took place primarily during the pontificate of Pope Damasus (366–84); the earliest textual evidence we have for the adoption of Latin in the Eucharistic Prayer comes in the years 360–82. Liturgical Latin continued to develop between the fourth and sixth centuries with the composition of collects and the eucharistic prayer—what we would call today "original texts." Popes Innocent (401–17), Leo the Great (440–61), Gelasius (492–96), Vigilius (537–55), and Gregory the Great (590–604) were largely responsible for those compositions.[3]

The East, on the contrary, never adopted Latin. Local languages like Syriac, Coptic, and Armenian were already well established when Christianity took root. When missionaries arrived in the East, one of the first things they did was to translate the Bible into the language of that particular country. Thus, the Bible was translated into Syriac as early as the second century, into Coptic in the third, and into Armenian in the fourth. Once biblical translations were completed, liturgical translations followed. National languages in the East continued to be employed for worship in those regions because quite frankly, there was no good reason for not using them. On the contrary, a continuation of vernacular usage assisted communities in contextualizing and appropriating what they were celebrating and also symbolized who they were both religiously and ethnically.[4]

The primacy of Rome and the influence of the Roman Empire, however, brought about different results in the West, which led both to the suppression of local rites in favor of a unified Roman Rite and a common language for its celebration. One exception comes in the seventh century when the Roman Church reintroduced some Greek into its liturgy—especially in the proclamation of the biblical lessons—as a cultural accommodation to Byzantine Christians. In general, however, Latin's force continued to hold sway in the West, thanks especially to the Carolingian reforms which followed. This classic Roman Rite that grew between the fifth and eighth centuries was—at least in its origins—expressive of the genius of the Roman culture known for its brevity and sobriety.[5] Indeed, the Latin prayer texts composed by Innocent, Gelasius, Leo, Vigilius, and Gregory reflected that classical style. Gradually, however, this localized Roman cultural form was transplanted into areas and regions that had a different cultural genius. And Latin remained as the *lingua franca,* leading to the extreme assertion on the part of some clergy that Latin liturgical usage was equitable with being Catholic—a position particularly offensive to Eastern Catholics whose local languages used in worship had remained in place even as local liturgical languages in the West were suppressed. A look at some interesting developments in the medieval period will make the point more explicit.

1.3 THE EIGHTH THROUGH THE FOURTEENTH CENTURIES

In the eighth century, a group of German clerics emerged who believed that it was proper to celebrate the liturgy only in those languages used in the inscription on the cross, namely Latin, Greek, and Hebrew. Known as the "trilinguists," this group rallied such support that in 794 the Council of Frankfurt condemned their teachings proclaiming that "to those who believe that God can only be adored in three languages, *anathema sit.*" Remnants of the trilinguists were the very ones who would oppose the vernacular efforts of Cyril and Methodius one century later.[6]

Elsewhere in Europe, as Carolingian reforms produced an ever greater uniform and clericalized liturgy in the West and as modern European languages began to develop, the liturgy remained in Latin. And as Latin became less accessible to congregations, lay popular devotions in the vernacular would emerge in the medieval period as a substitute for the liturgical participation which the use of Latin denied them. At about the same time, there was significant vernacular activity taking place in Eastern Europe, thanks to the efforts of Cyril and Methodius.

1.3.1 Cyril and Methodius: "Apostles to the Slavs"

In the ninth century, the brothers Cyril (+869) and especially Methodius (+885), missionaries to Moravia and Pannonia, led their Slavic communities in vernacular liturgies (both eucharistic and noneucharistic) in Old Slavonic.[7] Arriving in Moravia around 864, they began by translating the Gospels and some liturgical texts into the vernacular as an instrument for evangelizing those to whom they had been sent. Cyril, for his part, composed the Glagolithic alphabet which expressed the diverse Slavonic sounds spoken by the Moravians. Since the brothers had been reared in the Byzantine tradition, it is probable that the Liturgy of St. John Chrysostom was what Cyril and Methodius first used with their assemblies, but Methodius also knew another liturgy—the Liturgy of St. Peter—which was a shortened form of the Liturgy of St. John Chrysostom, with prayers translated from the Roman Mass (including the Roman Canon) which were then included in this hybrid rite. This is apparently what they translated from Greek into Slavonic.

These "Apostles to the Slavs," as they were called, were not the first Christians to have arrived in Moravia. The Germans had been there first, and Cyril and Methodius soon came into contact with those communities and their German clergy whose own missionary strategy would present challenges for the pastoral work of the two brothers, leading ultimately to Methodius' three year imprisonment when he returned from Rome in 870 after Cyril's death.[8]

As their missionary strategy continued to bear fruit and as they began to form future clergy for the region, the brothers needed to decide whether to have their candidates ordained in Rome or in Constantinople. They settled on Rome, and stopping off in Venice on their way to Rome in 867, en route, they encountered a number of "trilinguists" who opposed them, continuing to uphold the principle that God could only be worshiped in Hebrew, Greek, and Latin. By the time they arrived in Rome, the reigning pontiff Nicholas I (858–67) who had summoned them was dead, and Pope Hadrian II (867–72) had been elected. Since Nicholas was rather heavy-handed in his dealings with the East and a strong advocate of Roman centralization in all matters, it was perhaps fortuitous for Cyril and Methodius that they had not arrived in time. The reception they received from the new Pope was far better than they could have ever imagined.

Much to the disappointment of the "trilinguists," Hadrian II granted the two brothers full permission for the use of Old Slavonic in liturgy. Together they celebrated their vernacular liturgy in Hadrian's presence as he ordained presbyters and deacons among the most qualified Moravian men in the delegation. Cyril never lived to see his liturgy ratified by the Pope. He became ill during the Roman sojourn, moved to a monastery on the Esquiline Hill near Saint Praxedes, and died there on 14 February 869. One year later, in 870, Hadrian II formally ratified the liturgy for which Cyril and his brother had labored so intensely. That permission, however, was to be short-lived.

Hadrian died only two years later, and his successor, Pope John VIII, (872–82) forbade the liturgical use of Old Slavonic only one year after taking office and only three years after the original permission had been granted. John had come under the influence of the "trilinguists." Nonetheless, despite the papal ban on Old Slavonic in the liturgy, Methodius continued to celebrate in that language following his imprisonment in Moravia, leading to accusations against him of heresy. When Pope John heard reports of his disobedience and unorthodox views, he summoned Methodius to Rome in 879. After Methodius successfully defended himself, John VIII officially declared the accused "orthodox" and even came to appreciate the pastoral importance of the vernacular. This was the case to such an extent that the pontiff publicly defended Methodius and his vernacular cause against some German and Hungarian "trilinguists" who wanted to equate the use of Latin with being Catholic. John VIII wrote in the year 879:

"It is not opposed to the integrity of faith or doctrine that Mass be celebrated in the Slavonic tongue or that the Holy Gospels and the other lessons of the New and Old Testaments well translated in that language be used for the Mass and the Office, for He who made the principal languages, created all the others for His own praise and glory."[9]

To make his point even more explicit, Pope John placed Cyril and Methodius' translation of the Gospel on the altar in St. Peter's, and in the following year, he formally reactivated permission for the use of Old Slavonic in the liturgy, assisting at that very vernacular liturgy himself. Moreover, he condemned opponents of the Slavonic texts, saying that those who condemned use of Old Slavonic in the liturgy were to be "cut off from the Church."[10] The now supportive Pope did make one strategic error, though. At the request of several of his advisors, he consecrated a German named Wiching to be a suffragan bishop to Methodius, who was by then archbishop of Pannonia with pastoral responsibility for Moravia. Not surprisingly, Wiching was anti-vernacular to boot, and soon launched his campaign against Methodius and his ideas, this time with significant authority behind him particularly during the papacy of Pope Stephen V (885–91).[11]

Following the short-lived pontificate of Marinus I (882–84), the new Pope—Stephen V—was greatly influenced by the very same German clergy who had earlier opposed the missionary strategy of Cyril and Methodius. With such consultants at his side, it was hardly surprising that following Methodius' death on 6 April 885, the Pope restructured the Moravian Church according to the wishes of the German hierarchy. Relying on a letter said to have been written by John VIII which expressly condemned the liturgical use of Old Slavonic, Pope Stephen forbade all use of that vernacular language and appointed an administrator for that Metropolitan See who would likewise be influenced by the Germans. Ironically, Stephen relied on a faulty document for his decision. The letter had been forged by Bishop Wiching. In the words of Cyril Korolevsky, a former consultant to the Oriental Congregation in Rome:

"[W]here the pope praised Methodius, approved the use of Old Slavonic, and entrusted the carrying-out of the papal decisions to the archbishop, Wiching made the letter praise himself, forbid Slavonic, and make him independent of Methodius, with the duty of executing the pope's orders."[12]

Not surprisingly, Methodius' disciples found it very difficult to continue their own work within such a repressive environment, so they took refuge in Bulgaria where they were able to again worship in Old Slavonic. Thus were the foundations laid for a Slav-speaking Church that eventually included Russia and would move further and further toward Orthodoxy and away from the centralization of papal authority in Rome.[13]

1.3.2 Developments Elsewhere in Europe

The use of Old Slavonic continued in Bohemia and Dalmatia, but only as a local privilege reserved to specified Churches or pastoral centers. In the ninth century, for example, a Church council held at Split (Spalato) forbade the ordination of presbyters who knew only Slavonic. Nonetheless, local privileges did continue. Examples come both from parishes and religious communities. When the Benedictine monastery of Emmaus was founded at Prague in 1346, for example, the liturgical offices were celebrated primarily in Slavonic. In sixteenth-century Dubrovnik, there existed a complete missal in Croatian clearly intended for ministerial rather than devotional use by the way it was both printed and bound.[14] Thus in this period we find great diversity in practice even as Latin remained the predominant liturgical language in central Europe from the tenth through the sixteenth centuries.[15] It was only in the seventeenth century, in 1631, that the use of Slavonic in western liturgical rites was officially approved by Pope Urban VIII (1623–44).

As for the Byzantine liturgy, Patriarch Balsamon (ca. 1190) declared that those who did not understand Greek were to celebrate that liturgy in their own language, faithfully rendering the texts directly from the Greek *editio typica*. That principle of Balsamon continued to be applied for centuries, particularly as the Byzantine tradition found its way into countries like China and Japan.[16]

There were also some vernacular exceptions in western Europe, particularly in the area of preaching. In the twelfth century vernacular preaching emerged among Franciscan friars as a strategic means of attracting larger crowds and moving their hearers to greater faith. It must be acknowledged, however, that they were not the first to adapt their preaching to the local language. Augustine of Hippo (354–430) was the first known presbyter to take the bishop's place in preaching since Augustine was able to preach in the vernacular, unlike the bishop who was unable to preach in the local language of the people. By the time we reach the medieval period, bishops themselves were taking their own vernacular initiatives in preaching. Maurice de Sully (+1196), who was bishop of Paris, provided the models for sixty-four sermons in French; Abbot Samson (+1212) of Bury St. Edmunds preached both in French and in the local dialect of Suffolk.[17]

Medieval preaching in the vernacular also required a simplification of theological and biblical terminology so as to give the laity greater access to what they were trying to communicate. Latin remained normative when preaching to the clergy however. And when preachers wanted to preserve the homilies they had preached in the vernacular, those sermons were transcribed into Latin afterwards. Preaching in the vernacular became even more widely diffused by the thirteenth century and officially encouraged by the Church as a means of facilitating greater reception of the message.[18]

Medieval vernacular initiatives in western Europe were not limited to preaching. In an article that appeared in *Liturgiches Leben* back in 1936, Benedictine scholar H. Vehlen presents evidence of vernacular missals within western Europe in the late Middle Ages, well before the Council of Trent; examples exist of vernacular missals both containing and omitting the Canon.[19] In 1480, the *Messen singen oder lesen* included the full Canon whereas later editions of that text continued to include the Canon with the exception of the words of consecration.[20] Even then, the vernacular had its challengers. Johannes Busch, a reformer of German monasteries (+1479), lamented the fact that the laity had the missal with the Canon in German and went on a personal "search and destroy" mission within his monasteries to burn whatever copies of that text he happened to find.[21] Nonetheless, translations of the missal continued. A French translation of the missal is found as early as 1370 and then again in 1587, 1607, 1618, 1651.[22]

1.3.3 Vernacular Privileges for New Missionary Orders

Elsewhere around the world, newly founded missionary orders were requesting vernacular privileges to assist their own efforts at evangelization. When Pope Clement V (1305–14) nominated Franciscan missionary John of Montecorvino the first bishop of Peking, he granted special permission for the use of Mandarin Chinese in the liturgy as a means of evangelizing the Chinese. John also provided his own vernacular translations of the Psalms and New Testament. Later in the fourteenth century, Pope Boniface IX (1389–1404) conceded a similar privilege to the Dominican missionaries in Greece for the possibility of celebrating Mass in liturgical Greek. In Armenia, the "Friars of Union," a group associated with the Dominicans, were granted permission for the celebration of the Dominican liturgy in Armenian for the entire four-hundred-year period of their existence—from 1330 until 1794. Ironically, the Dominican Missal and Breviary they had translated into Armenian in the fourteenth century remained in manuscript form until 1713 when the Holy Office approved those liturgical texts for official publication.[23]

1.4 THE COUNCIL OF TRENT AND THE VERNACULAR QUESTION

Concern for the vernacular also found its way into discussions held during the Council of Trent (1545–63), and as we shall see, that council had its own vernacular proponents.[24] One is accustomed to limiting sixteenth century vernacular pioneering to reformers like Martin Luther, Ulrich Zwingli, and especially John Calvin, but the Catholic Church had its own supporters for the return to a vernacular liturgy.[25] In 1514, just thirty years prior to the opening of the Tridentine Council, Camaldolese monks Paolo Gustiniani and Pietro Quirini presented a *libellus* to Pope Leo X in which they recalled the vernacular liturgical practice of the patristic period and wondered why the Church of the sixteenth century continued to uphold a language the large majority of the faithful no longer understood. Those monks argued that pastoral need necessitated a return to vernacular liturgy and thereby made their plea to Leo X for an end to the impoverishment caused by Latin.[26]

During the council itself, some fathers would hold similar positions as those of Gustiniani and Quirini while others upheld Latin for its association both with mystery and Catholic doctrine. A first draft of the eighth chapter of the twenty-second session, which treated the vernacular issue, was presented to the council fathers on 6 August 1562. It read:

"The Latin language, too, which is used for the celebration of Mass in the Western Church, is in the highest degree appropriate, seeing that it is common to many nations. It seems beyond doubt that, were Mass to be carried out in each people's vulgar tongue, the divine Mysteries would be celebrated with less reverence. There would even be grave danger of various errors arising in many translations, with the result that the mysteries of our religion would differ, instead of being, as they are, one and unchanging."[27]

Discussion on that document continued through five assemblies from the eleventh to the twenty-fourth of August. Of the five bishops who spoke out in the aula, four of them were strong in arguing against any condemnation of the idea of vernacular liturgical celebrations. Only the bishop of Nîmes, a diocese which had a large Protestant population, spoke solely in favor of Latin, and only one theologian, Francisco de Santis from Spain, took the position of the "trilinguists," arguing that the sole languages worthy of Christian worship were Hebrew, Latin, and Greek. Interestingly no bishop who had experienced the use of Slavonic in the liturgy spoke against the vernacular. On the contrary, the bishop of Veglia whose diocese celebrated the liturgy in both Slavonic and Latin; actually spoke out against Latin, noting that at the Church of the Holy Sepulchre in Jerusalem, Mass is celebrated in many different languages. Concurring with the bishop of Veglia, the bishop of St. Asaph in Wales argued that there are many things which the liturgical assembly should be able to understand besides the gospel.[28]

With the best of intentions, some theologians and bishops errone-ously cited texts to defend their own positions on the issue. One theo-logian, Caesar de Ferrand, made reference to a *novella* of Justinian (no. 137) where he claimed the author spoke in favor of living languages. Justinian, as it turns out, was not talking about languages at all but rather against clerics who presided at Eucharists and baptisms silently so that their words were not heard.[29]

Attention then shifted to discussion on communion under both forms with the vernacular issue tabled. On the fifth of September, a revised, much more pastoral and conciliatory edition of the eighth chapter was presented to the council fathers, and it was approved. There was no further discussion on Latin. Those present simply made a pastoral decision that a shift from Latin to the vernacular would not be expedient (*non expedire*) but that liturgical readings and the mystery of the Eucharist should be explained to the people during Mass, at least on Sundays and feasts (no. 1554). The late Dutch Jesuit liturgist Herman Schmidt notes that this decision to retain Latin was largely a pastoral one of convenience since Latin was, in fact, the cultural-religious language of sixteenth-century Europe and a change to the vernacular would have been too abrupt an experience as imposed. Moreover, with the Protestant Reformers' call for vernacular liturgy, such a change might have been too easily interpreted as a concession to the opposition.[30]

In the end, the section entitled "Concerning Sacred Things to be Performed in a Foreign Language" condemned the view that the Mass should be celebrated only in the language of the common people.[31]

1.4.1 Post-Tridentine Vernacular Advances

There were, nonetheless, some vernacular advances even in the time of Trent. The Synod of Breslau held in 1592 decreed that vernacular hymns should be inserted at the Gradual and after the consecration wherever Latin singing was not the custom. The *Cantual of Mainz* (1605) offered a program for vernacular singing in German churches, both during a sung Latin Mass (with the option of replacing Latin chants of the proper with a German hymn) as well as at a "low Mass." The *Cantual* also included the option for a vernacular hymn to the Blessed Sacrament to be sung following the consecration. This mixing of vernacular singing with liturgical texts prayed in Latin was especially common in the Diocese of Trier. Jesuit theologian Peter Canisius (1521–97) was another advocate of vernacular music, calling for the singing of a German hymn by the congregation after the gospel as a means of introducing the homily. This German tradition of vernacular singing actually predated the Council of Trent since German synods of the fifteenth century discussed how to respond to this already existing phenomenon in numerous parishes especially in Bavaria.[32]

In 1624, Carmelite missionaries in Persia were granted permission to celebrate one Mass each day in classic Arabic "for the consolation of peoples recently converted." The issue was considered significant enough that it was discussed in full session by the Congregation for the Propagation of the Faith with Pope Urban VIII presiding over the meeting. The situation was somewhat different only three years later in Armenia when in 1627 Carmelites who had been granted permission for the use of Armenian in certain parts of the liturgy (e.g., the preface) were denied their request to extend the vernacular privilege to include the entire Mass since "concessions of this kind are a great hindrance to the communications of the Roman church."[33] This statement lacks logic as the Congregation must have known of the vernacular privileges already granted to the Dominican-inspired "Friars of Union" for their own missionary work in that same country.[34]

In 1631, however, full vernacular privileges were granted to missionaries in Georgia for the celebration of the Eucharist in either Georgian or Armenian as an instrument of evangelization. Permission for vernacular usage was granted again to the Capuchin missionaries in the following century (1757), but the use of Armenian was limited to the reading of the epistle and gospel.[35] This permission was granted as a response to the already existing Georgian practice where during sung Eucharist, the Capuchin friar celebrant first read the epistle and gospel *sotto voce* before chanting them aloud in Georgian or Armenian. Thus, the Holy Office conceded, provided the readings were first chanted aloud in Latin before any other language and that the translation used was a faithful rendering of either the Vulgate or the Greek text.[36]

Vernacular concerns were also on the minds of Jesuit missionaries in China. On the twenty-sixth of March 1615, Pope Paul V (1605–21) agreed to grant Robert Bellarmine's request for the liturgical use of Mandarin Chinese within the Chinese mission of Peking, allowing the translation of the Bible and permission for local priests to celebrate Mass and pray the Breviary in the vernacular. The privilege, in fact, was never used, probably because of the lack of prepared translations. Sicilian Jesuit Luigi Buglio spent twenty-four years translating the entire Roman Missal and Ritual, as well as a large part of the Breviary into Chinese which was finally printed at Peking in 1670.[37]

Jesuit missionaries again proposed a vernacular liturgy in Mandarin Chinese in 1665. It wasn't that the permission granted to Bellarmine had been revoked, but rather renewing the request for vernacular permission was considered the most prudent thing to do since fifty years had lapsed since the concession had been granted—a permission which, in fact, had never been acted upon. The Jesuits, however, were unsuccessful in reactivating the earlier permission granted them, largely due to Roman concern over the Chinese rites controversy.[38] The response was again negative in 1680 when Jesuit Philip Couplet made the request for permission to use Buglio's translation of the Missal. On several occasions, when Popes Alexander VII (1655–77) and Innocent XI (1676–89) referred the request to the *Propaganda Fide,* the response was consistently negative. Alexander and Innocent chose not to interfere with the final decision of the Congregation even though both Popes were personally in favor of the vernacular proposals.[39] The suppression of the Society of Jesus in 1773 put an end to further vernacular requests for the foreseeable future.

It must be noted that several minor concessions were granted. Just one year prior to the suppression of the Society of Jesus, the apostolic vicar of Szechwan wrote to the Congregation for the Propagation of the Faith, noting that the people regularly sang the *Veni Creator, Kyrie, Gloria,* Creed, *Sanctus,* and *Agnus Dei* in Chinese during Mass—texts which had been translated years before by missionaries. The Roman Congregation responded that this practice could continue provided that those texts were prayed in a low voice and never together in chorus.[40]

1.4.2 *Vernacular Translations in Western Europe*

Western Europe was engaged in its own vernacular proposals. By the sixteenth century, lay missals were already common among wealthier German, French, English, and Flemish Catholics, but in the summer of 1660, a particular edition of the French-Latin Missal called significant attention to the vernacular issue as it was caught in the middle of the Catholic-Jansenist debate. It is widely known that the French Church firmly resisted the decrees of Trent until after the French Revolution, well into the nineteenth century. Prosper Guéranger refounded the Benedictine monastery of Solesmes in 1833 precisely as an attempt to implement the largely ignored Tridentine reforms in France. Thus, the 1660 bilingual Missal must be seen in such a light.

A Parisian priest by the name of Voisin produced a four-volume French-Latin edition of the Missal with the *imprimatur* of Cardinal de Retz, archbishop of Paris. Even though the text was intended for use by the laity in better appreciating the richness of the liturgy, word soon arrived in Rome that this was one more attempt by French Jansenists to ignore Tridentine decrees and declare their autonomy from Rome in promoting a vernacular liturgy. As a matter of fact, there were already isolated cases of the vernacular liturgy being celebrated in Jansenist communities both in Germany and in Italy. The bilingual missal was condemned by an assembly of French clergy on 7 December 1660, during a scheduled session held in Paris. But their own authority to condemn such acts was quite limited. The real condemnation came from Rome one month later on the twelfth of January 1661, when the same Alexander VII who had been secretly sympathetic to the Chinese vernacular situation, issued the bull *Ad aures nostras.* Not only was the Missal of Voison put on the Index of Forbidden Books where it remained until 1897, but the Pope also threatened excommunication *latae sententiae* on all those who would print, read, or possess such vernacular missals. Moreover, all extant copies of the Missal were to be surrendered immediately:

"We therefore by special act and from certain knowledge and after mature deliberation condemn, disapprove, and prohibit for all time, and wish to be regarded as condemned, disapproved, and prohibited the above-mentioned missal in the French language, regardless of the author, no matter where and under what circumstance it may be in the future written and published, and to the faithful all and several of both sexes, of whatever rank, order, state of life, dignity, honor and preeminence, although in their case a special and individual mention had to be made, under pain of excommunication *latae sententiae* to be incurred by vigor of the law itself we forever forbid its printing, reading, and possession."[41]

Not surprisingly, the book continued to be found in Parisian bookshops. Indeed, condemnations of this sort make such books all the more marketable. Thus, four days later, the Council of State appealed to the king to search and destroy all copies of the vernacular missal still on the shelves. The archbishop of Paris, for his part, argued that the text was to help the laity better appreciate the Mass, and in a letter read during Sunday Mass throughout the archdiocese, his support for the Voisin Missal was reiterated, "for the instruction and consolation of all who wish to understand what is said in Latin in the holy Sacrifice of the Mass." On Monday morning, the Clergy Assembly gathered together in Paris renewed its condemnation of the book while the Holy See reaffirmed its own prohibition less than a month later on the seventh of February.[42] The idea, mistaken of course, was that members of the assembly would better reverence the sacred mysteries if they failed to understand on a cognitive level what was being said or, in the words of Joseph Jungmann, "if the veil of mystery were kept around it."[43]

Voisin was not alone in his translation pursuits. The French Jansenist Nicholas Le Tourneux (+1686) engaged extensively in the craft of liturgical translating, bridging the gap between serious scholarship and pastoral concerns shaped by his presbyteral ministry in working-class parishes and as a college chaplain. He wrote extensive commentaries on Advent and Holy Week which included translations of liturgical texts from Latin into French, but his most controversial work regarding liturgical participation and the vernacular can be found in his series *L'Année chrétienne* which he wrote in his retirement at the small priory of Villers-sur-Fère in Picardy and which was published after his death. Scholars debate on whether he managed to completed six or ten volumes of the work prior to his death; thirteen volumes were ultimately published and the series was completed in 1728.[44]

L'Année chrétienne was controversial not only because the work contained vernacular translations but also because Le Tourneux chose to employ the translations of biblical lessons from Voisin's already condemned missal. French bishops were further infuriated by the fact that he had included a translation of the Canon of the Mass. Fundamentally, they recognized Jansenist tendencies both in his translations and commentaries on the liturgical feasts and seasons. Thus, in 1691, it was put on the Roman Index of Forbidden Books. Despite the controversy, however, the book remained popular among ordinary French Catholics, not only because it contained the Ordinary of the Mass and Canon in translation but also because it gave the vernacular Scripture lessons for Sundays and feasts including weekday celebrations on saints' days. Not long after Le Tourneux and just across the English Channel, British vernacularist John Goder would use the work of Le Tourneux as a base text for his own liturgical commentary *Instructions on Hearing Mass*.[45]

Unimpeded by the French situation, if they had even heard of it, new vernacular missals were issued in England, Germany, and Holland without apparent condemnation from the Holy See. Even in France itself, new vernacular missals and breviaries were published without further Roman comment or interference. This continued well into the eighteenth and even the nineteenth centuries.[46] By the year 1830 only twelve dioceses in France were still using the 1570 Tridentine Missal of Pius V,[47] and the last diocese to give up its own breviary was Orléans in the year 1875.[48]

1.4.3 Vernacular Promotion in Britain

In his magisterial work, *The Stripping of the Altars: Traditional Religion in England 1400–1580*, Eamon Duffy describes how the laity assisted at Mass in England during the fifteenth and sixteenth centuries:

"The canon of the Mass was recited by the priest in silence . . . so that the people might not be hindered from praying. . . . It was not thought essential or even particularly desirable that the prayer of the laity should be the same as that of the priest at the altar. . . . These were the fundamental requirements for the laity at Mass: to kneel quietly without idle chatter, saying Paters and Aves, to respond to certain key gestures or phrases by changing posture, above all at the sacring to kneel with both hands raised in adoration, to gaze on the Host, and to greet their Lord with an elevation prayer."[49]

Devotional prayers like the "elevation prayers" and others were to be found in the wide assortment of lay primers which existed both in Latin and English and were used by wealthier Catholics who could afford those illuminated and elegantly designed texts.[50] Despite the beautifully adorned primers, however, the distance between laity and the liturgy continued, and they were deprived from a deeper level of participation in the Church's worship.

That the laity had some difficulty in following the Mass can be attested to in one classic text, the *Lay Folks Mass Book*, a manual containing prayer commentaries on the different parts of the Mass. The book was of Norman-French origin and had existed in English since the thirteenth century in many different forms and editions. Perhaps it was due to the indirect influence of the English Reformation or perhaps not, but in the seventeenth century the situation began to change. Pastoral reformers like James Dymock endeavored to create more than a text whereby the lay faithful could follow the Mass as they prayed privately, but rather a text which would assist greater liturgical participation in the Mass itself. He published *The Great Sacrifice of the New Law expounded by the figures of the Old* in 1676. By 1687, the text had been reprinted in eight editions. In his book, Dymock offers a complete English translation of the Ordinary of the Mass (including the Canon) along with the Proper for Trinity Sunday and a Mass for the Dead. Recently deceased British liturgist James Crichton notes that this is probably the first time ever we have the Canon translated into English.[51]

Equally significant in Dymock's text is his prescient theology of the laity with its inherent priesthood by virtue of a common baptism. Such an emphasis on the priesthood of the laity would explain why Dymock placed a high value on the ability to understand and participate in the Church's sacrifice which the congregation jointly offered together with the priest, "this sacrifice being ours no less than it is his." Dymock continues:

"It is our Host or Victim, it is our Oblation, which he offers with us, and we with him, and which he and we together with the Triumphant Church, offer to God the Father by His Son. . . . The people are to joyn as much as they can both with the Actions and Prayers of the Priest."[52]

Dymock was not the only English Catholic vernacularist of the era. He was succeeded in his efforts by a former Presbyterian, John Goter (+1704) of Southampton, who had become Roman Catholic in his youth. In 1678 he entered the English College in Lisbon where he was ordained a priest and served as prefect of studies. After returning to England in 1682, he found his way to Fishmongers Hall where he served on the staff of the Catholic Chapel and where Dymock was a colleague. Goter was as passionate about the poor, working-class folk of Britain as he was about the sanctity of Sunday and the care which should be devoted to the liturgy. This concern for ordinary people brought with it a concomitant concern for vernacular worship and for fuller liturgical participation on behalf of those who were present.[53] Goter presented his rationale for active liturgical participation in his text *Instructions and Devotions for Hearing Mass; for Confession, Communion, and Confirmation,* which served as a kind of liturgical guide for ordinary lay Catholics. He wrote:

"It is the priest alone that consecrates, but it is not to be imagined, it is he alone that is to offer the victim, no, the Mass is the sacrifice of the whole Church, that is, both of priest and people; therefore as the priest offers it to Almighty God, so ought likewise people offer it, both with the priest and by him."[54]

John Goter proposed four principal ways in which the faithful could "hear Mass." The first is geared toward children or adults who were recent converts. It is recommended that they go to Mass for eight to ten days (consecutively?) just to become comfortable and familiar with the celebration. They are expected to be attentive and observe, participating as much as they can, following along ideally with the help of a friend or family member who assists their understanding. His "Second Method for the Well Instructed" appears to be the mode of participation which Goter himself preferred. It included participating in the Mass as fully as possible using the translated texts provided (including the complete translation of the Roman Canon). On the pages opposite the liturgical texts, Goter places devotional prayers which correspond—more or less—to the action taking place. It is difficult to know why the liturgically minded Goter included such individually oriented devotional prayers in a liturgical text where he was attempting to foster more active corporate participation. Perhaps he did so simply to comply with what had become standard fare. The encouragement toward participation, however, cannot be denied.

The dialogue parts of the Mass are written as if they are intended to be prayed in dialogue form: "P" for "Priest" and "A" for "Answer," as in the Preface Dialogue. Conversely we find other instructions suggesting that the server prays the *Confiteor* in the name of the gathered assembly. The People are to say the Creed with the priest in English (presumably in silence) as he prays it in Latin. Throughout the Mass as described by Goter, it is difficult to assess what was prayed aloud and what was prayed in silence. Most of the texts were presumably prayed in silence especially since after the departure of James II there were no more public churches; only private (quiet) masses remained. Crichton suggests, however, that Goter, like his predecessor Dymock, might have been aware of the growing practice of vocal participation taking place in France thanks to Jansenist influences.[55] The third and fourth forms of "hearing Mass" are less liturgical and offer ways of including the devout who follow the Mass passively and pray privately (the third form) and for the "absent" who pray Psalm 83 and other assigned prayers.[56]

Goter translated the entire Mass into English including the Roman Canon. Called *The Holy Mass in Latin and English*, (later editions were called *The Roman Missal in Latin and English*), his text appeared in 1718. Richard Challoner, who had been a student of Goter's at Warkworth Castle and later became bishop and vicar apostolic of the London District (1758), followed in the master's footsteps. Challoner published his classic work *Garden of the Soul* in 1740. Taking his doctor of divinity degree at Douai, he became a prolific writer on matters of theology and catechetics and even produced his own revision of the Douai version of the Bible. Of all his publications, however, *Garden of the Soul* was the most popular. Despite the fact that Challoner had been a *protégé* of Goter's, his own approach was far more cautious. Unlike Goter, he did not print the translation of the Roman Canon despite the fact that he had done quite a decent job of translating that text and other liturgical texts privately. In another book, *The Catholic Christian instructed in the Sacraments, Sacrifice . . . of the Church,* published in 1737, only three years prior to *Garden of the Soul,* he does not support the idea of the congregation reading the Canon in the vernacular while at the same time, he directs his readers to Goter's *Instruction and Devotions for Hearing Mass.* Challoner also included vernacular parish Vespers and Compline for Sundays.[57]

However one interprets the vernacular promotion of John Goter, he was clearly well ahead of his time, and it was not surprising that some of his contemporaries or successors were more reserved in their own approaches. James Crichton contends that most probably Goter was unaware of Pope Alexander VII's prohibitions against vernacular translations of the Missal. Whether or not that was the case, Crichton concludes, "he saw the pastoral need and he met it."[58] Strangely enough, Goter's version of the Missal was never condemned and continued being published well into the eighteenth century, suggesting that it must have been used.

1.4.4 The English Catholic Enlightenment[59]

Goter's work became a sort of model for subsequent vernacular missals published during the English Catholic Enlightenment in the years 1780 until 1850. A classic example of such texts was the 1837 missal produced by Dr. Husenbath, *The Missal for Use by the Laity,* which offered a complete translation from Latin and continued being published until the end of the century. Husenbath relied substantially on Goter's work in his own vernacular edition. In the years 1809 until 1832, small pocket editions of the Missal began appearing in English as well.

John Lingard (+1851) was born in 1771 in Winchester and ordained a priest in 1795. He encouraged greater liturgical participation and use of the vernacular among his parishioners in Lancashire, greatly assisted through the publication in 1833 of his book *A Manual of Prayers on Sundays and During Mass.*[60] Fundamentally, Lingard was devoted toward the reunion of Anglicans with Roman Catholicism and so directed his vernacular efforts accordingly. He spoke positively of the Roman Catholic "assimilation" to Anglican worship as a means of drawing Anglicans back in, and at the heart of that assimilation was English. He took John Goter's reforms one step further and actually printed the *Confiteor* in English, allowing the congregation to say the "I confess" in the vernacular along with a vernacular absolution "May Almighty God have mercy . . . ," which would follow. Moreover, he argued in favor of the entire funeral liturgy taking place in English. On Palm Sunday, he insisted that the Passion be read in English by a lay lector while the priest read it in Latin from the sanctuary. Lingard was not merely a popularist but also a distinguished historian and Greek scholar. Less than pleased with the Douai-Challoner edition of the Gospels, he produced his own translation entitled *A New Version of the Four Gospels* (1836) which he used in his parish at Lancaster. Lingard's attempts at participative liturgy in the vernacular proved so popular that people came from as far as ten miles away just to attend those Masses. With his life given over so totally to ecumenism with a particular passion for reconciliation among the churches, he requested that his tombstone should read: "Here lies an advocate for the union of Christians."[61]

All of this liturgical publishing led James Crichton to remark: "The English Catholics were better provided with liturgical books to suit their needs than any other country in Europe or, unless these English missals were exported, than in the United States of America."[62] It re-mains to be studied just how much Anglican influence is to be credited for such a flurry of Roman Catholic vernacular translating that took place throughout Britain in the seventeenth and eighteenth centuries.

1.4.5 Eighteenth- and Nineteenth-Century Italy and the Vernacular

Eighteenth-century Italy bore witness to its own vernacular promo-tion beginning with the pastoral efforts of Sicilian Theatine cardinal and liturgical pioneer Giuseppe Maria Tommasi (+1713) and later through the work of Lodovico Antonio Muratori (+1750). Concerned that the lay faithful were too often excluded from the Mass and Office, Tommasi called for a thorough reform of both Missal and Breviary, re-moving excess material so as to better accentuate the essentials of the mystery being celebrated. At the heart of his reform of his liturgical books was a solid theology of liturgical participation where the entire Church as members of the Mystical Body of Christ offer and share the holy sacrifice together with the priest. Tommasi translated all of the as-sembly's responses into Italian, in addition to offering his own transla-tions of the *Gloria, Sanctus, Pater Noster, Agnus Dei*, and the Creed, where he clearly preferred the Apostles' to the Nicene. Like Muratori, who would follow a similar path to liturgical renewal in Italy, Tommasi recognized the limits of a frozen liturgical rite that was overly conscientious about rubrics and blocked almost all means of liturgical participation by the assembly.[63] Tommasi was canonized in 1986 by John Paul II, making him the first liturgical pioneer saint.

Tommasi's liturgical accomplishments in Sicily were soon matched by those of Lodovico Muratori in northern Italy. While best known for his scholarly works and discoveries at the Ambrosian Library in Milan and elsewhere, Muratori was equally devoted to the pastoral life and particular care for the poor which was reflected in his liturgical concerns. He was distressed that the contemporary liturgy he knew in eighteenth-century Italy was often a rather disorganized and haphazard affair with little dignity and care evident in the preparation and execution of liturgical celebrations. He was strong in his call for solid liturgical formation that would lead Italian Catholics to a better understanding of what the Mass was about and thereby free them from their disordered attachment to devotions and superstitions.[64]

Published in 1747, his first book, in which he dealt with liturgy and devotions, was called *Dalla Regolata Devozione dei Cristiani*. No devotion, according to Muratori, could compare with the celebration of the Mass itself, yet the average Italian was so far removed from it. The only solution was to promote greater use of the vernacular, at least for the proclamation of the Scripture readings. It was this radical proposal that caused Muratori the greatest difficulty, especially in traditionalist Italy where the sacrosanct words of the Mass pronounced in Latin were equivalent to preserving the dignity and inaccessibility of the holy of holies. But it was precisely the issue of accessibility and comprehension that troubled the Lombard scholar. He was convinced that it was, in fact, the inability to comprehend and grasp the liturgy's richness which led to unnecessary deviations and settling for inferior substitutes chosen from the Church's fare of popular piety. It was Latin, in fact, that separated the rich from the poor since it was the wealthier and more educated Church members who more easily grasped the Latin. His pastoral concerns for the poor and marginalized of eighteenth-century Italian society sustained him in his vernacular promotion even as he was roundly criticized by bishops, theologians, and members of the aristocracy.[65]

To defend his vernacular views against his critics, he recounted a personal experience of traveling in southern Austria near the Italian border. Going to Mass on one Sunday morning, he arrived at the local parish church just as the priest was leaving the sacristy to begin the liturgy. The Mass proceeded as usual until the gospel, which was read in Latin at the left side of the altar as was customary. What surprised Muratori, however, was that immediately following the gospel proclamation in Latin, the celebrant came close to the congregation and stood at the altar rail where he then proclaimed the same gospel in German in a loud voice. Muratori noted that the same practice had become normative in Dalmatia and Moravia. Reaction was fierce to his vernacular proposal, especially since Pope Benedict XIV (1731–58) had insisted that preachers should only quote the Sacred Scriptures in Latin. Bishops who opposed Muratori's reforms continued to equate Latin as inseparable from Church doctrine and dogma. Thus vernacular promotion was tantamount to touching the very soul of the Church's teachings.[66]

Frustrated but not defeated, Muratori then sought "the other way" and translated the entire Ordinary of the Mass into Italian, always keeping in mind the pastoral needs of the uneducated Italian Catholic. Speaking about the Mass itself, Muratori explained his logic:

"And since for many it is a grave obstacle to conceive and maintain devotion in their hearts and if ignorance of Latin prevents them from understanding the beauty of the holy prayers that the Church for just reasons continues to recite in that language, for the glory of God and the benefit of the ignorant here it is my desire to expound the Mass and its sacred and wonderful words for those who do not understand what the priest, in the name of all asks of God in the celebration of the Mass . . ."[67]

While Muratori's *Dalla Regolata Devozione dei Cristiani* was not appreciated in his native land, it received more positive attention outside of Italy after it was published in other European languages. Church historian Owen Chadwick called the book "a symbol of Catholic reforming ideals of the later eighteenth century," and he called Muratori himself "the finest type of Catholic reformer in the eighteenth century where critical intelligence assailed popular superstition at the same time as a pastoral heart longed for the well-being of a people's religion."[68]

Later in the eighteenth century and south of Lombardy in Tuscany, the Synod of Pistoia (1786) was strong in calling for the restoration of a vernacular liturgy where priest and people sang the Mass parts together, listened attentively to the epistle and gospel as they were sung, and where the presider proclaimed the Canon of the Mass "in a loud voice."[69] Led by the bishop of Pistoia-Prato, Scipio de'Ricci (+1799), and supported by Leopold, Grand Duke of Tuscany, this synod endeavored to restore the doctrine of the priesthood of the baptized where all members of the liturgy "can and should offer spiritual sacrifices of praise and thanksgiving to God, and because, even though all do not consecrate the body of Jesus Christ in the visible sacrifice of the altar, yet all who take part in it offer the spotless lamb."[70]

With the desire to restore the Church's liturgy as a corporate action shared together by the ordained minister and the liturgical assembly, it was not surprising that the vernacular figured prominently both regarding increased lay participation in the liturgy of the hours as well as the Eucharist. The issue was treated in the sixth session "On Prayer":

"Since we know that it would be a work against apostolic practice and against God's designs not to assist the simple people with the easiest means to unite their own voice with that of the whole Church, we believe that it is best to leave to the local bishop the responsibility of choosing certain venerable priests who will dedicate themselves to compiling a Ritual and Manual for use in the City and Diocese of Pistoia. Aside from the necessary instructions and explanations, such texts would offer both in Latin and the vernacular the prayers and rites of the Church in the administration of the sacraments and offices, principal feasts of the Church year, the Ordinary of the Mass, and all that would easily lead to a proper instruction and edification of the people."[71]

Consequently, the synod called for the preparation of a special text to assist the faithful in their prayer which would contain the offices of Sundays and feasts in Italian and the Ordinary of the Mass and other sacramental rites in Latin and Italian.[72] The bishop was deposed in 1791 and the synod was officially condemned three years later in 1794 with the papal bull *Auctorem fidei*.[73]

The Synod of Pistoia was hardly the last word on liturgical renewal. Only thirty-eight years after that synod was condemned, Antonio Rosmini (+1855) wrote his famous book *Delle Cinque Piaghe della Chiesa* (The Five Wounds of the Church) in which the third wound was the overly clericalized worship that kept the laity at a great distance from the celebration taking place. While the book was written in 1832, it was not published until 1848. Basing his liturgical principles on the

Mystical Body of Christ theology, the liturgy was fundamentally human activity in the sense that the invitation to "do this in memory of me" invites human response and action. Rosmini did not deny the fact that God reveals himself in the liturgy but emphasized the common baptism of all believers as necessitating a common response to God's initiative, and that response was corporate worship. To further assist this corporate action, members of the Church needed to be catechized through the liturgy itself so as to better appreciate the mystery inherent within the sacred action, to plumb the depths of Catholic ritual with its rich symbolic system so that those in the liturgical assembly understood that which they were celebrating. The vernacular was a fundamental instrument in the process and books should be provided for the laity with Italian translations of the Latin texts. What is unique about Rosmini, unlike other pastoral reformers of his day, was that he also called for instructing the laity in Latin so that they could better understand the Mass and sacraments.[74]

Rosmini was less than impressed with a catechism approach of questions and answers to better understanding the richness of Catholic worship. Rather, it was to be liturgy itself celebrated in the vernacular which would be the best teacher when properly celebrated. Accused of Jansenism, the author's book was placed on the Index of Forbidden Books in 1849, taken off the list one year before his death, put back on the list again twenty years later in 1887, and taken off the list more recently before the entire Index was abolished.[75]

1.5 THE VERNACULAR ISSUE IN THE MISSION OF JOHN CARROLL

Prior to the suppression of the Society of Jesus in 1773, Jesuit missionaries across the Atlantic had received permission from the Holy See for use of the Iroquois language in the liturgy celebrated with that Native American community in the area around modern-day Montreal.[76] But the more famous discussions on the vernacular in North America would take place toward the end of the eighteenth century in the mission territory of the United States of America thanks to the initiative of its first bishop, John Carroll (+1815). Carroll was born in Maryland on 8 January 1735 and studied in Europe at the Jesuit schools of St. Omer and Liège. Following his studies, he entered the Society of Jesus, spending several years on the continent and in England after his ordination as teacher and missionary, especially following the suppression of the Society. In 1784, he was appointed prefect apostolic of the mission in the United States by the Holy See. On the sixth of November 1789, Pius VI erected the Diocese of Baltimore and named John Carroll as its first ordinary, ratifying his election as bishop by the clergy of that region. He was consecrated by the Benedictine Bishop Charles Walmesley at Lulworth Castle, an estate of the wealthy English Catholic Thomas Weld on the fifteenth of August 1790, taking up his new see in Baltimore at the end of the year.[77] In 1808, he was named archbishop of Baltimore when four suffragan bishops were appointed to new dioceses in Boston, New York, Philadelphia, and Bardstown, Kentucky.[78]

Even before his nomination as bishop, Carroll needed to respond to a serious attack on the Church that came from Maryland-born former Jesuit Charles Henry Wharton who had left the Church. Wharton wrote a forty-page pamphlet entitled *A Letter to the Roman Catholics of the City of Worcester* (England) where he had been assigned for a number of years prior to returning to the United States in 1783. Wharton's attack on Catholic doctrine was well crafted and articulate and warranted an official Catholic response. Carroll was chosen as the most qualified for the task. He worked on the project during the summer of 1784 and the final product was a text three times the length of Wharton's polemic. Carroll entitled his response *An Address to Roman Catholics of the United States of America,* and it was published by Frederick Green of Annapolis, Maryland. A major source for Carroll's text was English priest Joseph Berrington's *State and Behavior of English Catholics from the Reformation to the Year 1780.*[79]

Several years after completing his own text, Carroll wrote to Berrington, who was already well known in England, both to express gratitude for his work and also to recommend future topics Berrington might study—among them, English in the Liturgy. Regarding the vernacular, Carroll wrote:

"I cannot help thinking that the alteration of the Church discipline ought not only be solicited, but insisted on as essential to the service of God and benefit of mankind. Can there be anything more preposterous than for a small district containing in extent no more than Mount Libanus and a trifling territory at the foot of it, to say nothing of Greeks, Armenians, Coptics, etc. to have a 'liturgy' in their proper idiom and on the other hand for an immense extent of countries containing Great Britain, Ireland, also North America, the West Indies etc., to be obliged to perform divine service in an unknown tongue;

and in this country either for want of books or inability to read, the great part of our congregations must be entirely ignorant of the meaning and sense of the publick offices of the Church. It may have been prudent, for aught I know, to refuse a compliance in this instance with the insulting and reproachful demands of the first reformers; but to continue the practice of the Latin liturgy in the present state of things must be owing either to chimerical fears of innovation or to indolence and inattention in the first pastors of the national Churches in not joining to solicit or indeed ordain this necessary alteration."[80]

Carroll's statement was so much in agreement with Berrington's own views on the vernacular that he quoted it in a publicized controversy in which he was engaged with his own superior, John Douglass, vicar apostolic of the London District. Carroll then received a number of protest letters from the British Isles—among them one from John Thomas Troy, o.p., archbishop of Dublin, who informed him that he had written a sixty-page pastoral letter against the vernacular proposal. Another letter of criticism came from Arthur O'Leary, o.f.m., chaplain to the Spanish Embassy in London.[81] Undaunted, Carroll responded to O'Leary:

"In a letter to him [Berrington] and before I had thought of ever being in my present situation, I expressed a wish that the pastors of the Church would see cause to grant to this extensive continent jointly with England and Ireland, etc. the same privilege as is enjoyed by many other churches of infinitely less extent: that of having their liturgy in their own language; for I do indeed conceive that one of the most popular prejudices against us is that our public prayers are unintelligible to our hearers. Many of the poor people, and the negroes generally, not being able to read, have no technical help to confine their attention."[82]

John Carroll was concerned about the credibility and intelligibility of the message, and like many other missionaries before him, he was employing the basic Jesuit missionary strategy of cultural adaptation or what is now called "inculturation."[83] He believed that the two greatest obstacles to a proper understanding of the Catholic Church were (1) the nature and extent of the spiritual jurisdiction of the Holy See and (2) the use of Latin in the Liturgy.

One year after his ordination as bishop, John Carroll called the first diocesan synod on the seventh of November 1791 with twenty-two priests of the diocese attending the four-day meeting. On the final day, the tenth of November, synod participants drafted regulations for the proper celebration of liturgical rites on Sundays and feasts. Carroll's earlier vernacular activism was greatly modified in this synod, and one notes an ever-greater caution regarding use of the vernacular the longer he is bishop. Nonetheless the Synod of 1791 allowed for some vernacular within liturgical celebrations. The gospel was to be read in English on Sundays and feast days; Benediction of the Blessed Sacrament was called for during Sunday Vespers with a catechetical instruction in English to follow; and sung hymns and prayers in English were also recommended during the services.[84] When preparations for Mass were completed, either the Litany of the Holy Name or the Litany of Loreto was to be recited unless the choir chose to sing in English. Following Mass, the whole assembly was to recite the Lord's Prayer, Hail Mary, Apostles' Creed, and the Acts of Faith, Hope, and Charity, all in English. In subsequent years, various attempts at unapproved liturgical translations on the local level abounded along with other abuses, causing Carroll to convene a bishops' meeting in November 1810 on the occasion of the ordination of new bishops. He and his colleagues in the episcopate addressed the vernacular issue squarely:

"It is being made known to the Archbishop and Bishops that there exists a difference of opinion and practice among some of the clergy of the United States concerning the use of the vernacular language in any part of the public service, and in the administration of the sacraments. It is hereby enjoined on all priests not only to celebrate the whole Mass in the Latin language, but likewise when they administer Baptism, the Holy Eucharist, Penance, and Extreme Unction, to express the necessary and essential form of those sacraments in the same tongue according to the Roman Ritual; but if it does not appear contrary to the injunctions of the Church to say in the vernacular language the prayers previous and subsequent to those Sacred forms, provided however, that no translation of those prayers shall be made use of except one authorized by the concurrent approbation of the Bishops of this ecclesiastical province, which translation will be printed as soon as it can be prepared under their inspection."[85]

Despite apparent attempts to close the door on vernacular experimentation as evidenced in the bishops' meeting of 1810, one should be careful to "read between the lines." Carroll and the other bishops did, in fact, imply permission for priests to make use of a maximum of English when celebrating the sacraments and seem to assume the use of the vernacular in sacramental administration except for the words embodying "the essential forms of the sacraments."[86] And U.S. priests stretched that permission even further as they continued to use English in the celebration of Mass and the other sacraments.[87] In 1822, Bishop John England of Charleston edited the first American edition of the Roman Missal in English, published in New York, taking much of the text from a Missal already being used in England with full approval of the English hierarchy.[88] This text produced its own share of negative reactions from ecclesiastical authorities, and it took a strong intervention by Archbishop Maréchal of Baltimore to block a threatened prohibition of the missal. His argument was simple: this was hardly a new text or a new translation of the Roman Missal. Rather, it had been used with great success and spiritual profit throughout England and Ireland. Any further threats of prohibition were dropped.[89]

1.6 THE NINETEENTH CENTURY

Abbot Prosper Guéranger refounded the French monastery of Solesmes in 1833 and restored usage of the Roman Rite in France using his monastery as a center. He discouraged vernacular usage as reflective of the French Jansenism he was trying to correct and promoted Latin as the unifying factor in his project of Roman restoration. Guéranger argued in favor of "the discipline of the secret," i.e., that the Canon of the Mass should not be translated, believing that in earlier centuries it was forbidden to reveal the core of the Christian mysteries. Thus, even in his famous pastoral series, *L'Année liturgique*, he paraphrased rather than directly translated the Canon.[90]

In 1850, the Catholic press in England was enjoying its own vernacular debates. John Henry Newman wrote to *The Tablet* responding to one who criticized the Oratorians' use of the vernacular in their liturgical celebrations:

"Sir: Will you allow me to correct a misapprehension concerning the Fathers of the Oratory, contained in the letter of your correspondent "s.M.: in last week's TABLET. He says 'if they are not exclusively bound to popular services *I cannot help thinking it a pity that they do not,* along with these, *cultivate the Ritual branch.*' On the contrary, *we are bound by our rule* to the Solemn Ritual services of the Church, *and*

SS Cyril and Methodius. Contemporary Bulgarian icon.

Cardinal Giacomo Lercaro

Archbishop John Carroll

we keep it. Both our own house here, and the Oratory in London, sings High Mass and Vespers *every* Sunday, and other principal festivals, besides observing the services prescribed for All-Souls, Candlemas, Ash Wednesday, Holy Week and other sacred seasons. The Congregations of the Oratory have been remarkable for their exact attention to the rubrics of the Ritual. . . . It is only because we have *daily* sermons and prayers and have thence been led to adopt vernacular and familiar services *also,* that we are supposed to neglect what in fact we scrupulously observe. People fancy we *substitute,* because we *add.* They assume we hold what we do not dream of holding, and then proceed to refute their own assumptions. Of course, in saying this, I am not alluding to the temperate and judicious writer who has given occasion to this note. I am, dear sir, Yours very truly, John H. Newman, Congr. Orat."[91]

As late as 1851 and again in 1857, the Holy See refused to allow liturgical translations in the vernacular, even as a tool for the laity in greater appreciation of the Mass: "It is not permitted to translate the Ordinary of the Mass . . . into the vernacular, and print the same for use of the faithful, nor can such a work get the approbation of the Bishop (6 June 1857)."[92] All that changed exactly twenty years later when, in 1877, the same Pope Pius IX (1846–78), who forbade vernacular translations, completely reversed his decision, allowing any bishop to authorize the translation and use of vernacular missals for use by the laity. Leo XIII (1878–1903) later put such missals on the ordinary *imprimatur* basis according to the judgment of each bishop.[93] The Church had come a long way from the Voisin affair of 1660.

Back in the United States, Belgian Jesuit missionary Pierre De Smet led his native American community in the Dakota Territory in eucharistic celebrations where hymns were sung not only in Latin but also in French and in Native American languages as well. De Smet's community was a very early example of multiculturalism. The Dakota had intermarried with the French; thus De Smet often presided over Mass at which French, mixed-race natives, and Native Americans were all present in the same liturgical assembly. Accordingly, he incorporated the use of several languages in worship as a way of responding to that diverse cultural reality.[94]

Some years later in 1884, the Third Plenary Council of the American Hierarchy gathered in Baltimore and appointed a committee of "liturgical experts" under the direction of the apostolic delegate to prepare a vernacular prayer book for American Catholic laity. The result was the 1889 publication of a 792-page *Manual of Prayers for the Use of the Catholic Laity*. Most of the prayers were translated from the Roman Missal, the Roman Breviary, and the Roman Ritual.[95] Meanwhile in Ethiopia the Roman Pontifical and Ritual were translated into *Ge'ez*, and the provisional text was approved on the fourth of February 1895, pending the revision and printing of Ethiopian liturgical books in that language.

1.7 TWENTIETH-CENTURY DEVELOPMENTS

In 1906, Pius X granted permission for certain areas of Yugoslavia to make permanent liturgical use of the classical Paleoslav language.[96] In 1920, Pope Benedict XV (1914–22) granted permission for the use of Croatian and Slovenian in Church rites and for sung epistles and gospels in the vernacular at solemn Masses and also legitimized the use of Czech in liturgical services in a specified region where that tradition had been customary since the early fifteenth century.[97]

In North America, the editors of the *American Ecclesiastical Review*, following a noteworthy correspondence in its pages, petitioned the United States bishops to issue an English Ritual in 1910. This petition was further advanced by the Rev. C. A. Campbell of Halifax, Nova Scotia. The bishops failed to respond to the request and the matter was dropped.

Pius XI was elected Pope on the sixth of February 1922, and his interest in and support of the missions was reflected in his openness toward greater use of the vernacular, especially in mission lands. Soon after his election Pius remarked that "the question of the vernacular is a grave one, but there can be no objection to its being discussed."[98] Some years later, there was an exchange between the Pope and a Roman-Rite priest from the Refuge of El-Abdioth about the need to chant the gospel in Latin prior to chanting it in Arabic. Pius responded:

"Don't use Arabic as a veneer on top of the Latin, but act as the Arab does. Attend carefully to what I say: You already sing the Gospel in Arabic after singing it in Latin, but understand clearly what I direct: Don't use Arabic as a veneer on top of the Latin.

"In order to make myself understood, I am going to tell you a story. The bishops of Estonia were complaining some time ago that all their people were joining either the Protestants or the Orthodox, because in those religions they could understand (the worship). They came to tell me: 'We have scarcely anyone any more: we ask you for permission to celebrate the Roman Mass in Estonian.' Among the consultors of the Congregation of Sacred Rites some said 'Yes,' and some said 'No.' But we said: 'Yes; let them celebrate Mass in Estonian.'"[99]

In that same period, national parishes like St. Stanislaus Kostka parish in Chicago (founded in 1867) and Native American communities in the United States were busy preparing prayer books and hymnals in the vernacular. In 1927, Jesuit Eugene Buechel wrote the 380-page *Lakota Wocekiye na Olowan Wowapi: Sioux Indian Prayer and Hymn Book*. More than 5,000 copies were printed, and the book was distributed among the reservations. The principal language for the text was Lakota, and it contained the weekly scriptural readings in the local language along with sixty Lakota hymns for Advent, Christmas, Lent, and Easter; ten hymns to the Virgin were also included. Morning and evening prayers, penitential prayers and prayers for the sick, litanies, and devotions completed the text.[100]

Aside from devotional texts in the vernacular, there were various concessions made toward greater use of the vernacular during the pontificate of Pius XI, as in the 1929 permission granted for a vernacular Ritual in the southern-German region of Bavaria, and the 1935 *Collectio Rituum archidioecesis Viennensis* which was used throughout Austria. The Austrian edition of the *Rituale* contained a preface by Cardinal Innitzer urging priests to reverently and clearly articulate that which they were praying:

"[O]f putting the proper reverence into the use of the vernacular in the sacred rites, of pronouncing the sacred words in a clear and distinct tone, without haste, in order that the prayers be more acceptable to our Lord, and in order that the minds of those listening be raised to heaven, and that bystanders be not scandalized by carelessness and irreverence in the pronunciation."[101]

As permission for the translation of the Roman Ritual continued to be granted, lay missals continued to be printed in different languages. In 1929, Abbot Emanuele Caronti of Finalpia first published his *Messale festivo per i fedeli*, in which the entire Canon was translated into Italian except for the words of institution; by 1954 the text had reached its seventh edition. Meanwhile in Belgium and France, Dom Gaspar Lefebvre's *Missel-Vespéral* (approved in 1920) translated everything into French, including the words of institution. Few missals were as widely distributed, however, as was *My Sunday Missal* by Brooklyn priest Joseph Stedman. First published in 1938, the book was eventually translated into Chinese, French, German, Italian, Polish, and Oticipwe Native American; more than fifteen million copies were sold. At the time of his death in 1946, he was working on a Latin-English Breviary. The book was popular because of its size, readable print, and layout, with the different parts of the Mass numbered sequentially. The Stedman Missal soon became known as the "if you can count to fifteen you can't get lost Missal."[102]

In 1941 and 1942, missionaries in various countries in Africa, China, India, Indo-China, Indonesia, Japan, and New Guinea were given permission to translate the Roman Ritual into the local language, retaining Latin only for the essential sacramental formulas. The vernacular editions of the Ritual were to be done by a commission of experts under the supervision of the apostolic delegate in the particular country. Once the texts were completed and approved by the delegate they were to be used for a period of ten years before they were to be sent to Rome for definitive approval.

Vernacular advances seemingly continued everywhere, except in the United States.[103] Concerned that individual German bishops might be giving too many local permissions for expanded use of the vernacular, the apostolic nuncio, in a letter dated the eleventh of January 1943, wrote that the Holy See would be glad

"to accord certain privileges (for example with reference to the Ritual), which could really have an advantageous consequence for the good of souls, in the instance that the request be presented to the Holy See by the entire German episcopate."[104]

Taking the Holy See at its word, the German bishops asked for some expression of confidence that it was, indeed, willing to grant permission for wider use of the vernacular. The response reiterated the nuncio's letter:

"[W]e can only repeat what we have already said on other occasions, namely that the question is being dealt with here in a calm and broad-minded manner by the cardinals charged with its clarification, and that the Holy See is prepared to meet, as far as is possible, the needs of spiritual ministration in Germany."[105]

At the end of that same year, on Christmas Eve 1943, a decree from the Sacred Congregation of Rites brought the Church in Germany approval of the largely vernacular *Gemeinschaftsmesse* (Dialog Mass) and the *Singmesse* which included the singing of German hymns at the "High Mass," which had already been the custom (e.g., *Treves* and *Mayence*) for several centuries.

While vernacular advances were being made in Germany, the English Liturgy Society (after 1945, the Vernacular Society of Great Britain) was founded in that same year (1942) by Samuel J. Gossling. Meanwhile, inspired by their episcopal counterparts in Europe, the bishops of Uganda had decided that they, too, would petition Rome for a vernacular Ritual which could be used in their country. Commenting on the Ugandan petition, Jesuit liturgical pioneer Gerald Ellard wrote:

"When this report went out from a newspaper in India, it was lauded in *Toronto's Social Forum* by an editor quoting Msgr. Fernando Cento, then Apostolic Delegate to Peru, as one who deprecated the 'Chinese Wall' between priest and people, and all this was reprinted in *The London Herald* (Jan. 21, 1944). The discussion was rapidly becoming world-wide."[106]

Ellard went on to recount a moving story of a vernacular liturgy celebrated at the Cathedral of Castres, France, in that same year, 1944:

"The cathedral was already full of people, and the crowd overflowed into the street. The whole congregation was composed of workers brought there by their fellow workers . . .

"Then Msgr. Moussaron, Archbishop of Albi, entered, garbed in his purple cassock. In full view of the congregation he was robed in his vestments while a priest explained their meaning. When midnight struck, the archbishop proceeded to the temporary altar and, facing the congregation, began the celebration of the Mass. By special dispensation of the Pope, this Mass, except for the Canon, was said in French. The effect on the congregation was instant and profound. For many it was as if they were hearing Mass for the first time. Numbers who had not practiced their religion for twenty or twenty-five years went to confession and received Holy Communion. The distribution of Communion lasted more than an hour. Three unbaptized workers, suddenly touched by divine grace, asked to receive Holy Communion. Two years later, when I returned to Castres, people were still talking about the ceremony, which had quickened for many a new view of faith and a return to the obligations of a Christian."[107]

Four years later, in 1948, the *Rituel latin-français*, provided a limited use of French in the celebrations of baptism, marriage, and anointing of the sick. Permission was granted the following year to China for the complete celebration of Mass in Mandarin Chinese, with the exception of the Canon which was to remain in Latin.[108] In that same year, when the bishops of Cameroon petitioned the Congregation for the Propagation of the Faith for permission to use the newly approved French Ritual for their Francophone constituencies, the response came back that the French Ritual could only be used by French citizens. The Latin Ritual was to be retained for the citizens of Cameroon, but they were to begin immediate preparation for a translation of the Ritual into the local language(s). A comment made in *Herder-Korrespondenz* clarified the Vatican's position on the matter:

"It is not a question merely that the liturgical text be understood . . . but that the Word of the liturgy be heard in the mother tongue—their Mother's voice is to be perceived in their mother tongue."[109]

India received permission in 1950 to use Hindi for the celebration of the sacraments in those regions where Hindi was spoken. The *Collectio Rituum I* was published at Regensburg in 1951 with authorized use for all the dioceses of Germany, providing for even more vernacular than was found in the French Ritual.[110] In that same year, the bishops of the United States directed their Committee on the Confraternity of Christian Doctrine to study the desirability of a bilingual Ritual; the text was finally proposed and approved for use by the Holy See in 1954.

In September 1953, the archbishop of Bologna, Cardinal Giacomo Lercaro, made the strongest plea on behalf of the vernacular since the Council of Trent:

"As Pius X made the Eucharistic Bread freely available for the Christian people, might not the Bread of God's Word be made more readily available by letting the people hear the readings at Mass in their own tongues, directly from the lips of the priest?"[111]

Lercaro's resolution was merely a summary of what he had already expressed in an extensive referendum on the subject. At that international liturgical congress held at Lugano, Switzerland, at which seventeen bishops and one representative of the Congregation of Rites participated, two of the four resolutions which came out of the meeting treated the vernacular issue. The first was Lercaro's. The second resolution, formulated by Bishop Weskaman of Berlin and Johannes Hofinger, s.j., completed the circle:

"The congress requests: so that the people may more easily and with more benefit take part in the liturgy, may bishops have authority to allow the people, not only to hear the Word of God in their own language, but to pray and sing in that language even in the Mass (*Missa Cantata)* and so make some sort of response."[112]

1.8 CONCLUSION

These examples throughout the Church's history, while not exhaustive of the vernacular debate, simply demonstrate the fact that a shift toward use of the vernacular within liturgical celebrations was hardly an idea limited to our own times or even to the years prior to the onset of the Second Vatican Council (1962–65). Just as Paul had argued for intelligibility in 1 Corinthians and the Church's liturgical language in the third and fourth centuries gradually shifted to Latin when members of the liturgical assembly no longer understood Greek, so does the history of liturgical language reveal numerous examples of *accomodatio.* Whether one points to the example of Cyril and Methodius in the ninth century or the missionaries and Church leaders of subsequent centuries, the issue was the credibility and intelligibility of liturgy so that the faithful might grow in their appreciation of that holy mystery they were celebrating.

Indeed, texts are more than words, and translated texts are more than a literal rendering of what is contained in the original. And texts are culturally conditioned. Thus, it would be simplistic to think that the same language could break through many different cultural barriers and convey with power the deep and multivalent levels of meaning inherent therein. This is well-articulated by Pierre-Celestine Lou Tseng-Tsiang who translated the Rule of Benedict into Chinese and called for a Chinese liturgy back in 1946:

"Between the Chinese language and those which use alphabets there is a difference of conception which is complete. In Chinese a man writes what the eye sees; in the languages which use alphabets a man writes what the mouth pronounces. In order to pass from the one to the others, or *vice versa* he must accept the labor of a new education, at once linguistic and literary. Only a limited number of men are capable of it."[113]

Scholar of liturgical language Gail Ramshaw reminds us that "theology is prose" and "liturgy is poetry."[114] Language has a way of including or excluding, as Paul reminds us in 1 Corinthians. It can either articulate and express the needs and desires of those who celebrate, or it can remain peripheral. It can disclose something of the holy and numinous or leave its hearers largely unchanged or disinterested because they remain "outsiders." The story which follows offers an interesting piece in the history of the vernacular, precisely because those "vernacularists" as they called themselves, recognized the power of words to dynamically transform communities of faith.

NOTES FOR CHAPTER 1

[1] 1 Cor 14:16-19. *The New Oxford Annotated Bible with the Apocrypha* (New York: Oxford University Press, 1991).

[2] Elisabeth Schüssler Fiorenza, "I Corinthians" in James L. Mays, ed., *Harper's Bible Commentary* (San Francisco: Harper & Row, 1988) 1186.

[3] Gilbert Ostdiek, O.F.M., "Principles of Translation in the Revised Sacramentary," in Mark R. Francis, Keith F. Pecklers, eds., *Liturgy for the New Millennium: A Commentary on the Revised Sacramentary* (Collegeville: The Liturgical Press/Pueblo, 2000) 18–19.

[4] Cyril Korolevsky, *Living Languages in Catholic Worship: An Historical Inquiry* (Westminster, Md.: Newman Press, 1957) 4–7.

[5] See Edmund Bishop, "The Genius of the Roman Rite" in *Liturgica Historica* (Oxford: The Clarendon Press, 1918) 1–19.

[6] Horace K. Mann, *The Lives of the Popes in the Early Middle Ages* III, 222, as quoted in *Orate Fratres* 24 (1950) 455.

[7] Josef A. Jungmann, S.J., *The Mass of the Roman Rite: Its Origins and Development* I (Blackrock, Ireland: Four Courts Press, 1950) 81.

[8] Korolevsky, 74.

[9] L. Eisenhofer, *Handbuch der Katholischen Liturgik* I (Freiburg i. B.: Herder, 1932) 154, as quoted in Gerald Ellard, *The Mass of the Future* (Milwaukee: The Bruce Publishing Company, 1948) 148.

[10] Horace K. Mann, 223, as quoted in *Orate Fratres* 24 (1950) 455.

[11] Korolevsky, 76–77.

[12] Korolevsky, 83.

[13] "Stephen V (VI)" in Richard P. McBrien, *Lives of the Popes* (San Francisco: Harper, 1997) 143–44.

[14] Korolevsky, 86, 88.

[15] J. M. Hanssens, S.J., "*Lingua Liturgica*" as quoted in Editor, "The Apostolate," *Orate Fratres* 27 (1953) 392.

[16] Josef A. Jungmann, *Pastoral Liturgy* (London: George Berridge & Co. Ltd., 1962) 96–97.

[17] Sophia Menache, *The Vox Dei: Communication in the Middle Ages* (Oxford: Oxford University Press, 1990) 22–23.

[18] Menache, 23; 69.

[19] H. Vehlen, o.s.b., "Geschichtliches zur Ubersetzung des Missale Romanum," in *Liturgiches Leben* III (1936) 89–97, cited in Jungmann, *The Mass of the Roman Rite* I, 143, n. 13.

[20] Jungmann, *The Mass of the Roman Rite* I, 143, n. 14.

[21] Jungmann, *The Mass of the Roman Rite* I, 143–44, n. 14.

[22] Jungmann, *The Mass of the Roman Rite* I, 143–44.

[23] Korolevsky, 94.

[24] For a thorough treatment of the vernacular debate as discussed in the Council of Trent, see Herman A. Schmidt, s.j., "*Le Concile de Trente*" in *Liturgie et Langue Vulgaire: Le problème de la langue liturgique chez les premiers Réformateurs et au Concile de Trente* (Rome: Analecta Gregoriana 53, 1950) 83–198.

[25] Vernacular promotion during the Reformation shall be treated in chapter 4.

[26] Parts of the *libellus* along with a detailed exposition of the argument can be found in Enrico Cattaneo, *Il culto cristiano in occidente: note storiche*, 282–85.

[27] Korolevsky, 98.

[28] Korolevsky, 98.

[29] Korolevsky, 98–99.

[30] Schmidt, 134.

[31] Section 7, Canon 4.

[32] Jungmann, *The Mass of the Roman Rite* I, 146–47.

[33] Archives of Propoganda Fidei, *Lettere della Sacra Congregazione* for 1777, fol. 81, as quoted in Korolevsky, 101.

[34] Korolevsky, 101.

[35] Hanssens, as quoted in *Orate Fratres* 27 (1953) 393–94.

[36] Korolevsky, 101.

[37] L. Pfister, *Notices biographiques et bibliographiques sur les Jésuites de l'ancienne mission de Chine* I (Shanghai, 1932) 240.

[38] The Chinese rites controversy, which began in the seventeenth century, was a debate primarily between Jesuit and Dominican missionaries on a proper strategy for evangelization and on how much of Confucian religious practices and traditional elements from Chinese culture could be permitted in Catholic worship. See George Minamiki, s.j., *The Chinese Rites Controversy: From its Beginning to Modern Times* (Chicago: Loyola University Press, 1985).

[39] George H. Dunne, s.j., "What Happened to the Chinese Liturgy?" *Catholic Historical Review* XLVII (1961) 1–14.

[40] Korolevsky, 104.

[41] Quoted in Gerald Ellard, *The Mass of the Future* (Milwaukee: Bruce Publishing Co., 1948) 127.

[42] Ellard, *The Mass of the Future*, 127.

[43] Jungmann, *The Mass of the Roman Rite* I, 144.

[44] James D. Crichton, *Lights in the Darkness: Fore-Runners of the Liturgical Movement* (Blackrock, Co. Dublin: The Columba Press, 1996) 53, 60.

[45] Crichton, 55, 60–62.

[46] Crichton, 127–28.

[47] R. W. Franklin, *Nineteenth-Century Churches: The History of a New Catholicism in Würtemberg, England, and France* (New York: Garland Publishing Co., 1987) 363.

[48] Simon Ditchfield, "Giving Tridentine Worship Back Its History," in R. N. Swanson, *Continuity and Change in Christian Worship*, Studies in Church History 35 (Suffolk, England: The Boydell Press, 1999) 203, n.10.

[49] Eamon Duffy, *The Stripping of the Altars: Traditional Religion in England 1400–1580* (New Haven: Yale University Press, 1992) 117.

[50] See Duffy, *The Stripping of the Altars*, 209–98.

[51] Crichton, 66.

[52] James Dymock, *The Great Sacrifice of the New Law expounded by the figures of the Old* (1676) 9, as quoted in Crichton, 66.

[53] Crichton, 67–68.

[54] *The Spiritual Works of Rev. John Goter* (16 vols.), vol. 10 (Newcastle Upon Tyne, 1792?) 4, as quoted in Crichton, 69.

[55] Crichton, 69–71.

[56] Crichton, 69–70.

[57] Crichton, 71–72.

[58] Crichton, 68.

[59] See Joseph P. Chinnici, *The English Catholic Enlightenment 1780–1850* (Sheperdstown, Pa.: Patmos Press, 1980).

[60] James F. White, *Roman Catholic Worship: Trent to Today* (New York: Paulist Press, 1995) 55.

[61] Crichton, 74–75.

[62] Crichton, 71.

[63] Enrico Cattaneo, *Il culto cristiano in occidente: note storiche* (Rome: C.L.V. Edizione Liturgiche, 1992) 368–69. See also Ildebrando Scicolone, *Il Cardinale Giuseppe Tommasi di Lampedusa e gli inizi della scienza liturgica* (Palermo, 1981).

[64] Cattaneo, 373–74.

[65] Cattaneo, 373–74; 376. See also Crichton, 19–21.

[66] Crichton, 20–21.

[67] As quoted in Cattaneo, 374. My translation.

[68] Owen Chadwick, *The Popes and the European Revolution* (Oxford: Oxford University Press, 1981) 400, as quoted in Crichton, 24.

[69] Fourth Session. "Decree on the Eucharist," as quoted in Cattaneo, 439. My translation.

[70] As quoted in Charles A. Bolton, *Church Reform in 18th Century Italy (The Synod of Pistoia)* (The Hague: Martinus Nijhoff, 1969) 79.

[71] "On Public Prayer," ch. XXIV as quoted in Cattaneo, 442. My translation.

[72] J. D. Mansi, *Sacrorum Conciliorum Nova et Amplissima Collectio*, vol. 38, 1040.

[73] Cattaneo, 445.

[74] Cattaneo, 471–74.

[75] Crichton, 25–29.

[76] Ellard, 255.

[77] John Tracy Ellis, "Archbishop Carroll and the Liturgy in the Vernacular," *Worship* 26 (1952) 549.

78 William R. Bangert, *A History of the Society of Jesus* (St. Louis: The Institute of Jesuit Sources, 1972) 407.

79 John Tracy Ellis, "Archbishop Carroll and the Liturgy in the Vernacular," in *Perspectives in American Catholicism* (Baltimore: Helicon Press, 1963) 128.

80 Archives of the Archdiocese of Baltimore, Special C, C-1, [1787] quoted in John Tracy Ellis, *Perspectives in American Catholicism*, 129.

81 John Tracy Ellis, *Perspectives in American Catholicism*, 129–30.

82 Carroll to O'Leary, Baltimore, undated, quoted in John Tracy Ellis, *Perspectives in American Catholicism*, 130.

83 See Minamiki, *The Chinese Rites Controversy*. On the theology of inculturation, see Aylward Shorter, *Toward A Theology of Inculturation* (New York: Orbis, 1988); on the inculturation of the liturgy, see Anscar J. Chupungco, *Liturgical Inculturation: Sacramentals, Religiosity, and Catechetics* (Collegeville: The Liturgical Press, 1992).

84 *Concilia provincialia Baltimori habita ab anno 1829 ad annum 1849* (Baltimore, 1851) as quoted in John Tracy Ellis, *Perspectives in American Catholicism*, 131.

85 As quoted in John Tracy Ellis, *Perspectives in American Catholicism*, 132–33.

86 John Tracy Ellis, *Perspectives in American Catholicism*, 133.

87 Jay P. Dolan, *The American Catholic Experience: A History from Colonial Times to the Present* (Garden City, N.Y.: Doubleday, 1985) 124.

88 John England, ed., *The Roman Missal Translated into the English Language for the Use of the Laity* (New York: William H. Creagh, 1822) iii.

89 Ellard, 128.

90 Korolevsky, 107.

91 John Henry Newman, "Letter to the Editor," *The Tablet* (28 October 1850), quoted in "The Vernacular Society Bulletin" (14 December 1950) 1. CVER 3/2.

92 Quoted in Ellard, 128.

93 Ellard, 128.

94 Ross Alexander Enochs, "Lakota Mission: Jesuit Mission Method and the Lakota Sioux 1886–1945." Unpublished doctoral dissertation, University of Virginia, 1993, 27–28.

95 William Busch, "From Other Times: The Voice of a Plenary Council," *Orate Fratres* 21 (1947) 454, 458.

96 Pius X, "Paleoslav use, Roman Rite" (8 Dec. 1906) *ASS* 40, 54–58.

97 Cited in Ellard, 152.

98 Quoted in Ellard, 152.

99 Ellard, 152.

100 Ross Alexander Enochs, 178–80.

101 Quoted in Ellard, 153.

102 Ellard, 128.

103 There were isolated calls for greater use of the vernacular, as in the inquiry about the possibility of celebrating baptism in the vernacular that surfaced in 1928. See "Substitution of Vernacular for Latin at Baptism," *Ecclesiastical Review* 79 (1928) 197–98.

104 Quoted in Ellard, 153.

105 Ellard, 153.

106 Ellard, 154.

107 Quoted in Ellard, 155–56.

[108] See S. Paventi, *La Chiesa missionaria. Manuale di missiologia dottrinale* (Rome, 1949) 388.

[109] Quoted in "Liturgical Briefs," *Orate Fratres* 27 (1953) 155.

[110] Korolevsky, 110–11.

[111] Jungmann, *Pastoral Liturgy*, 349.

[112] Jungmann, *Pastoral Liturgy*, 349.

[113] Pierre-Celestine Lou Tseng-Tsiang, o.s.b., "The Case for a Chinese Liturgy," *The Tablet* (2 February 1946), reprinted in *Orate Fratres* 20 (1946) 227. See also his autobiography, *Souvenirs et Pensées* (Bruges, 1945).

[114] Gail Ramshaw, *Worship: Searching for Language* (Washington, D.C.: The Pastoral Press, 1988) 110–11.

Chapter 2
The Origins of the Vernacular Society 1946–1956

2.1 INTRODUCTION: THE ST. JEROME SOCIETY

In 1945, German liturgical pioneer Hans Anscar Reinhold of Sunnyside, Washington, formed a small network of five lay Catholics from different parts of the United States to explore the possibilities of promoting the vernacular cause: T.C.P. Vermiyle of Redding Ridge, Connecticut; Walter Troy of New York; R. B. Heywood, a student at the University of Chicago; James Carey of Chicago; and John Kyne Granfield of Cambridge, Massachusetts. Together, the group contributed their resources (money, time, and expertise) to launching what would become the St. Jerome Society (later Vernacular Society) in the United States and to increasing membership to support their cause.

During the Liturgical Week held at the Shirley-Savoy Hotel in Denver, Colorado, from the fourteenth to the seventeenth of October 1946, Reinhold's network gathered together, joined by some of the key players within the liturgical movement: Godfrey Diekmann, o.s.b., Martin Hellriegel, Reynold Hillenbrand, Joseph Morrison, Bernard Laukemper, John K. Ross-Duggan, Gerald Ellard, s.j., and Michael Mathis, c.s.c., to name a few.[1] Prior to the Denver meeting, Reinhold's collaborators expressed frustration at his lack of organization despite his good ideas and their doubts that their cause would have much success under his leadership. Nonetheless, since the idea of a society to promote the vernacular came from Reinhold himself, he was unanimously elected the first president.

Two weeks after the Denver liturgical conference, the newly formed St. Jerome Society met on the twenty-ninth of October 1946 in Boston. The meeting was chaired by Boston liturgical pioneer Thomas Carroll, and Harvard law student John Kyne Granfield was elected as secretary. Seventeen new members were enrolled, bringing the total number of members to twenty-seven. Granfield was determined to increase membership and doubled the number from twenty-seven to fifty-five in the first year. Moreover, he began work on producing a "Vernacular Bulletin," which would further promote the cause. As with the liturgical movement itself, the vernacular cause drew a very mixed group of lay Catholics into its ranks. Granfield wrote: "I have graduated from Harvard Law School and taken the State Bar Examination, so that I now can devote myself wholeheartedly to the vernacular group."[2] Granfield's "wholehearted devotion," however, was short-lived. Within several months of his letter to Reinhold, he was enrolled in a seminary and no longer available to serve as secretary. Prior to his departure, however, he managed to produce one issue of his "Vernacular Bulletin."

In that bulletin, Granfield described the Society's goal as twofold: (1) to arrive at a fuller understanding of the Church's liturgy so as to foster better participation and (2) to study possible uses of the vernacular in liturgy so as to realize the goal of full liturgical participation. He then raised some foundational questions: What are the advantages and disadvantages of liturgical language as it now stands? How much vernacular is now permissible? How much vernacular should eventually be incorporated? What should be the prioritized order for such change to take place? As for those who opposed the vernacular, he suggested that their position should also be well considered and studied by his coworkers in the St. Jerome Society: What was their position and why? What were both the positive and negative aspects of their position? What methods of persuasion could be used to win them over to the vernacular? Finally, Granfield suggested that the goals of the Society could be carried out through research and study groups; lectures, articles and books; and translations themselves. Regarding translations, he asked: "What diction and style shall be used? How modern and colloquial shall they be? Shall an academy pass on the translations from time to time?" Interestingly, he was strong in calling for a separation between the Liturgical Conference and the St. Jerome Society:

"We must not confuse the two. We must, if we wish to succeed, stick within our boundaries. This distinction has been insisted upon by those who worked for the founding of this organization. To take an obvious example, they emphatically desire that the word 'liturgy' be left out of the Society's title, for they realize that such a word would becloud our real purpose."[3]

Put simply, unlike the Liturgical Conference which saw its task as reviving the pristine liturgical spirit of full and active participation within the mainstream of American Church life, the Vernacular Society was much more of a nonconformist lobbying group with the task of exerting pressure on Church authorities to move toward greater use of the vernacular. Thus, from the beginning, one notices a clear difference in approach: the Liturgical Conference working within a diplomatic and structured manner and the Vernacular Society as a more confrontative grassroots organization lobbying for change. This is not to suggest that members of the Liturgical Conference did not also lobby for change; they did, but in a much less aggressive way. This separation would grow as the vernacular issue was increasingly seen as divisive and its advocates as problematic.

Soon after Granfield's departure for the seminary in the autumn of 1947, Reinhold had lunch in Chicago with John K. Ross-Duggan (+1967) who would become a pivotal and colorful member of the Vernacular Society. Over lunch at the Lake Shore Club where Ross-Duggan had been residing, Reinhold, having already been turned down by four others, persuaded him to accept the position of "temporary secretary" which "The Colonel," as he was called, accepted. Reinhold then communicated the news to the entire Society:

"Since it would be inopportune for a me as a priest to hold a position in the Society I do not assume any official position except that of requesting instructions from our members. As I have no secretarial facilities in my place, I have asked Mr. J. K. Ross-Duggan, a member in good standing, for the time being to carry out the work of our secretary through his office, until we elect officers. He has kindly accepted the task. . . . I hope that we will soon equal our English brother organization in output of work."[4]

Reinhold might have considered it "inopportune" that a priest hold any office in such a Society, but he considered it quite "opportune" to continue writing strongly in favor of the vernacular in such journals as *Orate Fratres*! In commenting on an article which appeared in the French review *Le Maison-Dieu*, he challenged those who were rigid in their retention of Latin as the only suitable liturgical language: "One can make Latin a fetish and Latinity an idol, as has been done by Maurras in France, Belloc in England, and—Mussolini in Italy."[5] Reinhold's direct writing style brought about numerous "Letters to the Editor" criticizing the reformer's plea. The following example is typical:

"I have never heard of any vernacular-advocates being persecuted. It is they who want to 'persecute' the rest of us—to condemn us to being read aloud to all through Mass. . . . I am quite sure the majority would always be against the vernacular Mass. In theory it sounds well perhaps; and in a small intimate church with a pleasant-voiced priest with the right feeling for drama, it would go well for certain temperaments. But with the average priest, with his average voice and accent and mannerisms, shouting at the top of his voice the English words long threadbare with familiarity, determined to be audible (else why the vernacular at all?)—no, the prospect is unendurable. H.A.R. has a very active mind: good luck to him. But most people have not. They go to Mass for rest and refreshment, they want to use their hearts, not their minds. And so the Church has wisely soft-pedaled the instructional aspect. The present predicament of the Church of England is sufficient answer to the advocates of the vernacular."[6]

Predictably, H.A.R. responded, informing the writer that those who go to church for "rest and refreshment," completely miss the point.[7]

Ross-Duggan wasted no time in attending to his responsibilities as the Society's secretary. Spurred on by the recently promulgated papal encyclical *Mediator Dei*,[8] popularly called the "*magna carta* of the liturgical movement," he quickly began organizing what would become an annual meeting:

"I shall get out some publicity and an invitation to a meeting to be held during the first six months of 1948. It is important to have a much broader base than that on which the Society has previously operated. Meanwhile, by personal letters, word of mouth and the efforts of friends of the movement, the ground must be prepared for a good meeting. The previous technique of appointing somebody as secretary and then badgering him into accomplishing the impossible must be avoided. A solid foundation is essential to any progress. All members and friends will be asked to pray earnestly for the accomplishment of God's will in the Society. Every effort must be made to enlist the kindly interest of as many of the bishops as possible."[9]

2.2 THE VERNACULAR SOCIETY IS BORN

On the twenty-fifth of July 1948, seventeen members of the St. Jerome Society gathered together at the St. Benet's Bookshop in Chicago for what would be a historic meeting. Among other items on the agenda for the meeting chaired by Reynold Hillenbrand was the election of new officers. When H. A. Reinhold withdrew his name from the ballot arguing against his nomination this time because of writing commitments for *Commonweal* and *Orate Fratres*, Joseph Morrison, rector of Holy Name Cathedral, Chicago, where the first Liturgical Week in 1940 had taken place, was elected president, Ross-Duggan was elected secretary, and Rosemary Fitzpatrick, assistant secretary. Among other resolutions approved by those present was that the name of the Society would be changed to "the Vernacular Society"; that the president would appoint a committee of three to prepare a draft constitution; that the secretary would be requested to write to Samuel Gosling, secretary of the English Liturgy Society, for a copy of its constitution; that a newsletter would be issued occasionally and that H. A. Reinhold would oversee its publication; and that the official address of The Vernacular Society would be 39 East Congress Street, Chicago, 5, Illinois: the St. Benet's Bookshop.[10]

The Society met again several weeks later on the third of August 1948, during the annual Liturgical Week. At this meeting, the Society's constituency approved the proposed "Statement of Aims":

"In 'Mediator Dei,' [no. 60] Pius XII says: 'The use of the mother tongue in connection with several of the rites may be of much advantage to the people. But the Apostolic See alone is empowered to grant this permission.' This surely means that the matter of the use of the mother tongue in Catholic rites is a proper subject for discussion. In the words of the English Liturgy Society, the subject naturally falls under three headings:

"1. 'The rites of Baptism, Churching, Marriage, Visitation of the Sick, Reception of Converts, the administration of the last Sacraments, and Funerals, together with the Blessings contained in the *Rituale*. We feel that all these rites, as they have a special individual-personal significance, would immeasurably deepen and strengthen the spiritual life of the participants if the latter understood them better and were able to take their part in them easily and naturally. The Blessings, too, now largely neglected, would be much more sought after if the laity were more conversant with their meaning and use.'

"2. 'Vespers and Compline, to which may be added the liturgical blessings of candles, ashes and palms, together with an extension of the vernacular prayers and hymns now allowed at the service of Benediction.'

"3. 'The Mass. The Mass obviously stands in a category by itself for reasons that we need not enter into here. But even with regard to the

Mass it is clear that the mind of the Church is open to suggestions for the better understanding of the liturgy by the faithful, as shown by the movement for the Dialogue Mass.'

"Membership of the Society will be confined to Catholics who will admit of active promotion as well as general support, i.e.:

"a) Promoters, who will be expected to take an active part in conducting the Society and furthering its aims by research work, by writing articles, giving lectures, arranging study circles.

"b) Supporters, who are unable to take any active part beyond spreading the knowledge of its existence, purpose, and activities.

"Applications for membership ($1 per year) and all correspondence should be addressed to The Secretary, The Vernacular Society, 39 East Congress Street, Chicago, 5, Ill.

"At the outset, it is desired to emphasize the need for prayer. Priest members are invited to include the Society, in some general way, in their memento of the living in their Mass and to say Terce for its success. It is suggested to lay members that they make a remembrance at Mass and say a prayer to the Holy Ghost for the same intention."[11]

Anticipating critical reactions to the founding of such a Society, James Mallahan wrote a short article for *The Harvester* as an attempt to explain the importance of vernacular in the liturgy:

"The question of language in the liturgy is not essentially a matter of attracting Protestants or of beautifying our worship aesthetically; it is a matter which concerns the average Sunday Catholic, the weak Catholic, the lapsed Catholic, the Catholic who stands dumbly by listening to the leaden accents of Latin at the graveside where he has a right to understand the consoling words of joy and hope which Holy Mother Church holds out to him. It concerns the youthful bride and groom who need the encouraging prayers of the ritual to strengthen them against the pitfalls of married life, and it concerns the good mothers who bring their babies to be baptized and want to have the life of Christ in the souls of their children made real for them. It concerns the sick and the dying who listen so eagerly for comfort and encouragement as they prepare to face their God. It is these ordinary people in a world with little to remind them of God who are the living arguments for the vernacular. . . . "[12]

The Vernacular Society of Great Britain, for its part, was quick to voice its support and enthusiasm for the founding of the Vernacular Society in the United States.[13] In a letter written on the twentieth of December 1948, H. Francis Davis, vice-rector of Oscott Seminary, Birmingham, and president of the British Vernacular Society, wrote to Joseph Morrison, the newly elected president of the U.S. Vernacular Society:

"I was very interested to receive a report of the meeting of your VERNACULAR SOCIETY, and to hear that you had been elected President. . . . It is encouraging to us to hear that the movement is making progress in America. I suppose no section of the Church is more influential today than yours; and support from America will do more than anything else to further our interests.

"It always surprises me that the vernacular movement has received so little support in the English-speaking countries, compared with France and Germany. One would have thought that we would have been more eager. But for some reason we seem to be the most conservative section of the Church. I was in Germany during the summer, and I saw how much the people appreciate their vernacular practices."[14]

2.1.1 The Early Years of the Vernacular Society

Unable to attend the 1949 annual meeting on the eighth of August during the Liturgical Week in St. Louis because of his departure for Rome to lobby on behalf of the vernacular and participate in the 1950 Holy Year, Ross-Duggan sent his "Secretary's Report" read by a delegate. There he announced a total of 153 paid members (both clergy and laity) and that the total savings with the Continental Illinois Bank amounted to $291.15. He reported that it had been a year of "quiet work, prayer, and interest on the part of all members," and that another good year was anticipated with even greater numbers and support. The death of founding member and German liturgical pioneer Bernard Laukemper was announced, as was the absence of Reynold Hillenbrand due to illness. British liturgical leaders Clifford Howell, s.j., and Donald Attwater addressed the Society at their St. Louis meeting. Howell gave practical examples of vernacular usage in parish liturgies while Attwater spoke on "The many vernacular liturgies current in the Church and the need to stem Communism by a more intensive worship." Reinhold urged the collecting of the best articles on the history of and need for vernacular in the liturgy while Morrison encouraged new ideas and greater membership.[15]

The 1950 Annual Meeting was held on Wednesday, the twenty-third of August, at Conception Abbey, Conception, Missouri, and chaired by Joseph Morrison. Fifty-three members attended including The Colonel, freshly back from his European sojourn. Ross-Duggan reported a membership of 291 (four bishops among them) and $305.13 in the bank. Both in Europe and at home, he had distributed materials on the vernacular (along with a membership form) to over 2,000 individuals, some of whom were more receptive than others. The first of his "Notes on a European Trip" was also mimeographed and distributed widely, although the "Notes" often had more to do with The Colonel than they did with the vernacular!

During his visit to Rome, the secretary recounted how he had "rung all the doorbells" in the Vatican Congregations, particularly the Sacred Congregation of Rites where he was kindly received by Msgr. Enrico Dante, *sostituto* for the Congregation. While indicating opposition to a wholesale change in the liturgy from Latin to the vernacular, Dante said that such things as use of the vernacular in the Ritual, in the public parts of the dialog, and in sung Masses was a matter to be discussed by each local hierarchy. Dante affirmed that he anticipated little opposition in Rome to an English Ritual for the United States, along the lines of the German and French Rituals. And he regarded the matter of congregational participation as a very important one for the active consideration of the bishops.[16]

In the course of the Society's annual meeting, President Joseph Morrison outlined plans of action and promotion for the following year aimed at interesting the hierarchy in approving an English Ritual for submission to the Holy See and also toward increasing membership in the Society. Both the president and secretary were reelected for another term of office.[17]

One month later, Bishop Edwin O'Hara of Kansas City voiced his own support for the efforts of the vernacularists and in a letter to President Joseph Morrison, even enrolled himself as a member of the Society. Most significantly, he invited the Vernacular Society's participation at a National Catechetical Congress which had been planned for the following year:

"There is to be a National Catechetical Congress in Chicago in the first week of November 1951. We hope that the Liturgical Society [Conference?] will provide discussion of matters in the field appropriate to a religious instruction Congress. It seems to me that also the Vernacular Society could properly have a sectional meeting that would keep the Confraternity informed. . . . I am pleased to invite the Vernacular Society to hold at least a sectional meeting at that time."[18]

The annual meetings were times of support for vernacularists, offering a venue for the sharing of ideas, reports of vernacular successes and failures, updating on vernacular projects both nationally and internationally, and the organization of lobbying efforts. Those meetings usually took place conveniently during the annual Liturgical Weeks since most Vernacular Society members were also members of the Liturgical Conference. This relationship between the two organizations would grow increasingly tense in subsequent years. Indeed, when planning the 1955 annual meeting to be held during the Liturgical Week, Vernacular Society president Joseph Morrison chose to request permission to meet from the bishop of Worcester, John Wright, rather than from the Liturgical Conference itself.[19]

2.3 MEMBERSHIP

Growth in the Vernacular Society was constant, from 13 members at the first meeting of the St. Jerome Society in 1946 to a total of 2,753 only seven years later, in 1953. The year 1951 was an important one liturgically for the universal Church in the restoration of the Easter Vigil but also for the Vernacular Society in that it registered significant growth and recognition in American Church circles. Promotional efforts paid off as membership reached 837, including 6 bishops,[20] 12 abbeys, 6 diocesan chancellors, 7 vicars-general, 54 religious organizations, 15 sisters, 4 brothers, 149 pastors and 167 parochial vicars, 90 seminarians, and over 300 laypeople. More than 100 new members were enrolled at the 1951 annual meeting alone. Membership hailed from Canada, England, India, Italy, Puerto Rico, Mexico, Cuba, Jamaica, New Zealand, and Australia. And who were the lay members of the Society? Ross-Duggan described them in the Vernacular Society's "Bulletin":

"Laity—judges, members of state legislatures, fellows at Harvard, professors at Georgetown, Princeton, St. John's—Catholic University,

Duquesne, etc., doctors, lawyers, heads of big corporations as well as little business, editors, writers, students, mothers, wives, apostolic men and women, artisans, farmers, and plain ordinary guys like most of us."[21]

Moreover, another 20,000 individuals received mailings from the Vernacular Society in that year, many of whom responded with their support for the cause. In the Vernacular Society's "Bulletin" of 1952, it was reported that membership had reached 2,000 with about 25 percent who failed to pay their dues. The 1953 census of 2,753 included 43 bishops, including one from Chile and one from South Africa. Ross-Duggan wrote:

"I could say 3,000 if a few delinquent members would respond to our appeals. . . . We are a working crew and prefer to carry no passengers. The one thing I would like to emphasize is that the Vernacular Society is not a paper organization, but it is composed of active and apostolic members who pray and actively promote the aims and well-being of the Society."[22]

Indeed, in the one month of August 1953, 311 new members were added to the ranks alone. Following a talk given by British liturgist Clifford Howell, s.j., at the St. Benet's Library/Bookshop, Chicago, 55 new members were added; his subsequent lecture in Buffalo, New York, garnered another 23 members.[23]

By the time we arrive at 1955 with at least one major vernacular victory in the newly approved Ritual, the Society's membership roster and international mailing list reads like a Who's Who in Theology and Liturgy, including such names as Yves Congar, o.p.; Karl Rahner, s.j.; Herman Schmidt, s.j.; Dom Verheul, o.s.b.; Josef Jungmann, s.j.; Canon A. G. Martimort; A. Chavasse; Johannes Hofinger, s.j.; Louis Bouyer; Pierre-Marie Gy, o.p.; Theodor Klauser; Nina Polcyn; A.-M. Roguet, o.p.; and Johannes Wagner. One year later, the mailing list included such notables as Ade Bethune; Bishop Fulton Sheen; Avery [later Cardinal] Dulles, s.j.; Catherine de Hueck Doherty; Episcopal Bishop James A. Pike; Msgr. Frederick R. McManus; Gerard Sloyan; George Schuster; and Lancelot Sheppard.[24]

Despite the number of eminent clerics named in the previous paragraph, the movement remained dominated by lay people. Indeed, one of the concerns on the part of Vernacular Society members was that the Church had lost many of the working class members, both in maintaining "an outworn class structure" and also in perpetuating a liturgical language accessible only to the elite:

"In the matter of vested interest, the bureaucracy of the church is intrigued with the outward uniformity and ease of operation flowing from an all-over use of Latin in every phrase of church government and official worship. Thus the means is mistaken for the end which is the salvation of souls and not necessarily a smooth-running bureaucracy."[25]

Some Society members also played major roles in such organizations as the Christian Family Movement (CFM) and Catholic Action, while members of social movements such as Friendship House volunteered their services to help with organizational details, e.g., the mailing list. Total number of members reached 3,500 by 1955.

2.3.1 *The Role of Colonel John Kimbell Ross-Duggan*
The centrality of John Kimbell Ross-Duggan to the Vernacular movement cannot be overestimated. He was born in Scotland in 1888, and at the age of two, the family moved to Wellington, New Zealand, where he remained until completing university. With the onset of World War I, he joined the British Army as a private and fought from Messines to Flanders. It was during his military service that "the Colonel" had come into contact with Jesuit liturgist C. C. Martindale at Oxford in the academic year 1917–18. But his interest in English liturgy dates back even further—to his childhood days (1892–1904) in Wellington and to an English diocesan priest, Fr. Dawson, who had taught the children (with the approval of the archbishop) a complete set of English hymns related to the different parts of the Mass.[26] There, the seeds were sown for his later liturgical encounters in the United Kingdom.

Ross-Duggan maintained those liturgical contacts even after his arrival in the United States in 1919, settling first with an uncle in San Francisco before moving on to New York. In 1942 he became a member of the English Liturgy Society and three years later, in 1945, when the English Society decided to change its name to the Vernacular Society of Great Britain, was encouraged by its secretary, Samuel Joseph Gosling, to form a similar vernacular group in the U.S.A. Thus, when Reinhold asked Ross-Duggan to replace Granfield as secretary of the St. Jerome Society and to reorganize the St. Jerome Society with headquarters in Chicago, he willingly accepted. In fact, he accepted so willingly, that within two years (in 1949) he left his full-time job as publisher of the Chicago-based periodical *Quick Frozen Foods* to devote all his time to the vernacular cause. John K. Ross-Duggan was a networker, evidenced by his extensive correspondence from his European trips. His trip to the Lugano Liturgical Conference held from the twelfth to the eighteenth of September 1953 bears testimony to this. Rather than traveling directly to Lugano, he went to London, where he met with "his old friend," Canon Ronald Pilkington, chairman of the Vernacular Society of Great Britain. There, he was encouraged by "the unanimity of spirit, interest and action" between the two Vernacular societies. In Oxford, he met Christopher Dawson with whom he had good discussions on the vernacular and its role in liturgical renewal. In Lugano, he noted: "There was every evidence that the Holy Father, the Sacred Congregation of Rites and all higher authorities were very seriously interested in our deliberations."[27]

From Lugano, the Colonel traveled on to Bologna, where he met with Cardinal Giacomo Lercaro, the archbishop, who was a great supporter of the liturgical renewal and would later be one of the key players in Vatican II. In Rome, Ross-Duggan made his usual visits promoting the vernacular and getting new members for the Society: "As ever, I was graciously received wherever I went in Rome. I made calls at the Congregations where I was thanked—as on numerous other occasions—for sending copies of *Amen*."

It must also be noted, however, that the Colonel did not limit his visits and contacts to Vatican Congregations and members of the Episcopate. He was famous for calling at the North American College (NAC) soon after his regular arrivals in Rome, inviting open-minded seminarians over to his hotel in the evenings for discussion on the vernacular. Thus, given his association with the NAC, it was not surprising that after the Lugano Conference during his Roman sojourn, the Colonel managed to obtain a ticket for the papal blessing of the new North American College on the *Gianicolo*, "so there was at least one layman present from the United States."[28] More often than not, those vernacular "discussions" at the NAC were invitations to come and listen to "the Colonel" sermonize on the importance of English in the liturgy and gradually infiltrate some vernacularists into the seminary. Ross-Duggan was well aware that the brightest and best U.S. seminarians were sent to NAC with most of them taking their degrees at the Pontifical Gregorian University. The NAC was the training center for the American episcopate of the future; thus, careful strategic planning at such an early stage in clerical formation could bring about greater vernacular results when those seminarians were later given greater responsibility for the leadership of the U.S. Church. Like any other arranged meeting, the Colonel needed a "contact" who would assist him in granting access to the seminarians. The Colonel wrote to one pro-vernacular priest who knew the seminarians at the NAC, asking for the names of one or two of his vernacular "spies" whom he might call upon to organize a meeting. The priest responded:

"Spy no. 1 is a man who goes by the name of Steve Nolan and you'll find him at the old hangout up on the hill (North Amer. College). Knock three times and ask for Joe. I don't know whether I'm acting in a very priestly fashion exposing the young and innocent to your obstreperous personality, but . . . I suppose he'll be able to acquit himself quite well."[29]

From Rome, Ross-Duggan traveled to Paris where he met with French Dominicans Yves Congar and Pierre-Marie Gy at *Le Saulchoir*. He also met with Mr. Dubois-Dumee, editor of the Catholic French periodical *L'Actualité*, pleased to note that the editor had given coverage to the U.S. Vernacular Society in a recent issue. He returned to England before the trip home to the States, where he held meetings with Jesuit liturgist C. C. Martindale, Lancelot Sheppard, the officers of the Vernacular Society of Great Britain, editors of *The Tablet* and *The Catholic Herald*, Abbot Butler and the Benedictines of Downside Abbey—among them, Dom Gregory Murray.[30]

The Colonel returned to Rome the following year to attend the canonization of Pius X, paying his usual respects to the archbishop of Bologna, Cardinal Giacomo Lercaro, and using the time in Rome to meet with prefect of the Congregation of Sacred Rites, Cardinal Gaetano Cicognani, as well as other officials of that Congregation, e.g., Msgr. Enrico Dante and the Franciscan Ferdinand Antonelli. After the Roman canonization he traveled to France to participate in the liturgical congress organized at Versailles for French clergy. From Versailles, he went to Belgium for the Fourth International Liturgical Congress held at the Benedictine Abbey of Mont César near Louvain, later reporting on both events in the Vernacular Society's periodical *Amen*.

The leadership qualities of the Colonel cannot be denied. Despite his many contributions and his extraordinary capacity for networking both within the States and in Europe, he could also be quite stubborn and aggressive in his approach as is evidenced in much of the correspondence found in the Vernacular Society archives. Indeed, one wonders what might have become of the Vernacular Society had the Colonel been equally charismatic but more of a diplomat. There are numerous references to Ross-Duggan's "antics" and his tendency to treat all other Vernacular Society officers as his subordinates.

We know precious little about the Colonel's personal life. He married Catherine Thomas in 1920 of Hillsborough, North Carolina, just a year after his arrival in the States, but we hear virtually nothing about his wife afterwards. His European trips were almost always made alone, and there are no extant letters written to his wife during his long absences. They presumably separated at some point; his obituary in 1967 notes that she survived him in death. He remained in closer contact with his two children: a daughter, Remie (later married to Kenneth Fenske), in Rockaway, New York, and a son, Dr. John K. Ross-Duggan II, in Long Beach, California. Indeed, he seemed to spend a good deal of his time staying either with his son in California or his daughter in New York; the remainder of his time was largely spent "on the road" or at a hotel in Delray Beach, Florida. While working for Westinghouse and the American Steel Export Company, he traveled in India, China, and Japan. In 1930 he went to Canada where he worked for the McLean Publishing Company, being named its manager for Great Britain in 1933. He returned to Hillsborough in 1937 where he took a position in the stamp business and assisted in the restoration of the mansion that had housed Gen. Joseph Eggleston Johnson and Gen. Wade Hampton, and headquartered the Confederate Army. In 1940 he became a U.S. citizen and moved to Chicago where he joined *Time Inc.*, residing at the Lake Shore Club during that time. In 1944, he established Quick Frozen Foods where he remained until he became a full-time promoter of the vernacular in 1949.

2.4 THE VERNACULAR SOCIETY GOES INTERNATIONAL: THE LUGANO CONFERENCE

With the announcement of an international liturgical meeting called for Lugano, Switzerland, in 1953, Vernacular Society leaders geared their efforts both toward representation at the meeting and the chance to network with other vernacular activists in promoting the cause. In a letter to Reynold Hillenbrand, Ross-Duggan wrote:

"I believe I told you of my good interview with Cardinal Ottaviani . . . relative to the liturgy, use of the vernacular and lay participation. Forthwith, he invited me to the participated outside children's Mass in the Oratory of St. Peter. Do you sense the tremendous implication of Cardinal Ottaviani's request to Dr. Johannes Wagner that many laymen be invited to Lugano!

"I do hope that the USA has a representation *from* the mainland at Lugano. It is so very unsatisfactory when some (unwilling) person is pressed into service from the American colony in Rome or elsewhere. God willing, I will attend; and I hope you, too, and others.

"What further names should I suggest to Dr. Wagner for invitations? By all means, such men as Frs. Godfrey Diekmann, Thos J. Carroll, Shawn Sheehan, William Busch, Paul Bussard, Michael Ducey, Louis Putz, et al. Such laymen as Patrick Crowley, Willis Nutting, John Cort, Julian Pleasants, John Julian Ryan, John J. O'Connor and who else? Very few can go, but the inviting will stimulate interest at both ends and broaden knowledge of affairs liturgical. I thought also of suggesting that invitations be sent to our 34 bishop-members of the Vernacular Society, particularly Bishop Edwin O'Hara."[31]

Hillenbrand agreed with Ross-Duggan that bishop-members of the Society should especially be invited. Ross-Duggan was eventually delegated by Joseph Morrison to attend the Lugano meeting as representative of the Vernacular Society in the U.S.A.[32] When the Colonel wrote to Monsignor Hillenbrand encouraging his own attendance at the conference, he noted that he intended to "sell some of my books and give some lectures" to raise the money for the trip.[33]

2.5 *AMEN*

The Society's journal *Amen* was founded in 1950 with more than 10,000 copies printed in its first year of publication. The bulletin began as a mimeographed newsletter and grew into a periodical printed professionally two or three times each year. The byline of the magazine read: "How can one who holds the place of the layman say the 'Amen' to thy thanksgiving, since he does not know what thou art saying. (1 Cor 14:16)." As the magazine expanded its format, it went beyond simple reporting of membership activities to include articles on the progress of the liturgical movement in general, and the vernacular cause, in particular. Sympathetic magazines like *Commonweal* lent their support:

"A new publication, AMEN, a journal of study and discussion regarding the use of the vernacular in the liturgy and the rituale for parish churches (P.O. Box 1991, Delray Beach, Florida) carries 'A Plea to Our Hierarchy for Some English in the Liturgy,' written by Rt. Rev. Joseph P. Morrison, President of the Vernacular Society."[34]

Each issue of the magazine always set aside space for "Letters to the Editor," many of which came from hospital and military chaplains; pastors of parishes with large African-American constituencies; those who had contact with "borderline Catholics" or non-Catholics; former Anglicans and Lutherans who had recently joined the Catholic Church; farmers and immigrants. One of the first letters to appear was written by none other than pioneer and Vernacular Society founder, H. A. Reinhold:

"Dear Sir, Looking back over the years one cannot help but feel much better. The company the Vernacular Society is keeping looks pretty good. The last bit of odium has happily been removed by the profound and scholarly work of Father Herman Schmidt, s.j. *(Liturgie et Langue Vulgaire)* which appeared in Analecta Gregoriana.

"It would be a good idea now to become more aggressive especially among the clergy and religious, reassuring the latter in particular that we do not want to destroy what is dear to the hearts of all monks . . . but that all we are thinking of is where the great masses of lay people are concerned in parishes, schools, camps, and so forth . . . .

"As long as we need translations, missals are good, necessary, and to be multiplied. But when the blessed day arrives on which the gospel is chanted in English distinctly, worthily and with solemnity, or when for an Introit we sing a hymn, then the people are welded together in a common experience which would be destroyed by the reading of books. This day may be far off, much farther than we expect, but it seems closer than I hoped to see it when with the courage of despair I made my first pleas for the mother tongue in the liturgy of America.

"The greatest obstacle is not the Holy See, nor the Dogma professors, nor the Bishops, nor the tradition of the Church, nor dogma itself; it is

Bishop Fulton J. Sheen celebrates vernacular Mass (1955) at Pennsylvania shrine.

Col. Ross-Duggan, Fr. Michael Mathis, Fr. H. A. Reinhold, Fr. Godfrey Diekmann, o.s.b.; 1953 Liturgical Congress (Lugano, Switzerland).

in the ones who should welcome the blessing. . . . This becomes clear when it is reported that the 'older generation' instead of rejoicing over the restored Paschal Vigil . . . announced 'misgivings.' I am 'older generation.' They can't be much older or they would not be around. But I can hardly see how one can be so old as not to see the enormous possibilities opening up for our pastoral work, the return to trueness instead of performance in liturgy—in short, to all those answers that respond to the basic longing of our age as exposed in Yves Congar's magnum opus on the true and false reform of the Church (Paris: Cerf, 1950).

"I am quite sure that the same will happen the day after the American hierarchy solemnly announces the publication of an 'English Proper of the Roman Missal including those parts of the ordinary sung for or by the congregation in parish churches.' There will, in all the rejoicing, be some very worried elders, from 19 to 90, who will have misgivings and will wish to be left alone with their private prayers at mass, because 'all that singing really disturbs them and reminds them of Protestantism.' You just watch.

"Thus we should face realities and realize that besides reason, feelings are involved, stubborn, irrational ones. We need more discussion on the level of the people; in classrooms; in meetings; in diocesan papers; at deanery conferences and clergy conveniats. Those who do not want to pray for victory in this field, can still pray for light."[35]

The vernacular debate continued in subsequent issues of *Amen*, particularly in a lively exchange of letters between the cultural historian Christopher Dawson of Oxford, England (the first to hold the Chauncey Stillman Chair at Harvard), who argued for the continuation of Latin since it was the "universal giant" in Western Christendom, and vernacularists who opposed his views. One member of the Vernacular Society responded:

"The real question is whether Latin shall be allowed to become a *tyrant*, crushing the spiritual life out of the people who do not understand it and probably never will. In addition to our English-speaking peoples, there are the Chinese, Indians, Arabs, the natives of Africa, Oceania, in fact, every mission country, to whom Latin is something foreign; and, in some, is regarded as an instrument of imperialism.

There are many sad pages in past Christian history—the Crusades, the Portuguese in India, the French, Germans, and Italians also, where Latin—*merely as Latin*—has disrupted Catholic life.

"If I recollect correctly, Mr. Dawson in his book *Understanding Europe*, as also Mr. Josef Pieper in *Leisure, The Basis of Culture*, emphasize the necessity of worship of God as the principal means of restoring Western Europe to Christendom. May I ask Mr. Dawson how he suggests that this can be done in an unknown language?"[36]

Dawson responded by speaking of Latin as the "common liturgical language" and as "a sign of the Church's mission to reverse the curse of Babel and to create a bond of unity between the peoples." He continued:

"The introduction of an indefinite number of vernacular liturgies . . . would destroy this bond and would bring nationalism and nationalist rivalries into the sanctuary. And this is no small evil as anyone who knows anything of the strong feelings aroused by the language question in bilingual countries such as Czecho-Slovakia, Catalonia, Belgium, and Ireland must realize."[37]

Russell Young of Groton, Massachusetts responded:

"History is called into court to prove that a 'true religious unity without a common language' is impossible. Is this indeed the lesson of history? Presuming that the Church has enjoyed true religious unity throughout most of twenty centuries, the following queries come to mind: Has there ever been a common language for the liturgies and/or theology in a) the universal Church or b) the Western Church? Do not the facts include notable exceptions in the West?

"May I refer to what can only be Mr. Dawson's opinion namely, 'Without this (common language) the forces of nationalism and racialism became too strong for unity.' The principle involved is basic and exceedingly important, namely, the concept of the Mystical Body as a continuation of the Incarnate Christ. The Holy Father has said that the Church is neither Greek nor Slav, but Catholic. So that one might reasonably expect the Church in India to have a quite different garb from the Church in New York.

"Does this principle of the Church's incarnation in a multiplicity of cultures really jeopardize her unity; or is the principle wrong? Would it be better to Latinize the World?

"Mr. Dawson also argues that 'the existence of a common liturgical language . . . is a sign of the Church's mission to reverse the curse of Babel and to create a bond of unity between the peoples.' Where can this theory be found in Catholic tradition? Do all students of Catholic Oriental churches study theology in Latin? Will Latin be imposed on the Orthodox church if they return to unity (The Pope says not); or will the west re-adopt 'Greek' as a common language?"[38]

A final response to Christopher Dawson came from a sister who spoke from her experience of working with marginal Catholics:

"They (if they come to church at all) are dead tired from the daily struggle to make a livelihood; the pace of our times is most demanding, harassing. When the working people come to church, they are not ready for complicated mental exercises. Moreover, a quick hurried leafing through an English-Latin book, trying to keep up with a priest, does not fill their innermost needs.

"How often in my long years of labor among the 'border-line Catholics' have I not met people who, with every bit of good will, have attended our services and then have turned away in discouragement saying, 'I don't know what's going on.' . . . If I go to a Protestant church, there I gain something, even if much is missing of what I like in the Catholic Church.

"Frequently in explaining our services to border-line Catholics, it happened that so-called 'fervent Catholics,' practising Catholics, were listening in. Their questions and remarks showed an abysmal ignorance about the Mass. Our Catholic people bring such great sacrifices for their faith! Are they not deserving of the opportunity to grasp our treasures, to benefit by them?"[39]

Articles and "Letters to the Editor" found in *Amen* not only argued in favor of the vernacular but debated and discussed the type of English to be employed in the liturgy. This debate continues today as liturgical scholars argue in favor of the principle of "dynamic equivalence," where translators seek the nearest dynamic equivalent to the *editio typica* in a poetic English that speaks to the contemporary Church. Support for the principle of "dynamic equivalence" was significant immediately after the council represented in the official Vatican document on translations, *Comme le prévoit*, but is now opposed by those who prefer a literal translation from Latin to English, regardless of how the text reads or comes across, evidenced in the recent Instruction *Liturgiam Authenticam* issued by the Congregation for Divine Worship.[40]

It is interesting to note that even before a conciliar shift to the vernacular, there was a realization that liturgical texts prayed in English meant something more than a simple translation from Latin to English or the mere recitation of words. One of the earliest demonstrations of this discussion came over the usage of "Thou" or "You" when addressing God in worship. In 1952, former *Commonweal* editor John Cort wrote his opinion on the matter:

"I would like to cast one small vote for 'You.' If we are going to have some of the Sacraments in English, why not go all the way and put them into the actual English that they themselves use when they are speaking to God?

"I understand the Quakers sometimes address each other as 'Thou' and 'Thee.' It has a charming sound, but there is no question that it is not popular English. It has not been for several hundred years.

"When a man faces God directly and prays to Him in the secret fastness of his heart, he does not say 'O God, I beseech thee.' To use such language would make him self-conscious that his prayer would become almost worthless.

"Why therefore, when a man goes into church, must he speak to God with such archaic formality? It seems to me that this is simply another roadblock thrown up in the way of faith which is the same in church, at home, and at work, the Sunday, Monday, Tuesday, and forever. It is a holdover from the day when religion was strictly a Sunday affair.

"I do not suggest that the proponents of 'Thou' have any such design. I realize they are concerned to give God the dignity that is His due. But surely there is nothing undignified about 'You.' And certainly

God is concerned even more to be loved than to be held in awe by His people.

"For these reasons, I hereby petition our Bishops, when and if the Holy Father gives us English, that the English they approve will be the English of the 20th century, not the English of the 17th."[41]

Several years later, an Italian wrote to contradict the theory that the advantage of Latin lies in its universality, recounting his experience of attending Latin Mass in London:

"Latin the same everywhere! I must say, in spite of hearing through loudspeakers, that I could not follow many of the words of the Mass because the inflection and the accent are not the same as those of Italians, which made it hard to recognize what should be perfectly familiar to me. For all I knew it might have been in German or French or any other language with which I am not acquainted.

"It would have been easier for me to follow the service if it had been in English, even with my rather limited knowledge of your tongue. I may say that I know Latin very well, having studied it for years; but, even so, I cannot claim to be able to grasp every Latin sentence in Italian churches. You can imagine how much more difficult it is for the majority of my countrymen who are not in such a fortunate position.

"My conclusion therefore, is that the Vernacular Movement has a sound basis in both our countries."[42]

Amen continued its mission of spreading the vernacular message, despite occasional obstacles or even competition. In one letter, Ross-Duggan claimed that *Worship* "wanted to see *Amen* out of the way" but that since *Worship* refused to give the vernacular journal even a "modicum of publicity" when it was founded, it would have to simply deal with the competition.[43]

2.6 THE LATIN-ENGLISH RITUAL

A major step forward came toward the end of 1951 when the U.S. bishops authorized an episcopal committee to study and prepare a report on a Latin-English Ritual to be submitted to the plenary session of bishops in the following year at their November meeting. Vernacular

Society members were savvy. As a small, unofficial Society with a very large objective, they would need to get under the aegis of a larger authorized organization in order to present their plea to the whole hierarchy of the United States during their annual meeting in Washington. Since Bishop Edwin O'Hara was supportive and had the potential to influence the Episcopal Committee of the Confraternity of Christian Doctrine (CCD), the vernacularists petitioned that Committee during the 1951 CCD Congress in Chicago, asking them to present their request for an English Ritual to the plenary session of U.S. bishops as a concern of the CCD Committee itself; the strategy worked. Bishop O'Hara wrote to Morrison:

"The Episcopal Committee of the Confraternity of Christian Doctrine presented to the Bishops for consideration the use of English in the rites of Baptism, Marriage, Extreme Unction and Funerals. We recommended that a committee be appointed by the Bishops to study the desirability of applying to the Holy Father for permission for this privilege. The majority of the Bishops voted in favor of appointing such a committee. The presiding officer asked the Episcopal Committee of the Confraternity to make the study. Since the request originates with your group we shall expect your assistance in making the study. . . . Would it be convenient for us to fix a time to discuss these matters face to face? Perhaps yourself and Father Ellard could meet with me before the first of the year."[44]

Led by Gerald Ellard, s.j., and Michael Mathis, c.s.c., a commission of liturgists and literary specialists began their work, assisted by an additional sixty-four consultants including five from England, along with representatives from France, Germany, Italy, Canada, Africa, and Australia, to name a few of the countries represented. This mixed commission studied the initial request made by the Vernacular Society, composed English texts, and in 1952 presented a proposed revision of the Ritual in English and Latin. That proposal was well received by the bishops at their meeting in November 1952, but they called for several minor revisions: (1) that use of the term "Thou" be restored as the proper address in reference to the Divine persons; (2) that several of the longer prayers be broken down and divided; and (3) that special care be employed in the translation of Medieval Latin found in certain prayers within the Ritual.[45] The proposed ritual was returned to the commission of experts. The revised version was presented to the bishops and approved unanimously at their Washington meeting in November 1953.

The proposal was then sent by Archbishop Alter, chairman of the National Catholic Welfare Council (NCWC), to the Congregation of Sacred Rites, which ultimately approved the proposed Ritual the following year. The English Ritual was approved by the Congregation of Rites on the third of June 1954 and signed on the seventh. Not surprisingly, Ross-Duggan happened to be in Rome for the festivities, (he had been there for the canonization of Pius X) and wrote immediately to the Society's president, Joseph Morrison:

"Amen, Brother, Amen!!! Alleluia!!! Alleluia!!! Alleluia!!! The Constitution regarding the English Ritual for the United States is to be signed Monday, June 7, with three small amendments. Yesterday, I arranged a meeting with Msgr. Dante and Fr. Antonelli for Bishop O'Hara, Frs. Wilmes, Westhoff, Ehmann, Acerra, Shawn Sheehan with my friend Gunner Kumlien as interpreter. I stayed away to keep the party clean, as I had done my dirty work earlier. Meanwhile I have to step rather gingerly with regard to the vernacular in the scriptural readings and chants of *parish* Masses. We met Archbishop Muench and his Auxiliary (Dworshak) in the courtyard and they joined the party for photos. This afternoon, I have arranged for the above party with Bishop O'Hara to make a call on Cardinal Lercaro who is staying two days with the Assumption Sisters on Viale Romania. I also hope to see an old friend, Father Ettore Cunial, who was pastor of a very liturgical parish where I resided in previous years. He is now Archbishop Cunial, the assistant vice regent of Rome."[46]

In a letter written to Joseph Morrison the following month, Bishop O'Hara noted that the Sacred Congregation of Rites had granted vernacularists almost everything they asked for regarding the use of English in the administration of the sacraments. He then recommended that a telegram be sent to Pope Pius XII from the Vernacular Society's meeting in Milwaukee where the official announcement of the new Ritual was to take place, "thanking him for this privilege."[47]

The following month, on the seventeenth of August during the annual Liturgical Week held in Milwaukee, Archbishop Meyer officially announced the English Ritual and the telegram of gratitude was sent to the Pope. The new Ritual was, of course, seen as a great victory for the Vernacular Society, and this was well celebrated at its annual meeting on Wednesday, the eighteenth of August 1954 in Milwaukee, in the presence of noted liturgists Pierre-Marie Gy, o.p., of France, Johannes Hoffinger, s.j., of the Philippines, and Dr. George Montague of Ireland:

"Now that the English Ritual has been approved for the United States, it is the duty of the Vernacular Society to do its part in activating this splendid concession and reform. It is up to each and every member of the Society to play a part in *popularizing* the new Ritual, to reveal its beautiful meaning and sentiments, to lead parish priests to *use* this apostolic and catechetical instrument and to get our fellow laity to desire it and love it. This should be a No. 1 job for our good members."[48]

There was now fresh hope that the English Ritual would be a first step in wider use of vernacular within Church rites, helping Catholics to better understand what they were celebrating while serving as an instrument of evangelization. In an article entitled "The English Ritual: Is This Only the Beginning?" Theodore Vermilye wrote:

"It has long been evident that the exclusive use of a foreign and dead language in Catholic worship sets up a barrier which lessens our missionary effectiveness in an overwhelmingly non-Catholic land. And we know full well that understanding of the Faith and participation in public worship on the part of Catholics fall far short of what they should be because of the language difficulty."[49]

Other liturgical leaders were quick to voice their own enthusiasm for the newly approved text. Monsignor Martin Hellreigel of St. Louis welcomed the new ritual, saying that greater use of the vernacular in the liturgy will "awaken in our people a deeper understanding and appreciation of those sacred foundations from which flow that divine life which our Blessed Lord promised to pour out in abundance."[50]

Gerald Ellard, s.j., voiced similar sentiments on the issue:

"Almost every Catholic family has a Baptism, a wedding, or a sick call within a year. By means of the new Ritual, they suddenly will discover a wonderfully new and comforting aspect of their religion. We should recall that Latin originally was used for these rites when it was the spoken language of the common people."[51]

As always, the approval of liturgical texts and the issue of "reception" on the local level are two distinct matters, and it was no different regarding the new Ritual. The Vernacular Society made public a list of Midwestern dioceses which gave no approval, those which gave partial approval, and those which gave full approval:

"1. No APPROVAL for any part of the Ritual: Diocese of Owensboro;

"2. PARTIAL APPROVAL: All dioceses of Illinois, sc. Belleville, Chicago, Peoria, Joliet, Rockford, Springfield. In general, the new ritual may be used as it stands, but *all English* is *forbidden* in the following cases:

"a. nuptial blessing given at Mass. (The marriage ceremony itself may be in English as given in the new ritual);

"b. Administration of Communion to the sick, but it is allowable to use the English formula in the Administration of Viaticum (Rubric 7, p. 44; Rubric 16, p. 77);

"c. Imposition of ashes and Blessing of throats;

"d. Funeral Services. *Exception:* Belleville does not forbid use of English as given in the new ritual for funerals.

"3. FULL APPROVAL: All the (arch)dioceses of Indiana, Michigan, Ohio, and two of those in Kentucky s.c. Covington and Louisville. Therefore, in Cincinnati, Cleveland, Columbus, Covington, Detroit, Evansville, Fort Wayne, Grand Rapids, Indianapolis, Lafayette, Lansing, Louisville, Marquette, Saginaw, Steubenville, Toledo, Youngstown. In all these the new ritual may be used just as it stands, WITH THE SLIGHT EXCEPTION OF LOUISVILLE, that as regards prayers after funerals, approval is given to 'such prayers as have the sanction of usage.'

"N.B. In each and every one of the above (arch)dioceses the use of the new ritual is optional, not prescriptive, i.e. the old ritual may also continue to be used."[52]

News of the new English Ritual traveled quickly, as evidenced in a letter from the bishop of Samoa, which expressed gratitude for the new text as "the most valuable of the works I have gathered together in view of producing a Samoan Ritual." As it happened, the bishop of Samoa had just been notified by the apostolic vicar that the Holy See had approved his request to establish a liturgical commission to prepare a Ritual in Samoan. The new English edition would serve both as an inspiration and a model for their own project.[53]

Some members of the laity even wrote to the Pope himself to express their gratitude:

"Your Holiness:

"Our daughter, Ann Catherine, our third child, has just been baptized, in English. She was baptized in Assumption Church, our parish church, a suburb of Minneapolis.

"Father John F. Louis, O.M.I., visited our house after the Baptism. While we sat around the table with cake and coffee, we told him how happy we were that the ceremony was in English, and he told us that it was a great privilege that you recently granted.

"Therefore, we wish to tell you how much we appreciate this great favor. We were happy when our two other children were baptized in Latin. But we could understand this last Baptism. So we will always remember it, and it will help us to better live our Faith.

"It was so intimate, it made us feel at one with the earliest Christians; and the knowledge that you granted this privilege brings us closer to your own person.

"Again, your Holiness, thank you very much."[54]

One priest recounted the experience of one of his first Communion calls in the vernacular; the communicant was a retired army colonel:

"We noticed that he was silently praying right along with us. He took the 'I confess' by himself and in fine stride, his voice firm. He fought for control as we turned to him with the Host upraised while saying: 'Behold the Lamb of God . . . Lord I am not worthy . . .' Tears were trickling down his weather-beaten cheeks as we finished 'May the Body of our Lord Jesus Christ be the guardian of your soul into everlasting life. Amen.'"[55]

Lest the picture appear overly positive and upbeat, the new Ritual also had its critics—even enemies. Indeed, Ross-Duggan expressed concern about a certain group within the English-speaking world who were opposed to the renewal of the Church's liturgy in principle and were determined to have the decision approving use of the English Ritual reversed.[56] Undaunted by the opposition, Ross-Duggan and his colleagues traveled around the United States lecturing on the new ritual with Serra Clubs and other Catholic lay organizations, encouraging its study, and promoting its use. Those lectures were often widely publicized in diocesan newspapers, using the occasion of the visit as an opportunity to interview Ross-Duggan, Morrison, Hillenbrand, Reinhold, or one of the other vernacular activists who happened to the guest speaker.

2.7 STRATEGY AND TACTICS: TENSIONS BETWEEN THE VERNACULARISTS AND THE HIERARCHY

The victory of the Latin-English Ritual had not come easily. Among other things, the Vernacular Society had become increasingly marginalized as a credible voice for reform. This was due, in part, to individuals like Ross-Duggan who was often brash in his tactics and lacking in diplomacy, but it was also due to the very controversial nature of the vernacular issue itself. And the optimism of Vernacular Society officers was often tempered with the realism of those who were less directly involved. As one priest wrote to the secretary: "Well, if you have less than 1,000 priest-members out of a total of 45,000 in the nation, that is sure evidence they don't want the vernacular."[57]

Indeed, when the Society's officers tried to run a promotional add in *The Voice* (the magazine of St. Mary's Seminary, Roland Park, Maryland), they were denied because of the controversial nature of the vernacular issue and criticism the magazine had received in the past for running similar advertisements.[58]

The Liturgical Conference had worked hard at gaining the respect and acceptance of the U.S. hierarchy since its founding in 1940, whereas members of the Vernacular Society continued to be viewed as less acceptable because of their more confrontational stance. Interestingly, when Michael Mathis and Gerald Ellard had been commissioned to work on the English translation of the Ritual *[Collectio Rituum Anglicae Linguae]*, they did so independently of the Vernacular Society, basing their text on the German translation of the Ritual which had been approved on the twenty-first of March 1950. In fact, Mathis and Ellard were concerned that if the project of an English Ritual were too closely identified with the Society, it would mean the project's demise. For Michael Mathis, this problem was brought to the fore when the 1953 Liturgical Week (17–23 August) at Grand Rapids, Michigan, called for the reading of the epistle and gospel in the vernacular. Convinced that this would surely be interpreted as the Vernacular Society's influence on the Liturgical Conference, he withdrew his name from the list of those who endorsed those Liturgical Week resolutions on the twenty-eighth of August 1953.[59]

Mathis was not alone in his concerns. Numerous members of the clergy had anonymous memberships in the Society for fear of being discovered, and this continued even after the approval of the English Ritual. The Society's Chicago-based treasurer commented on this in a letter to Ross-Duggan: "The over-cautiousness of the clergy is, I am afraid, something one has to get to live with, frustrating as it is."[60] Such fear of association with the Vernacular Society is well-demonstrated in an exchange of letters between Bishop Vincent Waters of Raleigh and Joseph Morrison, president of the Vernacular Society. Waters wrote:

"I appreciate your letter of September 21st and your desire to have a picture of me in the next issue of *Amen*. I would ask you as a favor not to publish my picture . . . because as I understand it, the Liturgical Conference and the Vernacular Society . . . are two distinct organizations, and are in no way connected. I have received copies of *Amen* that were sent out to all the Bishops and on the last appeal for funds I sent in a couple of dollars to take care of the mailing expenses but I did not thereby join the Vernacular Society. I think publishing my picture in the issue would give the 3,000 readers the idea that I was a member and agreeing to all that the Society stands for, which is not entirely the case. To be entirely candid . . . the only real opposition to the new ritual in English came from those who confused the work done by the Liturgical Conference with the avowed aims of the Vernacular Society and this opposition is still prevalent among the hierarchy."[61]

Morrison responded that the two groups were, indeed, distinct organizations, and this was appropriate, but *Amen* had willingly carried publicity for the Liturgical Conference, and the Conference, in turn, had occasionally supported the Vernacular Society through paid advertisements in *Amen*. Waters responded:

"From my point of view as a member of the hierarchy, I think I could say that it is wishful thinking entirely to expect that many of the hierarchy at this time would subscribe to the Vernacular Society Manifesto especially in regard to English in the Mass. . . . It is not that I have anything against the Vernacular Society, it is just that I do not subscribe to all of their aims. . . . It is my opinion that the Liturgical Conference which seems to be a society that is taking leadership in this country in the Liturgical Movement should be of interest to every Bishop of the country and therefore, his interest should not be prevented, cooled or sidetracked by the thought that the Liturgical Conference might be too ultra-liberal in its views on the vernacular in the Mass, which to my mind seems to be the identifying characteristic of the Vernacular Society."[62]

Vernacularists were, in fact, seen as agitators, lacking in sense and understanding of the great unity of the Church brought about by Latin. Nonetheless, Morrison held his ground, further defending the Society and its manifesto in his response to the bishop:

"If you don't mind me telling you a little note of personal satisfaction, it seems strange to me that the Vernacular Society should have more Episcopal paid-up members than has the Liturgical Conference . . . Point 3 of our Manifesto is very cautiously and cleverly written. We do not advocate English in the Mass. We do subscribe to the Holy See where it is clear that it is open to suggestions for the better understanding of the liturgy of the faithful, as shown by the movement for the dialogue Mass; Congregational participation in High Masses; the reading of the Epistle and Gospel in English; the increasing use of a lector or reader; the addition of prayers in English for the conversion of Russia and for peace. My private information is this: No hierarchy will put in a petition for any Vernacular in the Mass.

"There is a commission now working in Rome and it has been working for some three or four years, for a reformation of the set-up of the Mass. I think, but I can't be quoted in the matter naturally, that the forepart of the Mass will be in the vernacular. . . . I think the whole set-up will be changed. I think there will be much Vernacular in the Mass; I think that this will come from the pen of the Holy Father himself, as we have had in late years the restored Easter Vigil, the Christus Dominus regarding the mitigated Eucharistic Fast. . . . I think that the Vernacular Society has to all intent and purposes accomplished its objective in carrying the vernacular into the Ritual. Cardinal Stritch has talked to me about this several times. I have assured him that I think it is absolutely unnecessary for the Vernacular Society to agitate for any vernacular in the structure of the Mass. As I understand and stated above, this will come out of Rome. I have also discussed it with him and it is a firm conviction with me, that it is senseless for us to agitate for the vernacular of the Divine Office. . . . As a matter of fact, I am coming more and more to the conclusion that the Vernacular Society has accomplished its work in the obtaining of the vernacular in the Ritual for this country."[63]

The exchange of letters concluded with the bishop's final response:

"It certainly is enlightening to me on the subject of what organization takes credit for getting the bishops to petition for the English Ritual. I have never been to a Vernacular Society meeting and last year was the first Liturgical Week I attended. It seemed to me on every occasion of the Liturgical Program as well as from a number of the priests individually that the Liturgical Conference was taking the credit for petitioning bishops for the Ritual in English. Now I understand from your letter 'this was done by the president of the Vernacular Society independent of any membership he holds in the Liturgical Movement.' . . . I am coming more and more to the conclusion that the Vernacular Society has accomplished its work in obtaining the Vernacular in this country."[64]

In fact, Morrison was correct about the number of bishops involved. When that exchange of letters took place between Morrison and Bishop Waters, there were fifty-three bishops enrolled in the Vernacular Society, and some were quite supportive. A major boost came in 1955 when Bishop Fulton J. Sheen celebrated a Byzantine Mass entirely in English at a shrine near Pittsburgh, Pennsylvania. Nonetheless, the impression remained that the U.S. hierarchy lagged behind episcopal conferences from other parts of the world in its support of the vernacular and that, in many respects, liturgical officials in the Vatican were often more open toward liturgical changes than the national hierarchies themselves. Ross-Duggan observed:

"On later visits to Rome, I judged that the higher authorities in the Church were moving faster in their liturgical thought and action than was the case with the national hierarchies, clergy and laity. I was credibly informed that the approval of the saying of the Epistle and Gospel facing the congregation as an integral part of the Mass without Latin equivalents was imminent. This, as usual, would be at the discretion of individual bishops. I also received a whisper that the reorganization of the entire Holy Week ceremonies might be announced in October. When at the Oriental Congregation, I put in my two-bits re: the authoritative request from the United States for an English Mass celebrated which is to be sung by Bishop (Fulton) Sheen on Labor Day, Sept. 5, in the Byzantine Rite."[65]

2.8 CONCLUSION

With the restoration of the Great Vigil of Easter on 9 February 1951,[66] the restoration of the entire liturgy of Holy Week on the sixteenth of November 1955,[67] and the arrival of the new Ritual itself, there was some sense that the Vernacular Society had completed its task and should thus be discontinued; this was apparently the opinion of Joseph Morrison himself. Ross-Duggan, however, was convinced otherwise. Opposed to Morrison's plans to disband the Society, he rallied the troops both to assist in popularizing the new Ritual and in pushing for further vernacular reforms in the liturgy. In writing about the matter to the Society's secretary, John Agathen, he cautioned "patience and obedience" and urged him to "keep the faith" and quietly express his disappointment to Morrison about the possible folding of the Society.[68]

Agathen did indeed write to Morrison but not quite in the way which the Colonel had recommended. His letter, written early in 1956, is ponderous, reflecting something of the soul-searching in which the Society's officers had been engaging:

"To me the issue is not so much whether objectives have been reached but rather the place which the Vernacular Society is to have in accomplishing them. In other words, has it a valid reason for existing? When I offered my services for whatever they were worth to the Society, it was with the conviction in my mind that I would not see the introduction (or restoration?) of the vernacular in my own lifetime, and I still feel much the same way. There would seem to be a long road ahead for this movement and in the meantime the idea has to be kept alive. The point about the Society is that it is an *organized* means of doing so.

73

"Father de Lubac says somewhere that it is the vocation of the Christian to be a witness to the truth but not necessarily to make the truth triumph. Possibly the function of the Society is something akin to that. At any rate, it seems to me that its role is not in the realm of the spectacular, and perhaps if the Colonel had had a keener realization of that he would not have felt so frustrated all these years. As I see it, we are concerned here with a movement the results of which are largely intangible, and so evaluation presents a real problem. But every time a seminarian writes in for material for a debate on the subject I think maybe we are accomplishing considerably more than we realize."[69]

How then are we to assess the success of the Vernacular Society's efforts in the first ten years of its existence? Clearly, progress had been made and their efforts had not been in vain; the new English Ritual bore testimony to that. But even with the enthusiasm of the restored Easter Vigil and Holy Week liturgies, key players within the Vernacular Society continued to grapple with its identity and purpose and to question its future. In the next chapter, we will have a look at how the Vernacular Society matured and how Agathen's musings and concerns about the Society's future played out.

NOTES FOR CHAPTER 2

[1] Others included Benedict Ehman of St. Bernard Seminary, Rochester, N.Y.; Thomas Carroll and Shawn Sheehan of Boston; Mary Perkins Ryan and her husband, John Julian Ryan, of the University of Notre Dame; William Busch; Michael Ducey, o.s.b., of Weston Priory; Leo Ruggle; Bede Scholz, o.s.b.; Gilbert Stack; Bernard Stanley; H. Velte; and Alphonse Westhoof.

[2] John Kyne Granfield, letter to Father Reinhold, 24 July 1947. CVER 2/32.

[3] "Elements to be Considered by A Vernacular Society" (1947) CVER 2/32.

[4] "Letter of Reverend H. A. Reinhold to Members, St. Jerome Society, 5 December 1947," St. Jerome Society Bulletins. CVER 2/32.

[5] "Timely Tracts: From the Vernacular Front," *Orate Fratres* 21 (1947) 460.

[6] Rev. N. N., "To the Editor," *Orate Fratres* 22 (1948) 92.

[7] H.A.R., "To the Editor," ibid.

[8] *Mediator Dei* (20 November 1947), AAS 39 (1947) 561–62.

[9] "A Brief Review of the St. Jerome Society," by John K. Ross-Duggan, Vernacular Society Secretary's Book Record 1946–53. CVER 2/14.

[10] "Meeting held at St. Benet's Bookshop, Sunday, July 25, 1948," Vernacular Society Secretary's Book Record 1946–53. CVER 2/14.

[11] "Minutes of the Vernacular Society Meeting held in Boston on August 3, 1948, Msgr. Morrison presiding," Vernacular Society Secretary's Book Record. CVER 2/14.

[12] James Mallahan, "Vernacular in Liturgy," *The Harvester* (1948).

[13] On the Vernacular Society in Great Britain, see James D. Crichton et al., *English Catholic Liturgy: Liturgical Renewal in England Since 1900* (London: Geoffrey Chapman, 1979) 63–64.

[14] Letter of Monsignor H. Francis Davis, vice-president of Oscott Seminary, Birmingham, England, and president of the English Liturgy Society, 20 Dec. 1948; Vernacular Society Correspondence: Monsignor Morrison 1948–1956. CVER 1/8.

[15] "Minutes of the Vernacular Society Meeting Held at St. Louis, Mo., August 8, 1949." Vernacular Society Secretary's Book Record 1946–53. CVER 2/14.

[16] "Annual Meeting held at Conception, Mo., Wednesday, 23 August 1950," Vernacular Society Secretary's Book Record 1946–53. CVER 2/14.

[17] "Annual Meeting at Conception Abbey." CVER 2/14.

[18] Letter of Edwin O'Hara, Bishop of Kansas City, to Monsignor Morrison, 21 September 1950. CVER 1/8.

[19] Letter of Monsignor Morrison to Reverend David Bushley, 8 July 1955. CVER 1/8.

[20] The bishops were O'Hara of Kansas City, Mo.; Willging of Pueblo, Colo.; Lane of Maryknoll; Greco of Alexandria, La.; McGuiness of Oklahoma City-Tulsa, Okla.; and Mullroy of Covington, Ky.

[21] Bulletin #1—Vol. 4 (5 March 1951). CVER 3/3.

[22] Report of Annual Vernacular Society Meeting, 20 August 1953, Grand Rapids, Mich. CVER 2/14.

[23] "Sectional Meetings," *Amen* 8/4 and 9/1 (1 Feb. 1954) 13.

[24] Despite clerical membership, however, the Vernacular Society remained staunchly a lay organization. Two lay members, John Lyon and Julian Pleasants, wrote their convictions about the importance of lay participation in the form of verse; they composed a song entitled "A Lay of the Laity" meant to be sung to the tune of "The Blue-Tailed Fly." Pleasants was a professor at the University of Notre Dame. Whether or not anyone sang the tune is another matter, but it does demonstrate something of the colorful membership constitutive of the Vernacular Society:

Let's hail the year 19-0-3, the year of Pius X's decree
That ev'ry Catholic from that date was going to participate.

The order of the liturgy had been based on this theory
That laymen should be seen, not heard—Pope Pius thought it was absurd.

The congregation simply sat while priest or choir went to bat,
Their own responses tossed back by two lacey-surpliced smaller fry.

Participation of this sort made liturgy spectator sport'
It taught folks just to hear and see and got them ready for T.V.

Pope Pius saw the laity were sinking in that apathy
That quickly starts to dominate the soul that can't participate.

He called for special efforts to give to the people what's their due,
Arousing the undying ire of ev'ry well-established choir.

Since he who sings prays twice, said he, all need the opportunity
When God has so much praising due, to multiply themselves by two.

Composers all had lent their art to dolling up the people's part
Which now the choir proudly sang and let the choir's part go hang.

He frowned upon the fancy tune, it takes professionals to croon;
If all cannot participate it's not Motu ap-Propriate.

He'd heard too many choirs croak a rather sublime Baroque;
Their shouts would fill the church's vault; he thought he'd better call a halt.

Plainchant, said he, is properer than something from an opera,
And if a concert's what you want, you'd better seek some other haunt.

The human voice with him was tops so when they pulled those organ stops,
They must, he said, just help along and never try to smother song.

Plainchant, said he, is just the song, plain folk aren't likely to sing wrong
But great feasts like Epiphany deserve to have Polyphony.

For modern music he found place if it has dignity and grace,
But he know how one type of hymn give shudders to the Seraphim.

He must turn over in his grave to see the way we still behave,
But fifty years is not too late, there's still time to participate.

Then may this year of Jubilo for his great Motu Proprio
At long last its fulfillment bring and swell the chorus that we sing.

Amen 8/4–9/1 (1 Feb. 1954) 13.

[25] "Some Thoughts on the Use of the Vernacular in Worship" (undated), CMRH 29/09.

[26] "Comments by Colonel John K. Ross-Duggan" (1962), Col. Ross-Duggan Correspondence #2. CVER 2/17.

[27] "News and Notes," *Amen* 9/2 (1 July 1954) 17.

[28] "News and Notes," *Amen* 9/2 (1 July 1954) 17.

[29] Letter of Rev. Rex Brown (London) to John K. Ross-Duggan, 4 October 1960. CVER 2/20.

[30] Letter of Rex Brown to Ross-Duggan. CVER 2/20.

[31] Letter of John K. Ross-Duggan to Msgr. Reynold Hillenbrand, 31 May 1953, CMRH 29/09.

[32] Hillenbrand to Ross-Duggan, 9 June 1953, and Ross-Duggan to Hillenbrand, 17 June, 1953, CMRH 29/09.

[33] Letter of Ross-Duggan to Hillenbrand, 16 February 1953, CMRH 29/09.

[34] *Commonweal* (1951) as recorded in the Vernacular Society Secretary's Book Record 1946–53. CVER 2/14.

[35] "A Letter from Father Reinhold: More Confidence Needed" *Amen* 6 (15 May 1951) 2.

[36] Senex, Letter, "Mr. Christopher Dawson," *Amen* 8–9 (1 Feb. 1954) 2.

[37] "Mr. Christopher Dawson and the Vernacular," *Amen* 8–9 (1 Feb. 1954) 12.

[38] Russell Young, "Mr. Young in Reply," *Amen* 8–9 (1 Feb. 1954) 12.

[39] Sister Hildegrade, "A Sister Talks Up," *Amen* 9 (1 July 1954) 2.

[40] One example comes from a doctoral defense in which I participated, where the student continually referred to the "agency of the Apostles," attempting to

translate the Latin as literally as possible. Of course, the "ministry of the apostles," while not a literal translation of the Latin, would have been a far better rendering in English of what the text was intended to convey.

[41] John C. Cort, "Favoring You," *Amen* 7 (May 1952) 2.

[42] Giulio Balocco (Turin, Italy), "An Italian Visitor Writes," *Amen* 10 (1 Nov. 1955) 2.

[43] Letter of Ross-Duggan to John Agathen, 30 July 1954. CVER 1/2.

[44] Letter of Edwin V. O'Hara, bishop of Kansas City, to Monsignor Joseph P. Morrison, 20 November 1951. CVER 1/8.

[45] Letter to Edwin V. O'Hara to Joseph P. Morrison, 2 December 1952. CVER 1/8.

[46] Letter of Ross-Duggan (from the Casa Santa Brigida, Rome) to Monsignor Morrison, 4 June 1954. CVER 1/2.

[47] Letter of Edwin V. O'Hara, bishop of Kansas City to Monsignor Morrison, 23 July 1954. CVER 1/13.

[48] "The Secretary's Report," *Amen* 10/1 (1 July 1955) 4.

[49] Theodore C. P. Vermilye, "The English Ritual: Is This Only the Beginning?" *The Christian Family* (December 1955) 2.

[50] Vermilye, 4.

[51] Vermilye, 4.

[52] *The New Latin English Ritual* (undated). CVER 1/8.

[53] Letter of Louis Beauchemin, s.m., to Archbishop O'Hara (undated). CVER 1/8.

[54] Letter of Mr. and Mrs. Robert Boeser, Richfield, Minnesota (undated), to "Your Holiness," reprinted in *Amen* 10 (1 Nov. 1955) 3. CVER 5/1.

[55] The Priest, "The New Ritual," *Amen* 11 (1 June 1956) 19.

[56] Letter of Ross-Duggan to Rev. Michael Ducey, o.s.b., 4 December 1955. CVER 2/5.

[57] "The Bulletin" (1953). CVER 3/3.

[58] Letter of Carroll J. Noonan, s.s., to Monsignor Joseph Morrison, 28 March 1952. CVER 1/8.

[59] Robert L. Tuzik, "The Contribution of Msgr. Reynold Hillenbrand (1905–1979) to the Liturgical Movement in the United States: Influences and Development," unpublished Ph.D. dissertation, University of Notre Dame, 1989, 88–89.

[60] John Agathen to Ross-Duggan, 24 November 1954. CVER 1/3.

[61] Letter of Vincent S. Waters, bishop of Raleigh (president of the Liturgical Conference), to Monsignor Joseph P. Morrison, 4 October 1954. CVER 1/8.

[62] Vincent S. Waters to Joseph P. Morrison, 22 October 1954. CVER 1/8.

[63] Letter of Morrison to Waters, 2 November 1954. CVER 1/8.

[64] Waters to Morrison, 8 November 1954. CVER 1/8.

[65] John K. Ross-Duggan, "Off-the-Record Account of European Trip 1954–55." CVER 3/5.

[66] Sacred Congregation of Rites, *Dominicae Resurrectionis*, 9 Feb. 1951: *AAS* 43 (1951) 128–29.

[67] Sacred Congregation of Rites, *Maxima redemptionis nostrae mysteria*, 16 Nov. 1955: *AAS* 47.

[68] Letter of Ross-Duggan to John Agathen, 30 July 1954. CVER 1/2.

[69] Letter of John Agathen to Monsignor Morrison, 29 February 1956. CVER 2/5.

Chapter 3
Pressure for the Vernacular Mounts: 1956–1962

3.1 INTRODUCTION

In 1956 a new wave of Vernacular Society officers appeared on the scene: Benedictine Michael Ducey of Weston Priory, Vermont, as president; Robert Sherry of Cincinnati and John Connorton of New York as vice presidents; Edgar T. Groark of Washington, D.C., as recording secretary; Aelfred Berger of Cincinnati as corresponding secretary; and Ed Wintermute of Hasselt, Michigan, as promotional secretary. The Colonel continued his reign as general secretary. A small committee headed up the several regional chapters that existed around the United States: J. Carothers Jr. in Los Angeles; W. Daly in Boston; and Dr. Joseph Evans in Chicago.[1] Meanwhile, Patrick Crowley of Chicago, who cofounded the Christian Family Movement (CFM) with his wife, Pattie, offered his services as a lawyer and helped the Vernacular Society become legally incorporated. Thus, the Society expanded despite continued internal problems and the organization's uncertain future.

While the Colonel alienated many of his coworkers, he often succeeded in pulling out all the diplomatic stops when meeting with members of the hierarchy. Not only did he have extraordinary access to high-ranking prelates both in the United States and in the Vatican, but they would write the Colonel afterwards, thanking him for his visit and the conversation. One such letter came from the archbishop of Cincinnati, Karl J. Alter:

"It was a genuine pleasure to have you visit me at my home and I not only enjoyed the discussion but found some of your comments quite informative. I hope that the coming Conference in Assisi in September will be productive of some practical results."[2]

That Assisi Congress offered Ross-Duggan and his colleagues the opportunity for more vernacular networking and gave fresh hope to those concerned about liturgical renewal in the Church.

3.2 THE ASSISI CONGRESS

Acknowledging the significant liturgical advances registered around the world, the Sacred Congregation of Rites convoked an international congress on pastoral liturgy from the eighteenth until the twenty-second of September 1956 in Assisi, which was to conclude with a private papal audience in Rome on the twenty-second. The meeting was organized by Bishop Carlo Rossi of Biella, Italy; Johannes Wagner of the *Liturgisches Institut* at Trier; Pierre-Marie Gy of the *Centre de pastorale liturgique* in Paris; and Luigi Agustoni of the *Centro di liturgia pastorale* in Lugano, Switzerland. In many ways, the prior international liturgical meetings held at Maria Laach in the Rhineland (1951), Saint Odile near Strasbourg (1952), Lugano (1953), and Louvain (1954) were, by comparison, preparatory meetings for the much larger congress scheduled for Assisi. Major talks were given by Josef Jungmann, s.j: "The Pastoral Idea in the History of the Liturgy"[3] and Augustin Bea, s.j., "The Pastoral Value of the Word of God in the Sacred Liturgy."[4] Those talks were significant in that they presented ideas that would later be developed in Vatican II's liturgy constitution *Sacrosanctum Concilium*.

There were over thirteen hundred participants at the meeting and its emphasis as stated in the opening address given by Cardinal Cicognani, prefect of the Congregation of Rites, was to be "pastoral liturgy." Cicognani's address was consistent with the recent papal encyclical *Mediator Dei* (promulgated in 1947) expressing both praise for the accomplishments of the liturgical movement and caution against acting erroneously or too quickly. Thus, there were to be no "debates" during the Assisi Congress although "private and unofficial discussions might well result in . . . conclusions to be submitted to the ecclesiastical authority."[5] Predictably, Cicognani upheld the continuation of Latin in the liturgy not only as "a splendid sign of unity and universality" but also to "clothe the sacred truths in their magnificence . . . effectively safeguarding them against the corruption of true doctrine."[6] He continued that even though those in the assembly do not normally understand Latin, that is no reason for substituting it with the vernacular since they did not participate in the ordained priesthood:

"The faithful are not the hierarchical priesthood, a chosen class who alone offer the sacrifice in the true and proper sense and who for that reason should understand fully the sacred formulas and expressions. In their 'royal priesthood' the faithful take part *aequo modo,* according to their station, in the sacrifice and the divine mysteries."[7]

This strong reaffirmation of the unqualified use of Latin in the liturgy came as a shock, and the translators at this point fell silent.

Cicognani was well aware of the grassroots support for the vernacular around the world and did his best to see that the topic would carefully be avoided in the course of the meeting; he did not succeed. There may have been no official "debates" at the congress, but unofficial debates and discussions abounded with the prefect himself. And the topic, not surprisingly, was the vernacular. This was so much the case that when the cardinal abruptly departed from Assisi, rumors quickly spread among the participants that Cicognani had been so infuriated by the pro-vernacular stance of the gathered assembly that he had returned to Rome to inform the Pope himself so that a strong rebuke could be prepared for the papal audience on the twenty-second. The real reason for his departure was apparently much more benign. During the congress, the prefect was housed in the "Cardinal's Suite" within the bishop's palace in Assisi. In the absence of regular guests, the bed in the royal suite had become infested with fleas that took a liking to Cardinal Cicognani. After several nights of no sleep, combined with swelling where he had been bitten along with a mild fever, he returned to Rome. Pro-vernacularist Cardinal Lercaro of Bologna then stepped in to preside over the congress in place of the Prefect.[8]

Despite Cicognani's attempts to avoid the vernacular topic in the congress, every major speaker addressed the importance of the vernacular indirectly—and even at times directly—in their presentations. Beginning with liturgical developments in the early Church, Jungmann carefully demonstrated how pastoral need brought about use of the vernacular as a way of making worship intelligible: "the living liturgy actively participated in, was for centuries the most important form of pastoral care."[9] As Jungmann traced the history of the vernacular, he was interrupted several times with sustained and enthusiastic applause, much to the chagrin of Cardinal Cicognani. In fact, translators had been forbidden to translate anything regarding the vernacular during the public talks and discussions. Thus, when the topic was broached, the translators paused in shock not knowing what to do; the audience began to applaud; Jungmann looked up rather confused as to what had transpired; and Godfrey Diekmann, who was in one of the translators' booths at the time, "began jumping up and down and saying: 'it's a revolt! It's a revolt!'"[10]

Each country was allowed only a certain number of delegates since space at Assisi was limited. Among the participants at Assisi, there were three American bishops: Annabring, Wright, and Dworschak. Archbishop O'Hara, who had long supported the vernacular cause and planned on attending, died in Milan en route. He was to have been the designated head of the American delegation representing the apostolate delegate in Washington, D.C. The apostolic delegate's first choice had been Francis Cardinal Spellman of New York, a great opponent of the vernacular. When Godfrey Diekmann heard that Spellman was soon to be nominated, he traveled immediately to Washington to change the delegate's mind, since Spellman "knew nothing about liturgy."[11] Diekmann succeeded, and O'Hara was announced, only to die on his way to the meeting. His voice was heard, nonetheless, in that he had already prepared a report for the Assisi meeting. While the report dealt ostensibly with how the revised Holy Week rites were being received in the U.S. Church (more than ninety archdioceses and dioceses had responded to the questionnaire), the vernacular issue was also treated. He reported that most respondents agreed that "a greater use of the vernacular would be most desirable" and that only a few indicated opposition to more vernacular in the liturgy.[12]

Together with the three U.S. bishops, liturgical leaders Godfrey Diekmann, o.s.b., Gerald Ellard, s.j., Martin Hellriegel, Reynold Hillenbrand, William Leonard, s.j., Michael Mathis, c.s.c., Frederick McManus, and Joseph Morrison led the American delegation of one hundred, Colonel Ross-Duggan among them. Morrison had been delegated by Cardinal Stritch to attend. Stritch wrote:

"I shall be very pleased if you attend the Liturgical Congress at Assisi in September of this year. . . . If the question of the use of the vernacular in the Liturgy should be discussed I am sure that you know my mind and that I am convinced that the admirable unity in the official worship of the Church which the use of Latin gives us is something that must be treasured and safeguarded."[13]

As for Ross-Duggan's presence, Diekmann and Mathis as comembers of the American Subcommittee on Organization for the Assisi Congress had originally attempted to block the Colonel's participation. Exploring alternatives, Ross-Duggan had written them requesting a list of the USA delegation, hoping to find at least several on the list who might support his petition for access to the meeting; Diekmann and Mathis refused.[14] Undaunted, Ross-Duggan then tried his luck again—this time with Prior Michael Ducey of Weston Priory:

"I have heard from Fr. Mathis that no list of USA delegates is being officially issued; and Archbishop O'Hara wrote me that he did not expect to have the list. Can you supply me with an unofficial list of USA delegates which will not be attributed to you?"[15]

The Colonel succeeded in the end by making his presence known at the congress, much to the consternation of many. Among other things, he was not pleased with the choice of Assisi as the venue for such an important international meeting, complaining that "there is hardly a level spot; one must leap from crag to crag." He also complained about the way he was treated by the other delegates:

"I did not receive much help from Fr. Ducey or Msgr. Morrison at Assisi or later; the average cleric seems to think that a layman is made only for work. As one of the very few laymen at Assisi, I have formed a very low opinion of the attitude of the clergy towards lay workers."[16]

Ducey, for his part, wrote to Joseph Morrison that "the Colonel's behavior continues to be distressing, as at Assisi."[17]

A good example of Ross-Duggan's behavior at the congress comes from the final session with the Pope himself. The twenty-second of September arrived and congress participants were bused down to Rome for the papal audience. It had been rumored that during the audience the Pope would announce major vernacular concessions, so there was great enthusiasm as participants arrived in the Sistine Chapel for the audience. Pius XII was solemnly carried in on the *sedia gestatoria* and spoke for forty-five minutes on the importance of the liturgical movement, praising the efforts of those who brought it about. But to everyone's surprise, he said nothing about further changes in liturgical language. Rather, he upheld Latin as the language of the Church and reaffirmed its permanent place in the liturgy:

"On the part of the Church, the liturgy today entails a concern for progress but also for conservation and defense. She returns to the past without slavishly copying it and creates anew in the ceremonies themselves, in the use of the vernacular, in popular song and in the building of churches. It would be superfluous, nevertheless, to recall once again that the Church has serious reasons for steadfastly retaining in the Latin rite the unconditional obligation of the celebrating priest to use the Latin language and, likewise, for insisting that the Gregorian chant in the holy sacrifice to be in the language of the Church."[18]

Ross-Duggan was less than amused by the Pope's remarks, as re-counted by William Leonard in his autobiography: "When he was being carried out the Colonel cried in a loud voice, 'Take him away!' I was sitting beside him and I said 'Sh-h-h, Colonel!' 'No, no' he shouted, 'He'll never do us any good. Take him away!'"[19]

Diplomacy was not one of the Colonel's strengths, and with such comments, one understands why there were so many personality clashes among officers of the Vernacular Society, especially when Ross-Duggan was present. Nonetheless, he continued to "make the rounds" and spent some time in Rome after the Assisi Congress visiting various cardinals and Vatican offices. Following his visits, he concluded:

"I am afraid that the matter of the use of the vernacular is becoming a *political* matter in certain Roman circles especially by those who op-pose the "intrusion of foreigners" into the Roman Curia or Civil Serv-ice. There has been a big movement for an internationalized Curia in the best interest of the Church, especially in Great Britain and other English-speaking countries.

"I was received most kindly by Cardinals Cicognani, Ottaviani, and Tisserant . . . and I believe I did help to break down the prejudice that some conservatives like Cardinal Cicognani hold against any popular liturgy."[20]

3.3 "SOUL-SEARCHING" AND THE CALL FOR AMALGAMATION

The years 1956–62 registered some success but also a significant number of disappointments. On the one hand, vernacularists were en-couraged by recent victories such as the approval of the Roman Ritual in the vernacular, and they were busy in popularizing the Ritual for parishes and dioceses. On the other hand, there were also the low points: personality clashes in the organization mostly centered around Colonel Ross-Duggan; challenges to sustaining momentum in the ver-nacular cause; and newly promulgated pro-Latin Church documents like the Instruction on Sacred Music (1958) and *Veterum sapientia* (1962). In an unpublished doctoral dissertation, William Wiethoff dis-cusses the public debate over the vernacular as recorded in the press and notes wide-ranging views on the subject. Even *Sports Illustrated* commented on the subject.[21] Dismissing the pastoral value of English, calling it a "Donald Duck language," some traditionalists attacked the

vernacular reform as "pathetic" or "artificial" and an attempt to "sabotage . . . America's humanistic scholarship."[22] Moreover, while the
Assisi Congress was a great boon to those advocating liturgical renewal with public recognition of the liturgical movement on the international level, it was a great disappointment as far as the vernacular
issue was concerned.

The situation was not helped by one minor official of the Roman
Curia who wrote a series of articles in the review *Monitor Ecclesiasti-
cus* attacking the Assisi Congress for its promotion of the vernacular.
Predictably, Ross-Duggan expeditiously wrote his own critique of
Monsignor Romita's articles.[23] When diocesan bishops began to hear
about what transpired in Assisi, especially as viewed through the lens
of curial officials like Monsignor Romita, they became concerned that
supporting the vernacular might well be viewed as either disrespect-
ful or disobedient toward the Holy See and its wishes; the results
were palpable. The Vernacular Society's request to Archbishop Karl
Alter for permission to meet in Cincinnati following the 1958 Liturgical Week demonstrates the point:

"His Grace, (the Archbishop of Cincinnati) has given permission to
hold the meeting of the Vernacular Society *after* the close of the 19th
North American Liturgical Week with the direct understanding that
there is to be no intermingling between the two groups. Furthermore,
he strongly advises against a lot of publicity in connection with the Vernacular meetings because of the delicate situation that has arisen since
the Assisi Congress relative to the whole vernacular movement."[24]

The Assisi Congress came off as being too "pro-vernacular" and
"anti-Latin," and at least some bishops were concerned that "intermingling" meetings of the Liturgical Conference and the Vernacular
Society would mean death to both. Michael Ducey typed his own
notes that he recorded during the congress, and they express something of the dilemma faced on the vernacular question. In particular,
he cited three major reasons why the Vatican was opposing the vernacular: (1) "scandal" to those who were unaccustomed to it; (2) fear
of nationalistic churches and loss of centralization; and (3) the problem of translating prayers into "GOOD" vernacular while at the same
time maintaining the orthodox and doctrinal elements of the prayers
themselves. He drew the conclusion: "Wait and See, more usage may
come," thinking especially of mission areas where the vernacular was

most necessary as a tool for evangelization, and finished the sentence: "meanwhile, make best of what we have—low Masses, Rituals, etc."[25] Ducey then made some jottings about the Vernacular Society itself and his own role within it. After strategizing about how the Society might best continue its work given the new challenges from Assisi, Ducey wrote:

"Patience regarding further changes, don't be revolutionaries—spirit of loyalty and obedience. Charity regarding persons who disagree with us. In a word, EXEMPLIFY THE SPIRIT OF THE LITURGY. Our desire is to operate within the framework of church organization, i.e., not a lay organization, private-owned and operated, responsible to no one. Confining ourselves to areas clearly open for vernacular. . . . Await publication of Assisi proceedings for further comment on future possibilities."[26]

Ducey's call for patience and forbearance was also felt in other sectors of American liturgical renewal. The early numbers of *Orate Fratres* and *Worship* contained numerous articles on the vernacular, whereas in 1957—the year following the Assisi Congress—Volume 31 does not even carry one article devoted to the vernacular itself; there are, however, several articles that treat the Assisi meeting more generally.

In his reflections on the international gathering, Godfrey Diekmann wrote that Assisi offered liturgical scholars the possibility to "think out loud." He continued: "This is not the language of 'revolution' or of 'extremism.' There was freedom of thought and expression, within the bounds of unquestioning obedience."[27] Diekmann called for the importance of viewing Assisi as a project to be carried forward rather than as an end of liturgical reform. To see the Assisi meeting as a *"terminus"* would be "irresponsible superficiality."[28]

As Ross-Duggan continued his travels throughout Europe after the congress, there was an increasing amount of soul-searching going on back in the United States, and at least some in the Society felt that its work had been accomplished and should be discontinued. Others suggested that while there was more to be done in the promotion of the vernacular, the Liturgical Conference should take the lead according to their own plan and style. The Vernacular Society could be discontinued and members could then lend their support to the Liturgical Conference as they chose to do so. Such talk tended to infuriate Ross-Duggan for whom there was simply no other cause worth fighting for. As soon as he would hear of such recommendations he would write a strong letter to the individuals involved, questioning their loyalty to the Society, accusing them of having "sold out" to the system or of sheer apathy. One of the newcomers on the scene was the Rt. Rev. Robert Sherry of Cincinnati, and his call for the Vernacular Society's amalgamation with the Liturgical Conference was met with a sharp rebuke by the Colonel. Sherry responded:

"The remark attributed to me 'the Vernacular Society should be amalgamated with the Liturgical Society' was made by me at a meeting of the Board of Directors of the Liturgical Conference in an effort to forestall its complete disappearance from the scene. Most of the members present at this meeting were very dubious about its future. I thought that by combining the two organizations into one, each would be strengthened. However, upon second thought, I believe they would mix like oil and water."[29]

The changing of the guard continued as founders of the Society grew older and newcomers were added to the ranks. And there were occasional moments of light. John Agathen, who had earlier been discouraged with the direction in which the Society was heading, wrote to Joseph Morrison early in 1957: "I think we have a fine organization; one we need not be ashamed of."[30] Morrison's own contribution to the Society would last only several months longer; he died unexpectedly on the fourteenth of August 1957, less than a year after the Assisi Congress he attended.

The post-Assisi caution against the vernacular continued to hold sway. Only several weeks after Morrison's death, the Vernacular Society was scheduled to hold its annual meeting during the Liturgical Week at Collegeville, Minnesota, but it was denied permission to meet at Saint John's Abbey. Abbot Baldwin Dworschak wrote to the Society's president:

"The lateness of this letter replying to yours of March 23 in which you request approval of the Vernacular Society holding its annual meeting in conjunction with the 1957 liturgical week at St. John's reflects the difficulty your request posed for me, and my hesitation in arriving at a conclusion.

"The reason for my hesitation derives from the fact that confidential but urgent information has reached us from trusted persons in Rome that it would be most unwise, and also prejudicial to the cause itself of more vernacular in the Liturgy, to stress the vernacular question at the present time. It would seem that the Holy See was seriously disturbed by what it considered the too hearty demonstration for the vernacular demonstrated at Assisi, despite the restraining words of the Cardinal Prefect of the SRC in his opening address. We have therefore been advised, by persons in high position who are themselves not unfavorable to the vernacular, not to give any publicity over which we may have control, nor to give any prominence to the vernacular question for the time being. . . .

"Even if no notice of the Vernacular Society's meeting were to be contained in the week's program, you would very likely wish to announce the meeting to your members in the next issue of *Amen* after the event. And since your periodical is sent to all the American bishops, and to the officials of the competent Roman Congregations, the impression would surely be taken—although erroneously—that the Week in some way sponsors the Vernacular Society. Because of the reasons cited above, such an impression would be embarrassing to me as host to the Liturgical Week, and would necessitate letters of explanation that would perhaps not be convincing to the recipients in Rome. Under the circumstances, I would much prefer if the Vernacular Society would not hold its annual meeting here at St. John's. . . . Perhaps it would be possible to convoke the annual meeting prior to, or immediately following the week either in St. Paul or Minneapolis, or in St. Cloud?"[31]

In fact, no annual meeting took place. Rather, the Society's board met privately in St. Paul on the twenty-first of August. At that meeting, Michael Ducey stepped down as president due to leadership responsibilities at Weston Priory but agreed to stay on as vice president. He was replaced by Robert Sherry of Cincinnati who was in attendance. Sherry's tenure, however, was brief; he resigned the following May because of pastoral responsibilities. Also present at the meeting in St. Paul were Alfred Berger of Cincinnati, Joseph Evans of Chicago, and Ross-Duggan.

The secretary reported a total of 4,008 members of the Society, 75 of whom were bishops; 12 abbots; 1,837 priests; and 1,587 laity. The rest were either seminarians, religious sisters, or brothers. Two new board members were added: Rev. Father Sergius, O.F.M., of West Chicago, and

Rev. Walter Le Beau of St. Paul, Minnesota. All board members recognized the urgent need for an increase in membership but expressed a certain frustration about how to succeed in bringing that about.[32]

That same frustration had already been experienced on the local level. It had been the desire of the Society's officers to form local chapters, believing that grassroots support for the cause would be more easily obtained through local organizing. But this was easier said than done. A decade after the founding of the Society, in 1958, there were only three active local chapters: Chicago, Los Angeles, and Washington, D.C. In writing to John Agathen to congratulate him on the success of the Chicago chapter where the monthly meeting always closed with Compline prayed in the vernacular, Ed Groark noted how difficult it was to sustain interest in and support for a Maryland chapter of the Vernacular Society.[33] Groark was not alone in his frustration. Indeed, the Society's archives contain numerous letters of vernacular promoters who expressed frustration at advertising and promoting a product that people were simply not enthusiastic about.

Even numbers at the annual meeting decreased. Whereas some meetings drew as many as five hundred people, the 1958 annual meeting in Cincinnati drew only seventy-five. And during that meeting, all were not equally enthusiastic about continuing to plead for more vernacular. Some attending the meeting questioned whether it might not be better to deepen the influence the group already had rather than to continue lobbying for further liturgical changes. Others suggested that *Amen* regularly publish "progress reports" on vernacular gains throughout the world. Several publicly expressed their disapproval of the Vernacular Society's aims and goals, to which a newcomer from Spokane, Washington, Fr. John O'Brien, responded: "We thrive on opposition." He continued that the Society needed to further its mission of preparing the U.S. Church for the day when the liturgy would be fully celebrated in the vernacular.[34] Meanwhile, Theodore Vermilye reminded vernacularists that despite diminishing numbers, they had come a long way from the early days of the Society when they were regarded as "heretics."[35]

3.4 "INSTRUCTION ON SACRED MUSIC AND SACRED LITURGY"

Vernacular hopes were dashed in September 1958 with the publication of the Congregation of Rites' "Instruction on Sacred Music and Sacred Liturgy"[36] which seemed to stifle further vernacular developments. While the document was presented as a follow-up text to *Mediator Dei* (1947) and *Musica sacrae disciplina* (1955), it was seen as an attempt to promote uniformity in the liturgy and diminish local liturgical adaptations, which would, of course, include the vernacular. In his commentary on the new document, Fernando Antonelli, o.f.m., relator of the Historical Section of the Sacred Congregation of Rites, attempted to present the text in a positive light, stating that the Instruction was not meant "as a floodgate for the liturgical movement" but rather "as a dyke to protect it."[37]

Antonelli was well acquainted both with *Amen* and the Vernacular Society and had received delegates from the Society in his Vatican office on several occasions. A report from one of those meetings offers a positive impression of Antonelli:

"The overall impression . . . was that Fr. Antonelli is a very balanced man and sympathizes with the aims of the Vernacular Society, to which he gave a categorical approval as containing no errors.

"The highlight of the interview was the unqualified support Fr. Antonelli gave *Amen* (with which he was already acquainted) and the Vernacular Society. . . . He advised that the sanity of the aims of the Vernacular Society be more publicized, because here in Rome, where the Society or its paper may not always be personally known, there is a tendency to frown on liturgical reforms as being all of them extremist. In this situation, reasonable movements suffer. If it were made more evident that the Vernacular Society seeks only reform within the limits of what is permissible much would be done to remedy the state of things."[38]

Despite the positive reading of Antonelli, members of the Vernacular Society were less enthusiastic in welcoming the Congregation's document on music and liturgy than he was, rather, they were convinced that it was a Vatican ploy to stamp out vernacular usage in the liturgy. Pius XII died one month later on the ninth of October and the future of the vernacular seemed grim. The Society's Executive Committee met in special session several weeks later on the twenty-eighth of October—the very day in which John XXIII was elected pope. In the absence of the Colonel and in the spirit of good Vatican diplomacy, they drafted a resolution that mentioned only those items in the document the Society could applaud:

"RESOLVED, that the Vernacular Society welcomes with joy the new directive of the Holy See, calling for active vocal participation by the laity in liturgical worship, and also its recognition of the value of the vernacular in extra-liturgical devotions. We pledge our fullest cooperation to further the program therein outlined."[39]

Several weeks later, Michael Ducey sent a memo to the Society's officers and executive committee, suggesting a careful strategy in accepting the new Instruction:

"The 'Instruction' seems to close the door to any further vernacular usage in liturgy. . . . May I suggest your consideration of what action, if any, our Society should now take? Personally, I believe we should immediately adopt a policy and program of complete conformity with the various provisions of the decree so as to leave no doubt in the minds of all concerned regarding where we stand in relation to it. The policy could be formulated . . . as follows:

"(1) That our society should take immediate steps, as our legal expert Mr. Patrick Crowley may advise, to change its name to that of 'The Pius Twelfth Society of America Incorporated.'

"(2) That we revise our statement of policy to coincide as closely as possible with the letter and spirit of the 'Instruction,' substituting for all references to 'the vernacular,' with corresponding references to 'active participation in the liturgy.'

". . . Getting behind the new legislation will not only present us with a wider field of activity, in close conformity with the express wishes of the Holy See, but also promote the vernacular cause by indirection. Surely if the laity are now required by law to *participate actively in Latin,* the desire for permission to do this in their own tongue will become more widespread than it is now."[40]

When the executive committee met once again in special session on the sixth of December, they invited *Worship* editor Godfrey Diekmann, o.s.b., to come and explain the document. Basing his opinion on his interview with Fr. Joseph Loew of the Sacred Congregation of Rites and on his own study of the document, he surprised them by stating that the Instruction represented a major advance for more active participation of the laity in the liturgy. Moreover, he stated that there had been no intention on the part of the document to forbid the vernacular but rather to legislate a norm for a uniform, maximum participation. He noted the distinction within the document between direct participation for which only Latin could be used and indirect participation in which the faithful do not pray along with the celebrant and for which they could therefore use their own vernacular tongue. This distinction between the parts of presider and assembly marked something new of this kind and was referred to six times in the document. When one board member asked Diekmann if it would be tactful to lobby for the vernacular also in direct participation, he replied that the German bishops had recently discussed the document in a plenary session and believed that the new document would do much to hinder progress within the liturgical movement. When two German cardinals went to Rome to represent the other bishops and discuss the matter, they were assured by the Congregation that the Instruction would not be enforced in Germany. Arguing for a less confrontational position, Robert Sherry suggested that much could still be done in promoting the vernacular in indirect participation while remaining within the bounds of the Instruction.

In Diekmann's presence, the board then discussed Ducey's proposal to change the Society's name so as to make it appear less controversial. It was decided unanimously not to change the name, rather they discussed how the efforts of the Vernacular Society might continue in actively promoting its aims. Diekmann suggested a revision of the resolution agreed upon at their previous meeting; the suggested revision was approved unanimously. It read:

"RESOLVED, that the Vernacular Society welcomes with joy the new Instruction of the Holy See calling for active vocal participation by the laity in liturgical worship and also its clear statement in regard to the value and legitimacy of the vernacular in liturgical services. We pledge our fullest cooperation to further the program therein outlined."[41]

Sherry, however, remained concerned that his colleagues on the board be grateful for what was already granted and not agitate for too much vernacular. He was very much in line with conservative American Catholics who considered the Dialogue Mass in Latin to be the end of any discussion for liturgical renewal.[42] In fact, Sherry was one of the more cautious members of the Society, calling for moderation and temperance in promoting the vernacular while maintaining a balanced appreciation of Latin. But as Sherry continued to express his reservations, others in the Society were more determined than ever to win their cause. Attempting to promote the new document in a positive light, he wrote an article which was featured on the front page of *Our Sunday Visitor* on the twelfth of July 1959. It was entitled: "Your Part in the Mass: Wide Use of the Vernacular Authorized by New Instruction on Liturgy, Especially in Low Masses." The article began: "At first blush it might appear that the new Instruction on Sacred Music and the Sacred Liturgy is heavily weighed in favor of Latin. A careful reading of the document, however, demonstrates that the use of the vernacular in liturgical worship is by no means lightly regarded or merely tolerated."[43] The article then proceeded to explain the document.

Sherry was not the only vernacularist attempting to explain the document. Rev. Joseph T. Nolan (then at St. Margaret Mary Church in Wichita, Kansas; currently professor of theology at Boston College) wrote his own thirteen-page pamphlet entitled, "Vernacular in the Liturgy." Nolan took the 1958 Instruction as his point of departure, stating that the document itself "should lead us to reexamine the whole question of the vernacular." He then stressed the advantages of Latin: (1) it emphasizes the role of the priest; (2) it produces a dialogue between the presider and assembly; and (3) the prayer between presider and assembly is unified when they pray aloud together. But he continued "we will not have *complete* participation in our parishes until we use English."[44] Nolan's pamphlet was anecdotal, recounting how liturgical leaders like Gerald Ellard and William Leonard came to be "converted" to the vernacular. And his writing style is quite direct: "Ask the Glenmary Fathers if their backwoods converts are going to be at ease with 'the simple Latin phrases.' Ask your own friends and family what *'O salutaris'* means."[45]

Nolan continued:

"There are no quick solutions to these difficulties. But it is long past time that we begin earnestly working for a permanent solution. Mass in the vernacular can only come from Rome. It will never come at all unless we think out the case with all its historical arguments and immense pastoral usefulness, and then present the desired petitions to Rome through our hierarchy."[46]

Lamenting the fact that the vernacular movement in the United States was lagging behind that of other countries, Nolan faulted the Liturgical

Conference in their annual Liturgical Weeks for less than whole-hearted support of the Vernacular Society and the issue itself:

"At the various Weeks, discussion was left, for the most part, to the Vernacular Society, and certainly there was nothing like the excellent arguments and sound enthusiasm shown by the official speakers at the most important gathering of all, at Assisi. Neither have there been any petitions such as Cardinal Lercaro and other members of the hier-archy have thoughtfully prepared and presented; neither have there been any concessions, except for the Ritual, such as the German and missionary bishops have gratefully won for their people."[47]

He opposed proposals which called for a bilingual Mass which would combine Latin and English calling it "patchwork" with a procedure which would move from "now you understand it; now you don't."[48] Nolan concluded: "Until there is a world language that the majority understand, we have need of the vernacular tongues to instruct and pray well."[49]

The "patchwork" of a bilingual Dialogue Mass was also criticized by members of the laity who found such a solution less than satisfac-tory. One corporate executive from Ann Arbor wrote to Archbishop John Dearden of Detroit:

"This is a respectful protest against the 'Dialogue Mass' in which the faithful are expected to respond in Latin, a language virtually meaning-less to the vast majority of them. . . . To expect ordinary Americans to pray in a foreign tongue is, to say the least, a most unreasonable imposition on them. And to assume that this process will, in any way, increase their faith and devotion is no more than wishful thinking. I respectfully suggest that as a comparison you mentally put yourself in the position of now being required to "Say the Mass" in Chinese or some other language completely meaningless to you, and being told that this will increase your devotion."[50]

The archbishop's secretary, the Rev. (later Bishop) Joseph L. Imesch, re-sponded that since the Pope called for the Dialogue Mass it was a good thing for the Church, and all should comply with his request. Imesch concluded: "I am sure that if you make every attempt to pray the Mass with the priest and try to understand the Latin words, your devotion will be increased."[51] Discussions of this kind took on an even greater urgency in mission territories.

3.5 THE VERNACULAR AND THE MISSIONS

In September 1959 an International Study Week on Liturgy and the Missions took place at the Uden Retreat House near Nijmegen in southern Holland.[52] Thirty-seven bishops participated—many of them Africans and Indians—along with more than one hundred priests, mostly from mission countries, and, of course, Colonel John K. Ross-Duggan. The meeting was organized by missiologist Johannes Hoffinger, s.J., of Manila and led by Cardinal Gracias of Bombay.[53] In calling for the active promotion of the liturgical movement in mission lands, the vernacular surfaced as a fundamental issue for the renewal. Commenting on the meeting in the London *Catholic Herald*, Jesuit liturgist Clifford Howell wrote: "speaker after speaker maintained that the all-Latin liturgy not only labels the Church as an alien institution but is also a grievous handicap in the work of evangelization."[54] Some working in mission territories noted the complexity of the vernacular issue in regions where there was no common language. Eugene Hillman, c.s.sp., from the Tanganyika Territory of East Africa, wrote to John Agathen:

"We talk a lot about the necessity of adopting Christianity to indigenous cultures, but I do not see how this can be done effectively without the use of the vernacular. Much thought will have to be given to this problem in Africa where the multiplicity of languages might be a strong objection to the use of the vernacular."[55]

Other letters of interest in and support for the Vernacular Society came from such far-flung places as Acapulco, Mexico; Buenos Aires, Argentina; Khartoum, Sudan; Manresa, Spain; and Queensland, Australia.[56] Meanwhile, Bishop Lawrence Nagae of Urawa, Japan, urged that the entire Liturgy of the Word be celebrated in Japanese as a help to Japanese converts:

"The liturgy of the Word has a catechetical goal, and serves, in a mission country like Japan, not only in the instruction of Christians and catechumens, but also as the first enlightening of the non-Christians who perhaps come to the services out of curiosity."[57]

And while one does not normally think of New York City as "mission territory," a similar point was made regarding the Episcopal Church's use of the vernacular in the growing Puerto Rican community.[58]

3.6 SOCIETY MEMBERSHIP AND NEW VERNACULAR INITIATIVES

The Vernacular Society's Pittsburgh meeting in August 1960 was wrought with tensions and personality clashes. Robert Sherry had resigned as president several months prior to the meeting leaving his successor, John P. O'Brien of Newport, Washington, with a very difficult meeting to chair. The revelation of major economic problems both with *Amen* and the Society itself further complicated matters. One of the few positive outcomes was the election of William Storey as second vice president, collaborating with English professor John F. Mahoney of Ann Arbor, who accepted the editorship of *Amen* after Irwin Tucker's resignation. Storey, then a young professor at Duquesne University, was both bright and balanced and added a necessary boost to the struggling organization. He later became a well-known liturgical scholar and professor at the University of Notre Dame. O'Brien resigned as president following the Pittsburgh meeting and was replaced by Joseph Fischer of Kansas City.

Despite so many upheavals—unsteady leadership, economic problems, and personality clashes among the vernacularists—the movement continued to attract notable interest. For example, in the same year as the difficult meeting in Pittsburgh, Senator Eugene McCarthy wrote to the Society to express his continued support and interest in the vernacular issue and the work of the Society,[59] and new members surfaced on both sides of the Atlantic. Ross-Duggan, for his part, continued his networking among members of the hierarchy in the United States, meeting with Cardinals McIntyre, Spellman, Cushing, Ritter, Meyer, Muench, and the apostolic delegate, Archbishop Egidio Vagnozzi, when the Colonel was not in Europe or some other part of the world.[60]

The growth in new membership for the Society also meant new members for the board. Estelle Kissner of Passaic, New Jersey, was elected corresponding secretary. She became a leader in promoting the work of the Society in the New York metropolitan area and moved the secretariat from Chicago to Passaic. One of Kissner's first tasks was to invite two hundred fifty members in the New York metropolitan area to a meeting to be held on the thirty-first of January at Leo House on West 23rd Street in Manhattan; Irwin St. John Tucker was the featured speaker. A major snowstorm that paralyzed New York did not deter them and the meeting went ahead as scheduled with only seventeen people attending: eleven from New York, and six from New Jersey.[61]

That same year brought further vernacular support from Catholic women as noted in an article which appeared in the *Chicago Sun Times*: "Catholic Women Acclaim Eastern Liturgy in English." The article noted that the biennial convention of the National Council of Catholic Women at Chicago's newly opened exhibition hall, McCormick Place, chose to celebrate the liturgy in English, led by Maurice F. Meyers, s.j., who had worked at the Russian Studies Center at Fordham University in New York, assisted by Demetrius Kowalchik of St. Procopius Abbey in Lisle, Illinois, who headed up the Russian Reunion Center in Chicago. Old Slavonic was employed in the Mass only for the words of consecration. That Eastern vernacular liturgy followed the Latin-English "Dialog Mass" which had been celebrated at the same convention on the previous day.[62]

The mission of promoting a vernacular liturgy continued to be carried out in varied ways according to the ingenuity and creativity of the vernacularists themselves. Two vernacular enthusiasts were Alfred and Florence Berger who began a "tape of the month club" in Cincinnati, Ohio, using their parish as the pilot project. The tapes were exchanged among club members and contained various lectures on the liturgical reform and the vernacular given by liturgical leaders around the country. From their parish in Cincinnati the club soon spread out across the country. Steered by twelve members scattered throughout the United States, the club grew in one year from forty members in January to seventy-five in March, to one hundred seventy-five in April, to two hundred seventy-five in May.[63] Tapes were sent free of charge to those who requested them—except for the 4-cent return postage. The local leader convoked the monthly meeting where members listened to the tape and discussed it afterwards, sometimes stopping the tape during the audio presentation for questions and discussion.

Within three years, more than a thousand tapes were dispatched to every state in the nation and to several foreign countries as well, with the help of eighteen regional distributors. Tapes were sent out between the first and tenth of the month and could be held by the borrower until the twenty-fifth, allowing for several different groupings or hearings in the same geographical area. More than two hundred convents of sisters and nuns were receiving the tapes, many of whom began duplicating copies for other convents; duplication was, in fact, encouraged by the organizers. Some convents began their own monthly mailings. More than seventy-five seminaries took up membership in the club. Some seminary groups, like the one formed at Mount St. Alphonsus

Msgr. Joseph Morrison, Fr. Benedict Ehmann, Col. John K. Ross-Duggan, and Fr. Gerald Ellard work out Vernacular Society bylaws during a Liturgical Week.

Clifford Howell, s.j., leader of the Vernacular Society of Great Britain

Archbishop Karl J. Alter

Fr. Godfrey Diekmann, o.s.b., Archbishop Dennis Hurley, o.m.i. (Durban, South Africa), Archbishop O'Neil (Regina, Saskatchewan), Cardinal G. Lercaro, Msgr. Annibale Bugnini.

in Esopus, New York, distributed outlines of the lecture beforehand to assist those who would gather to hear the presentations.[64]

3.7 *AMEN* AND INTERNATIONAL SUPPORT FOR THE CAUSE

Ross-Duggan continued consolidating relationships, making use of his trips abroad to spread the vernacular message and gain support. When he was not traveling, he would write to his foreign contacts— often members of the hierarchy—to update them on the Vernacular Society's activities and send a complimentary copy of *Amen*. In some cases, some of these individuals responded by sending a donation to join the Society while in others, the individual responded with a letter of gratitude for the magazine and support for vernacular efforts. One such letter came from the archbishop of Peking, Thomas Cardinal Tien:

"My dear Colonel,

"Accept my hearty thanks for the courtesy you have shown me by sending me a copy of your fine publication *Amen*. I am convinced that, when the situation in China renders possible the resumption of normal Catholic activity, many important changes will be introduced into the liturgy, and that one of them will be the use of the vernacular to a large extent in the Mass, the Divine Office, and in the ritual of the Sacraments. I have no doubt regarding the urgency of such changes.

"It is heartening to know that a start has already been made towards facilitating the use of the vernacular for liturgical purposes in China. The Missal has already been translated and the text of the whole Bible in Chinese is nearly completed. Please pray that conditions in China may soon improve sufficiently to make it possible for the work of Christianization of the Chinese race to be resumed and pushed ahead with renewed zeal.

"Your sincere well-wisher in Christ,
+Thomas Cardinal Tien, s.v.d.
Archbishop of Peking"[65]

Similar letters of support were received from such notable figures as Dom Helder Camara in Brazil; Dorothy Day and Jesuit John LaFarge in New York; Dominican theologian Yves Congar; Jesuit theologian

Karl Rahner; Trier liturgists Balthasar Fischer and Johannes Wagner; Archbishop Roberts in England; and Cardinal Lercaro of Bologna. Roberts had been archbishop of Bombay and understood the need for the vernacular because of his missionary experience as a Jesuit. Thus, in retirement living at the Jesuits' Farm Street Residence in London, he maintained a steady correspondence with the Colonel about the vernacular. One letter, in particular, merits citation:

"As for the vernacular, you have every reason to thank God for the success of your efforts at a time when you were a pioneer and liable to suffer much! Here we have reached the 'reductio ad absurdum' of the Scottish bishop asking for the Irish ritual as much better than the English. Your battle is nearly won, and I pray that God may reward you with better health and the fulfillment of your hopes for your family and friends."[66]

True to form, Ross-Duggan was seldom a team player on the international front; he often worked independently, failing to consult the other officers on his strategies and plans until well after those plans had been executed. His good friend, Monsignor Reynold Hillenbrand, was perhaps the only one who had some idea of what Ross-Duggan was up to on his "Round-the-World Liturgical Tours" as the Colonel would call them, paid for, as he always noted, "at my own expense." Writing from Spain on yet another European trip back in 1959, he wrote of his upcoming meetings where he would seek support for the vernacular:

"I have already arranged to revisit Cardinals Ottaviani, Tisserant, Montini, Lercaro, Robert, Valeri, Cicognani, Wendel, Frings, and Feltin (quite a variegated list you must admit). Also Pere Congar, Father Martindale, perhaps Canon Cardijn, and many more."[67]

Theodor Klauser of Bonn and Josef Pieper of Munster were later added to the list. Ross-Duggan reported back that among the many cardinals and bishops with whom he spoke during his six weeks in Rome, there was "considerable confusion" over how much vernacular would or should be allowed in the Mass itself. After listing the conservative cardinals with whom he disagreed, he praised those avant-garde cardinals like Tisserant, Lercaro, Agagianian, Montini, and the French and German cardinals: "May the Lord strengthen their number and their stout hearts!"[68] He continued that at the Congregation of Rites where "I stood up for my personal convictions as to the place of English in the worship of all English-speaking Catholics," he was "urged to be patient ('Pazienza!') as there were to be new and mitigating instructions issued by the Congregation of Rites in the near future."[69] He was encouraged and supported by meetings held in Innsbruck with Josef Jungmann, Yves Congar in Strasbourg, and Johannes Wagner and Balthasar Fischer in Trier.

As the Colonel continued living out of suitcases for months at a time on his "Round-the-World Liturgical Tours," officers of the Vernacular Society and editors of *Amen* were busy at home trying to keep the organization afloat and get the magazine out on time. *Amen*'s mailing list continued to expand with monthly additions of new names, including such notables as composer and head of the St. Paul's Choir School in Cambridge, Massachusetts, Thedore Marier; Mother Kathryn Sullivan, R.S.C.J., cofoundress of the Pius X School of Liturgical Music in Riverdale, New York; U.S. liturgists Martin Hellriegel, Robert Hovda, John Miller, C.S.C., and Eugene Walsh, S.S.; liturgical architect Barry Byrne; European liturgists Romano Guardini, Louis Bouyer, and A. M. Roguet, O.P.; U.S. Senator Eugene McCarthy; Mary Travers (of "Peter, Paul, and Mary"); Msgr. (later Cardinal) William Wakefield Baum; Auxiliary Bishop (later Archbishop) Mark McGrath, C.S.C., of Panama; Luigi Ligutti of the Rural Life Conference; Edward Skillin of *Commonweal*; Richard McSorley, S.J., of Georgetown University; Monsignor Jack Egan of Chicago; Monsignor (later Archbishop) Paul Marcinkus of the Vatican Secretariat of State; Bishop (later Cardinal) William H. Keeler; and Arthur Hull Hayes, president of CBS Radio in New York. While their level of support for the Vernacular Society and the cause itself cannot be easily measured, what is certain is that these individuals were regularly receiving copies of the magazine in the years 1956–62.

Amen continued to receive interesting and varied "Letters to the Editor," expressing hope for greater use of the vernacular. One such letter came from John Bennett Shaw in Tulsa, Oklahoma:

"Dear Sir:

"I am not a theologian, a liturgist, a pious old body, nor am I a young revolutionary. I am a run-of-the-mill layman, a businessman. I love the Mass which I feel compelled to attend daily. I am firmly, seriously, and vocally supporting every effort being made that will give us of the Church-in-the-world this great boon of hearing and assisting at Mass in our language.

"Let me tell you why I feel so strongly about this. I am by profession a mortician and I deal with families who are of all faiths. I often overhear or discuss with them the things they consider different or odd about Catholics. I have seen the success locally, that the Episcopal Church has had by their increased use of the traditional liturgy—especially the Mass.

"I recently directed a funeral which consisted of the Requiem Mass as we know it but which was said in English. Naturally, I listened closely and I could not help but be drawn to the stately beauty of the prayers. How can this not impress the average Protestant to whom our liturgy is foreign. Just think, they knew what was being said and how it was a solace to the saddened family.

"John Bennett Shaw, KHS
Tulsa, Oklahoma"[70]

John Cogley, editor of *Commonweal* from 1949 until 1955, wrote along similar lines when he said that, fundamentally, the vernacular issue was one of understanding and rights:

"As it happens, I personally know enough Latin to understand what the priest's words mean. I am fortunate. Most people are not.

"I think they have a right to expect that the prayers addressed to them (e.g., *Orate Fratres*), the prayers spoken in their name (e.g., *Suscipiat*) and above all the prayers addressed to God in their name should be in a tongue they understand. I think they have a right to expect that when the Word of God is proclaimed in the Epistle and Gospel they will understand what is being proclaimed.

"It is a question of understanding. Understanding seems to be paramount."[71]

In another letter to the editor, one American Benedictine archabbot suggested that it was inappropriate to speak of Latin as a liturgical language since all languages should be liturgical. He then included excerpts of a letter which he had written to Pius XII asking for the entire Mass in English:

"If our dear Lord mingled among people in Italy today, He would surely speak Italian. If he mingled among us in the United States, He would surely speak English. But the mystical body of Christ is here, constantly using an interpreter because so few of the people understand Latin."[72]

Others wrote privately to the editor of *Amen* or to officers of the Vernacular Society itself, asking advice on how best to promote the vernacular in their own countries and regions. João Konzen of Viamao, Brazil, wrote one such letter, seeking counsel as to how the newly founded Cardinal Lercaro Liturgical Center in Brazil might best be developed; Konzen also requested more information on the vernacular movement.[73] Another letter came from seminarian (later Archbishop) James Lyke of St. Joseph's Seminary, Westmont, Illinois, asking for "some authoritative arguments in defense of the use of the vernacular in the liturgy for a class speech."[74] An interesting letter came from Pietersburg, South Africa. K. F. McCurtis was the general physician at the Benedictine abbey there and had become interested in the vernacular through his association with the monks in South Africa. McCurtis helped to promote the vernacular cause by producing his own monthly newsletter, "Jottings from an African Abbey," informing friends and associates throughout Africa of the work of Ross-Duggan and of the Vernacular Society in the U.S. and Great Britain, raising consciousness on the vernacular in South Africa and beyond. Commenting on the 1958 "Instruction on Sacred Music," he wrote to the Colonel:

"I have always been opposed to the two-way traffic Mass in which the priest goes his way (mumbling in Latin) and the lector and people go their way in the vernacular. This is not community worship; the priest and people are traveling on parallel lines (which never meet!) instead of traveling together. Yet this two-way traffic is now authorized apparently as far as the Epistle and Gospel are concerned. How much more dignified was the Papal concession to France that priest and people were united first in the Latin text and then in the vernacular text of Epistle and Gospel.

"I want to see the people join in the dignified official liturgy of the Church (in whatever language they understand), not merely in non-liturgical pious devotions. I don't trust the local bishops (any more than Rome does) to deal with changes in the official liturgy. They have proved themselves quite untrustworthy by failing to see that priests make low Mass largely an audible act of worship as the rubrics prescribe."[75]

Almost one year later, he continued his argument on behalf of the laity who were left with popular devotions in the vernacular as a poor substitute for liturgical participation:

"Priests (even here) seem to think that it is presumption for the laity to have any ideals higher than the gabbling of the Rosary for non-eucharistic worship. I totally disagree, but as a layman, I cannot push myself and my views forward *too* arrogantly. I think concentration *only* on Eucharistic worship is wrong; the Office is necessary too, otherwise worship becomes lop-sided and resembles a sandwich from which the bread and butter have been removed, leaving the meat in icy isolation (and indigestible)."[76]

Amen continued to expand in the years immediately preceding the council despite steady economic problems in keeping the magazine afloat. Such problems often led to delayed publication because the Society was unable to pay its bills. On several occasions *Amen* was on the verge of folding, but like the proverbial phoenix it would rise from the ashes and be revived with enthusiastic support. The journal often came under fire for its strident views on the vernacular and left no room for the tolerance of any Latin whatsoever. This was a concern of Archbishop Karl Alter of Cincinnati who took issue with the magazine's aggressive tactics. He jotted a note to Robert Sherry: "Msgr: To speak of certain advantages of the vernacular is good, but there is *no* need or good reason to devaluate Latin or downgrade it. Too much tendency in this direction."[77]

In light of the 1958 Instruction on Sacred Music, the editorial board of *Amen*, under the leadership of its new editor, Irwin St. John Tucker, considered adapting a more general approach to the type of articles treated, broadening the appeal to consider such areas as Scripture, ecumenism, and understanding the liturgy itself. Tucker was an interesting character. A former Hearst newspaper journalist, "Friar Tuck" as he was called, rivaled the Colonel in his direct and uncompromising approach. He had been an Episcopal priest, ministering at St. Stephen's Church in Chicago on Sundays while serving as full-time copy desk editor for the Chicago *American* during the week until his retirement in 1951. Thereafter, he remained active in ministry at St. Stephen's until he joined the Catholic Church in 1954 after attending a large Mass in Chicago that closed the Marian year. Steeped in *The Book of Common Prayer* and in the importance of English liturgy, Friar Tuck soon became involved in the Chicago Vernacular Society and in the publishing of *Amen* of which he became editor in 1958. A man of strong opinions and aware that the acclamation "Amen" was part and parcel of the vernacular movement, Tucker was bothered that Catholics failed to pronounce it properly. Thus, he advocated—among other things—the proper pronunciation of the term, preferring "Ah-men," rather than the pronunciation which would rhyme with "lay-men," reminding him too much of Southern Baptist services with their oft-repeated, "Amen, brother."[78]

Influenced by his career as a journalist, Tucker had already intro-duced some stylistic changes into the magazine that received mixed reviews; the board even discussed making the magazine available in Braille or on tapes for the visually-impaired. However, while some praised Tucker's innovations—especially the inclusion of more his-torically based articles on the vernacular—others criticized the ap-proach as too sensationalistic, claiming that Tucker's headlines often contained an overly "evangelical" tone. Reactions to Tucker's pro-posal for a more general approach in the magazine were less than fa-vorable, fearing that the vernacular message would be too diffused in such a context. Moreover, with periodicals such as *Worship, Common-weal,* and *America,* there was hardly need for yet another periodical treating similar issues.

Tensions escalated between Ross-Duggan and Tucker, reaching their climax at the Society's annual meeting held in Pittsburgh in August 1960, when a resolution was put forward criticizing the conduct of *Amen.* Tucker's resignation as editor of the magazine soon followed de-spite failed attempts on the part of some board members to convince him otherwise.[79] He began his own vernacular journal "The Briefery" as a protest, although it never amounted to anything more than a mimeo-graphed newsletter of several pages stapled together. "The Briefery" was most famous for initiating a petition in favor of the vernacular, which was sent to the Second Vatican Council, signed by thousands of Catholics from the U.S.A. and also Europe and South America.[80]

Editors of the magazine would come and go, but it was always the Colonel who remained at the helm, albeit unofficially, making it rather difficult for those who were in charge. Tensions were especially evident in the Colonel's angry letters regarding the style and format of *Amen*. He wrote to Michael Ducey, for example, accusing him of trying to turn *Amen* into "an Irish liturgical journal" and "planning to dissolve the Society."[81] Ducey was not the lone recipient of the Colonel's missives.

Only months after Friar Tuck's resignation, the magazine was on the verge of collapse yet again. William Storey wrote to his fellow vernacularist, William Crowley:

"What now of the future of the paper *[Amen]*? It would be a pity for it to cease publication at this crucial moment in the history of the vernacular movement. Now more than ever, I feel that we should press on in pursuit of our laudable goals. So much depends on the coming Council and on the formation of public opinion before it convenes!

"Permit me to suggest that we offer the editorship to John Mahoney. As you possibly know by now, he is moving to the University of Detroit this fall . . . and since this will relieve him of many responsibilities, he would be free and willing to assume the burden of editor. In his hands, I feel confident that the paper would assume a new tone and could be used as a vehicle for something more than mere agitation in favor of English. A scholarly journal? Not that, perhaps, but at least a periodical which suggests concrete proposals and examples of what may and can be done now and in the future."[82]

Storey was wise in his advice. Following the somewhat aggressive and sensationalistic reporting of Tucker, Mahoney brought the magazine to new levels, consistent with the Society's overall desire of gaining credibility and being viewed more in the mainstream. When Mahoney assumed the post as editor, he wanted to make it clear to the magazine's readership than a new age had dawned:

"This issue of *Amen* marks the beginning of a new series of the Vernacular Society's publication, begun not in any rejection of the old, which by this becomes Series I, but begun instead in recognition that part of the principle of the labors and prayers of the Society's membership have come to fruit.

"It remains rather the privilege of the 'vernacularists' now not to assume so much the position of the distant and sometimes rebellious
voice but rather that of the contemporary and at least tacitly approved
scholar. We say this out of no pride, for the accomplishment . . . was
due to the commendable scholarship and eloquence of the Liturgical
societies around the world, and to . . . those members of the hierarchy and Church commissions who forwarded its cause.

"Moreover, it may also be true that many efforts which 'vernacularists'
made have deterred the success of the common liturgical goal. . . .
Amen Series II will attempt to offer itself as a journal open to the publication of information, study, and experiment which its several de-
partments suggest.

"The section called 'Chronicle' will present the combined commentaries and journeymen researches of Col. Ross-Duggan, the Vernacular
Society's oldest supporter, and of Professor William G. Storey, whose
article on the Vernacular Psalters and Breviaries in this issue represents the articulate advancement he has offered the liturgical vernacular movement continually. . . . 'The Chronicle' hopes to become a
fairly reliable quarterly index of activity in the vernacular interest on
a scene as wide as its reader locations.

"The section of 'Reviews' wishes to provide the very sorely needed
department which would make its readers aware of at least the major
examples of . . . books which bears on the vernacular question."[83]

Mahoney continued that articles in "Series II" of *Amen* would include
(1) reporting on vernacular experiments taking place; (2) reports on
assorted materials available in promoting the vernacular (books and
articles, tapes, etc.); and (3) historical articles on the vernacular.[84] His
own editorial efforts succeeded in raising the quality of the magazine
and they were timely with the onset of the Second Vatican Council.

3.8 NEW CHALLENGES TO THE PROMOTION
OF THE VERNACULAR

Despite the fact that a number of Catholic lay organizations began
experimenting with vernacular liturgies at their meetings and conventions, some lamented the apathy on the part of many laity in the Church
regarding full vernacular concessions; many became pessimistic that

the day for a full vernacular liturgy would ever come. One priest from Illinois, Frank Troesch, wrote to the Society's secretary, John Agathen:

"People are funny. All want vernacular but few are willing to help get it. Despairingly they say: 'What's the use? It will never come in our time; the Church will never change.' Some are against the vernacular because it will take too long to get Mass over with; or because the Church is becoming Protestant."[85]

Agathen responded to Troesch about the matter:

"Your observations about the lack of support for the movement among the people generally, even though all agree we should have the vernacular, bears out our experience to the nth degree. In this city (Chicago) which harbors numerous apostolic groups of very dedicated persons, all agree wholeheartedly with our aims, but it is most difficult, indeed, to get any active support from any of them. It is a most curious phenomenon. To me, liturgical reform is basic to all their efforts yet they remain aloof, seemingly content to till their own gardens without realizing that unless the laity, by and large, begins to function actively and intelligently at the altar, it is not going to function apostolically in the marketplace either. After all, it all begins there. Of course, there will always be the specially dedicated to whom this does not apply; I am thinking of the masses who, in the most important activity to which they are called—their worship—have everything else done for them under present conditions. It is hard for me to see how a sense of individual responsibility, for which the Bishops are pleading, is really going to develop in such a climate."[86]

Later that year, Agathen engaged the Society's president, Joseph Fischer, in a similar discussion. He expressed his own disappointment with the leadership received from those with authority in the Church, and acknowledged "grave misgivings" about the Society's future. Agathen noted that every president of the Society, except for John O'Brien, had called for the Society's dissolution. And as for all the talk in the Catholic press about that period being the age of the "lay apostolate," he was not convinced: "This is simply the century in which we are doing a lot of talking about the lay apostolate." In expressing his frustration with the Society's progress, Agathen again reaffirmed the convictions that had drawn him to the Society in the first place:

"If the layman does not stand on his own two feet, say his own Amens, and know what he is saying Amen to, he is, by and large and with notable exceptions, not going to be imbued with a very keen sense of apostolic responsibility in the market place. Muteness at the altar means the bungling, inarticulate Catholic in his social relationships. It all goes together."[87]

Agathen continued that the stand which Church authorities had been taking on the vernacular would prove to be as embarrassing one hundred years hence as the prohibition against missal translations one hundred years before. As for Tucker's idea of a vernacular petition, he expressed serious reservations that such an initiative would make a difference since members of the hierarchy were already well aware of the desire for the vernacular on the part of many Catholics in the United States:

"Will petitions change the mind of a hierarchy which is already aware of the trend among the laity and which shows no inclination to acknowledge it? We have seen argument after argument for the vernacular put forth, often with the utmost conviction and logic, only to be told Latin is indispensable, and that with no acknowledgement or refutation of the vernacular position. Over the years this becomes quite frustrating, and in anything but an authoritarian Church would result in severe disrespect for our leadership."[88]

John Agathen was a man of integrity and conviction, and despite frustrations with the running of the Society and with the apathetic response of many, he did not lose his passion for vernacular reform. He was convinced that the liturgical reform was the most important problem facing the Church and that the vernacular issue was at the heart of the problem. At the same time the Vernacular Society needed to respond respectfully to the criticisms voiced by those individuals and groups who wished to maintain the status quo. Nonetheless, Agathen and the other officers were strengthened in their convictions by the many other letters received offering support and encouragement for their vernacular initiatives. One such letter came from a Minnesota seminarian:

"I pray daily that the Council will be able to overcome the Latinist for the good of the Church and the greater glory of God. May God deliver us from the bondage of a language which none of the faithful understand. Actually, only about five percent of the student body here can speak Latin. May God bless your work and strengthen you to face those who would keep us from the liturgy.

"P.S. I ask please that you *not* publish this letter since the opinions expressed would surely displease some who have authority over me."[89]

Agathan was not the only one receiving letters. Even more significant than individual letters was the eventual acceptance of Irwin Tucker's proposal to launch a petition pleading for the vernacular.

3.9 THE VERNACULAR PETITION

In August 1961, Vernacular Society president Dr. Joseph Evans was invited by the Liturgical Conference to address the annual Liturgical Week scheduled for Oklahoma City. The speech received significant press coverage, and at least one report that appeared in the *Chicago Sun Times* noted how such an invitation was a major step forward for diplomatic relations between the two Societies raising Evans "beyond the lobbyist category" while reflecting "a growing willingness by Catholic liturgists to discuss the value of a liturgy in the language of the people participating."[90] In his speech entitled "The Vernacular Question and the Liturgical Apostolate," Evans argued that the laity "have a right, indeed a duty, to let the bishops hear our needs." And that the bishops themselves "have the obligation of listening carefully and respectfully to our opinions." He continued: "Such assertion by the laity is not a challenge of authority nor is it a mark of disrespect but rather an evidence of deep concern for the welfare of the Church."[91] Evans succeeded in motivating his hearers to action. A "Layman's Plea for Vernacular Liturgy" was circulated among the participants at the Liturgical Week following his speech, and more than 8,000 individuals signed it. The petition called for an all-English Mass and would be sent to delegates at the Second Vatican Council.[92]

Dr. Jack Willke of Cincinnati was one of those who took responsibility for initiating the petition. Willke was a graduate of Xavier University, Oberlin College, and the University of Cincinnati Medical School. He was also the father of five children and had a general family medical practice. In the free time which remained from his sixty-hour workweek, he and his wife campaigned on behalf of the vernacular. Commenting on the importance of the issue in the *Cincinnati Enquirer*, Willke said:

"Christian truths cannot and will never change, but the world we live in is constantly changing. To be most effective in bringing the message of Christ to our world today . . . to allow our public worship to be most effective . . . the external, non-essentials of form and language of public worship must change at times to meet changing needs of the modern world. . . . If Christ were living among us today and would offer the Mass (the Lord's Supper) with us, I believe he would do it in the language that we think and speak in: English."[93]

Willke continued that Catholic laity throughout the world were being given a unique opportunity to speak out on behalf of the vernacular before the upcoming ecumenical council. Prior to launching the petition in Cincinnati he wrote to the archbishop, Karl J. Alter, and the archbishop's secretary responded promptly:

"This will confirm my telephone conversation of today, indicating, in response to your inquiry, that His Grace would not object to laity of the Archdiocese expressing to the Holy See, according to some suggestions that have been made, their desire for a fuller use of the vernacular in the Sacred Liturgy."[94]

One month later, Willke received a letter from the archbishop himself:

"The experience which you have had with regard to the petition for signatures concerning the use of vernacular in a forepart of the Mass indicates clearly that our Catholic people would prefer the use of their mother tongue, at least for this part of the Mass. . . .

"It is well to include in the petition the sacraments and sacramentals. I am inclined to think that they also might be rendered in the vernacular."

Archbishop Alter concluded the letter, stating that he hoped "some favorable response may be obtained from your petition as well as from any others which have reached the Holy See."[95]

Alter was correct in his reference to other vernacular petitions which might have been sent to Rome. Only two months after the archbishop's letter to Willke, the secretary of the Council's Preparatory Liturgical Commission, Annibale Bugnini wrote to Msgr. Robert Sherry, also of Cincinnati:

"I have received many thousands of petitions for English in the Mass and sacraments. Others continue to arrive every day. I can assure you that so extensive a desire of the Catholic people to participate more actively in the liturgy of the Church will be submitted to the Fathers of the next Vatican Council."[96]

Curiously, the idea to contact Bugnini directly came not from the Vernacular Society but, as we shall see in the next chapter, from the Vatican's Secretariat for the Promotion of Christian Unity.[97]

Willke, for his part, was tireless in his promotion of the vernacular petition. With the support of the Rev. George Gude who pastored St. Clare's parish in Cincinnati, he began by speaking to a joint meeting of the Holy Name and Rosary Altar Societies; about eighty people attended. He spoke on the history of the Eucharist itself, highlighting developments in liturgical language over the centuries. His presentation also treated the liturgical movement and recent liturgical innovations, as well as the possibility of further changes. He concluded with the proposal of a vernacular petition and sought volunteers to assist in collecting signatures of parish members. On the following Sunday, the pastor and parochial vicars explained the vernacular issue and the petition during the homily, inviting those in the assembly to sign the petition as they left church. More than two-thirds signed. With 1,500 people attending the Mass, 922 people signed the petition and 578 abstained. Willke wrote in *Worship*:

"All of us will await with intense interest to see what degree of cooperation we will find among the clergy and laity elsewhere in the diocese. It seems to us that the people of God of this country do desire the vernacular in our public worship. If this is true, such a mass expression of opinion, as this could conceivably become, would certainly be given serious attention at the General Council. It is our deepest hope that we have been instruments of the Holy Spirit in this activity."[98]

Different dioceses and institutions amended and adapted the petition as they judged best. Vernacularists in Oklahoma for example, circulated the following petition:

"We, the undersigned priests, religious and laity of the Diocese of Oklahoma City and Tulsa, deeply conscious of the urgent need for praying attentively, devotedly and with dignity, hereby and formally request that we be allowed to fulfill this need by saying all the prayers of the liturgy in English."[99]

The National Federation of Catholic College Students offered their own version of the document which was circulated on college campuses throughout the United States in the spring semester of 1961. In that particular edition, university students petitioned the Episcopal Moderator of the National Federation to represent their desires for a vernacular liturgy at the council. The bishop was also a member of one of the council's Preparatory Commissions.[100]

After the pro-Latin Vatican document *Veterum sapientia* was published the following year in 1962, the vernacular petition moved out from the typical parish setting into other sectors of American life. Ed Groark, an active member of the Vernacular Society and chairman of the U.S. Board of Appeals, did his own lobbying in Washington, D.C. Thanks to Groark's efforts, the list of supporters of the petition came to include U.S. Attorney General Robert J. Kennedy; U.S. Civil Service Commissioner Frederick J. Lawton; the Honorable Eugene McCarthy, senator from Minnesota; the Honorable Mike Mansfield, senator from Montana; John J. McCormack, Speaker of the House of Representatives; Walter Kerr, New York playwright and drama critic; and Claire Booth Luce.[101] Ross-Duggan sent his own memorandum to potential signers of the petition with the call:

"Now is the time to ask all those interested in this important matter to consider *prayerfully* the enclosed Petitions to the Fathers of the Second Vatican Council, get them signed and returned in time to be forwarded to the Council for consideration and recommendation to His Holiness, Pope John XXIII."[102]

Vernacularists in the United States were not the only ones sending petitions to Rome. The Vernacular Society of Great Britain (founded in 1942) sent its own petition on the twenty-seventh of September 1961. It received even more attention than expected when the Society's secretary resigned in protest over the fact that the embargoed text had been leaked to the press prematurely. The petition read: "We humbly ask, therefore, as the principle to be adopted, that the normal liturgical language of the Roman rite in Great Britain be English, except where the local Ordinary considers Welsh more suitable."[103] In that petition we can also note the call for the careful preparation of liturgical texts necessitating a commission which would later be known as the International Commission for English in the Liturgy (ICEL):

"Likewise it would be an advantage if the Hierarchies of England and Wales and of Scotland were jointly to commission and approve an official order, a lectionary, and musical accompaniments, for use throughout the whole of Great Britain."[104]

The vernacular petition also had its opponents. Some criticized English as "less solemn and mystical" than Latin and argued that vernacular worship would "bring God down to the common level."[105] Letters and articles continued to debate the "pros" and "cons" of Latin or a vernacular liturgy, as did university lectures. In a series of lectures delivered at The Catholic University of America, the great Latinist Christine Mohrmann was unwavering in her advocacy of liturgical Latin. Summarizing the content, Gerard Sloyan wrote:

"I was properly impressed with her learning (had read her little Canon book with Bernard Botte (L'Ordinaire de la messe), but came to conclude from her talks that the cause of pastoral liturgy has no warm friend in her. She is for the mystery of language for the sake of that mystery (a sacrament of awe, so to say); she thinks that vernacular departures from Greek in the East in the centuries after the 5th made heresies; she thinks that, having hammered out a Christian Latin for the necessary purpose of praying it in the 3rd–5th centuries we have somehow done a perfect work. In a word, she has no conception of what the last Mass crowd is like in its total incomprehension and would, I think, be shocked to be told that Wyclifites and Lollards had a good measure of success because they shared the mystery rather than kept on mumbling Latin. I guess what I minded most was that, in a community of learned folk, she was not in any mood to be a learner. There were even a few bemused smiles at 'liturgists.'"[106]

Even stronger than Sloyan's defense of the vernacular, one Benedictine wrote an article in *Theology Digest* several years later suggesting that Latin was at the root of "our liturgical malaise." In listing the shortcomings of the liturgical reforms of the Council of Trent, he noted, "a prolongation of the medieval spirit, a quasi-definitive consecration of Latin, and a pastoral separation of clergy and laity."[107]

Meanwhile, the Vernacular Society continued to experience a certain degree of instability in its leadership, and a number of the officers and members remained uneasy with their own involvement since the vernacular topic was considered so controversial. Theodore M. Hesburgh, C.S.C., president emeritus of the University of Notre Dame, who was a member of the Society, recalls that vernacularists were considered "borderline heretics" by some in those preconciliar years.[108] Indeed, some traditionalists would have omitted the word "borderline" in their description of vernacular reformers since they "dared to tamper with God's own words." This was the opinion of an editorial which appeared in *The Wanderer*.[109] A certain level of popular resistance to the vernacular was further complicated by pressure on some members of the Society to resign because of a conflict of interest due to other responsibilities. This was the case with Chicago members Monsignor Reynold Hillenbrand and Patrick Crowley, both of whom resigned from the Society in 1961. It was not clear whether the pressure to resign came from Cardinal Meyer. Both were founders and key players in the Christian Family Movement (CFM), and whatever the reasons, it was clearly a resignation which they had discussed and decided upon together.[110] Joseph Nolan and several others also called for the ending of the Vernacular Society, suggesting that it would be better to have a well-written article on the vernacular included in *America* or *Worship* or to use the Liturgical Conference as the proper means of vernacular lobbying.[111]

3.10 MORE CHALLENGES FOR VERNACULAR WORSHIP

On the twenty-fifth of March 1961 when *L'Osservatore Romano* ran an anonymous article, "Latin, the Language of the Church," in which the continuation of Latin was upheld as a language which is "universal, immutable, and not vulgar." That article had been written by the president of the Pontifical Institute of Sacred Music, Monsignor Anglés Pamies, and would later serve as the base for the apostolic constitution *Veterum sapientia*. The article's attack against the vernacular was quite specific when it referred to "the campaign underway against liturgical Latin," using words like "speciousness, disloyalty, iconoclastic, fanaticism, and intemperance."[112] It concluded by admonishing all clergy to obediently respect and observe the words of Pope Pius XII at the end of the 1956 Assisi Congress where the pontiff upheld the continuation of liturgical Latin for the universal Church.

Several months later, the vernacular issue was not helped much with the baccalaureate address of the apostolic delegate, Archbishop

Egidio Vagnozzi, given at Jesuit-run Marquette University in Milwaukee, Wisconsin. Speaking about the discontented Catholic intellectual, Vagnozzi singled out the vernacular and the liturgical movement as evidences of what he saw as a disturbing trend.[113] Chicago's archdiocesan newspaper, *The New World,* published an editorial praising the apostolic delegate's speech, stating that if this is anti-intellectualism (as it had been criticized in the secular press), "then let's have more of it."[114] Needless to say, the talk infuriated vernacularists but also a number of U.S. bishops. Fundamentally, Vagnozzi was against change in all its forms whether the topic was vernacular, liturgy in general, or the renewal of Church life. Tucker wrote to Joseph Evans expressing his frustration:

"How much of this can one stand? . . . This man Vagnozzi sneers at intelligence, at the vernacular, at about everything the Holy Spirit is trying to accomplish in this hour of acute peril. . . . It is as though the money changers have taken the whip and are trying to drive Christ out of the temple. . . . I do not see how the Vernacular Society or even the Liturgical Conference can keep on living unless they take some vigorous action to repudiate the Vagnozzi utterance."[115]

Bishop Mark Carroll expressed similar frustration in a subsequent letter to Ross-Duggan:

"I need not tell you that I have little or no regard for the Apostolic Delegate. I shall not be uncharitable and tell you what I think of his backward and archaic views of many things. Archbishop Vagnozzi belongs to the old school which has outlived its usefulness and is not in contact with the world today. I presume that he is a good man but I do not like his actions."[116]

Months later, on the eighth of December 1961, Pope John XXIII wrote to Monsignor Anglés Parmies on the occasion of the fiftieth anniversary of the Pontifical Institute of Sacred Music. He praised the Institute for its promotion of Latin in the liturgy since Latin "is inseparably bound to the sacred melodies of the Church of Rome and is, in fact, a manifest and splendid sign of unity. It is the noble and venerable mother tongue of the sons of the Church."[117]

3.10.1 Veterum sapientia

On the twenty-second of February 1962, John XXIII issued the apostolic constitution *Veterum sapientia* that put an end to attempts to suppress the use and study of Latin in seminaries around the world. Moreover, the Pope affirmed that the new document was to be the definitive response to the recent debates over Latin usage and also to the numerous bishops around the world who had requested some type of papal statement on the matter. In the first two of eight norms issued in the document, bishops were admonished both to implement the papal prescriptions on Latin and to be sure that no priests or seminarians in their jurisdictions, "eager for novelties," would make public statements against Latin "either in teaching the higher sacred disciplines or in the liturgy." The other six norms in the document addressed the importance of solid Latin formation in seminaries.[118]

Liturgists and vernacularists were devastated by news of the document, particularly since the Preparatory Commission of the Second Vatican Council was already meeting in Rome. And the media did not help the situation. The News Release of the National Catholic Welfare Council was entitled "Liturgists, Seminary Educators See Broad Significance in Holy See's New Declaration on Latin." The article stated: "The document plainly put a crimp in any all-out agitation for the use of vernacular in the liturgy. . . . One veteran liturgist commented that, in view of the new document, there is 'very little likelihood that any further vernacular will be allowed in any foreseeable future.'"[119] The article noted, however, that liturgists like Godfrey Diekmann were quick to point out that the papal constitution contained only one reference to the liturgical use of Latin and that the new document needed to be interpreted in light of the Vatican's actions in the years prior to 1962 when it had granted permission for the increased use of the vernacular. This was also the position of veteran canon lawyer and liturgist Frederick McManus. The question had been raised:

"Does the Apostolic Constitution *Veterum sapientia* suppress existing concessions of the vernacular in the liturgy, affect the simultaneous reading of English lessons at Low Mass, inhibit the use of common English hymns and recitations at low Mass, or prevent future concessions of the vernacular in the liturgy by the Holy See or the Ecumenical Council?"

McManus responded with a resounding "No," writing that "only the most farfetched interpretation of the constitution on the promotion of the study of Latin would create such impressions."[120] McManus continued:

"The single reference to the sacred liturgy in the constitution was incidental to its basic purpose, to stem the grave deterioration of the study of Latin among the clergy of the Western Church. There is a further and almost inescapable conclusion with regard to the sacred liturgy: that neither present nor future vernacular concessions for the sake of the faithful excuse the clergy from a thorough knowledge of Latin for purposes of theological and other study, communication, etc."[121]

As for future concessions of vernacular in the liturgy, McManus had this to say:

"It seems unlikely that the Holy See would discontinue its policy of extending gradually indults already enjoyed widely, for example, the bilingual lessons at solemn, sung, and low Masses. On the other hand, it would be rash to predict whether new and different concessions will be forthcoming from the Holy See or from the Second Vatican Council. Nothing in the constitution *Veterum sapientia* gives any indication one way or the other; its lengthy discussion of reasons favoring the study of Latin does not even touch on liturgical considerations."[122]

Nevertheless, many liturgists spoke privately about their disappointment with *Veterum sapientia* and how it did represent a reversal of the trend toward the "gradual admission of some vernacular in the liturgy."[123] Few published articles commenting on the text were as strong as one which appeared in *The Christian Century*:

"One pre-eminent service this document has accomplished—a service it without any doubt was designed to perform—has been to quash the current liturgical movement in the Roman Church. It expressly forbids all clerics to criticize the use of Latin in the liturgy. A veteran liturgist in Mexico has declared, in view of the document, that there is 'very little likelihood that any further vernacular will be allowed in the foreseeable future.' . . . A liturgical movement which cannot look forward to the eventual use of the vernacular in the sacred rites is just silly. This is the point to which the liturgical movement in the Roman Church has now been reduced. In short, *Veterum sapientia* has actually succeeded in cutting the ground from under the feet of the exponents of a living liturgy."[124]

On the pastoral level, the document opened an entirely new debate as bishops and pastors, seminary professors, liturgists, and especially vernacularists began to discuss what the liturgical implications might be. Predictably, traditionalists called for an end to any further discussion of the vernacular and even discontinuing use of the vernacular where it had already been conceded.

Despite the measured statements of Diekmann and McManus, many bishops began to fear further discussions of vernacular in the liturgy, interpreting *Veterum sapientia* as the press had been portraying it, i.e., a final condemnation of a full vernacular liturgy. The result was drastic. Clergy were forbidden to continue their association with the Vernacular Society, and the Episcopal patron of *Amen* along with the president of the Vernacular Society were the first two to start the ball rolling. Bishop Mark Carroll of Wichita made a public statement on the matter:

"In view of the issuance of the Apostolic Constitution *Veterum sapientia* of Feb. 22 1962 by His Holiness Pope John XXIII, I am asking that my name be taken off the masthead of *Amen* magazine . . . published with the ecclesiastical approval of the Bishop of Wichita. . . . At the same time, the Rt. Rev. Msgr. Joseph N. Fischer, who has been acting as president of the Vernacular Society . . . is not only asking that his name be taken from the masthead of *Amen* but is also . . . tendering his resignation as president of the Vernacular Society.

"Even though there is much that is debatable about this Apostolic Constitution as it affects the Liturgy, we feel that in the spirit of obedience and submission to the Holy See, the above request and resignation be made.

"At this time we wish to reaffirm our allegiance to the Church in such an important matter, especially in opposing anyone and anything that would militate against, or worse still supplant Latin as the official language of the Church, as well as those who are 'moved by an inordinate desire for novelty' to write against the use of Latin in the teaching of the sacred disciplines or in the liturgy."[125]

On the same day as his public statement, Bishop Carroll wrote privately to Ross-Duggan revealing his true sentiments on the matter "off the record":

"Msgr. Fischer seems to think that for the time being, at least, it would be prudent for the clergy interested in the vernacular to discontinue their apostolate. Without the clergy, I am confident that *Amen* magazine could be run probably by the devoted laymen. I think the work of the vernacular would be hurt very much if only the laity were promoting the sacred cause.

"I am certain that the magazine, if published without the imprimatur of a Bishop, would lack authority and approval. Msgr. Fischer thinks that we should wait until the first session of the Vatican Council is over when we could align ourselves again if an opening has been made and the liturgy discussed."[126]

As discussions surfaced between Bishop Carroll and Vernacular Society officers regarding the future, some questioned whether the Society should continue to exist depleted of its clerical members. This was a question on the mind of Fischer's successor as president, Joseph Evans, M.D., professor of neurology at the University of Chicago Medical School. Evans wrote to Bishop Carroll, "whether or not it is appropriate to follow the injunction of Pope Pius XII at the Second World Congress of the Lay Apostolate: 'Where the fundamental rights of the Christian are concerned, he can assert his demands.'"[127]

Meanwhile, infuriated by the National Catholic Welfare Council's "News Release," Ross-Duggan decided that in conscience, he needed to write privately to Pope John XXIII on the matter, which he did. He also called on the laity of the Catholic Church to mobilize and support the vernacular petition being sent to the Second Vatican Council.[128] He lamented the bad reporting on *Veterum sapientia* which obviously had significant influence on some key players in the Society and in the U.S. hierarchy. He called it "an American plot" to undo the work of vernacular activists, saying that "it will make quite a story after the Council." He concluded: "In conscience, I am proceeding as formerly."[129] And proceed he did, until his death in 1967.

3.11 CONCLUSION

Given the repressive climate following *Veterum sapientia*, Joseph Evans, in his capacity as president, made it his aim to present vernacularists as being in the mainstream of Church renewal rather than renegade dissidents. In an interview given to the *Seattle Daily Times* during the Annual Liturgical Week in August 1962, Evans tried to smooth out old tensions between the Liturgical Conference and Vernacular Society over the years. He stressed the common goals of the Conference and Vernacular Society in renewing Catholic worship and admitted that an overdue emphasis on the vernacular during the Liturgical Conference gathering itself could easily "overshadow the more significant work of the week."[130]

Meanwhile, the anti-vernacular influence of *Veterum sapientia* could be seen even in such secular journals as *Time* which predicted the continuation of Latin as the perduring liturgical language of the Catholic Church:

"The Council will not abolish Latin as the liturgical language of Western-rite Catholics, but will probably let regional or national councils of bishops make vernacular translations for the parts of the Mass specifically addressed to the congregation—the Epistle and the Gospel, for instance."[131]

But the vernacularists continued circulating their petition for English in the Liturgy. And those who "sowed in tears"—with documents like *Veterum sapientia* impeding their efforts—would soon "reap with joy" as plans for the Second Vatican Council took shape across the Atlantic.

NOTES FOR CHAPTER 3

[1] "Current Topics: Annual Meeting of Society," *Amen* 11 (1 Dec. 1956) 2.

[2] Letter of Karl J. Alter, archbishop of Cincinnati, 13 July 1956. CVER 1/4.

[3] In *The Assisi Papers. Proceedings of the First International Congress on Pastoral Liturgy, Assisi-Rome, September 18–22, 1956* (Collegeville: The Liturgical Press, 1957) 18–31.

[4] *The Assisi Papers*, 74–90.

[5] Quoted in William J. Leonard, s.j., *The Letter Carrier* (Kansas City: Sheed and Ward, 1993) 167.

[6] Leonard, 167–68.

[7] Leonard, 168.

[8] Annibale Bugnini, *The Reform of the Liturgy 1948–1975* (Collegeville: The Liturgical Press, 1990) 12–13.

[9] Quoted in Leonard, 168–69.

[10] Remarks made by co-translator Shawn Sheehan in Kathleen Hughes, *A Monk's Tale: A Biography of Godfrey Diekmann* (Collegeville: The Liturgical Press, 1991) 164–65.

[11] Quoted in Hughes, *The Monk's Tale*, 161–62.

[12] The Most Rev. Edwin V. O'Hara, D.D., "The Assisi Report on Holy Week in the United States in 1956," *Worship* 30 (1956) 551.

[13] Letter of Samuel Cardinal Stritch to Rt. Rev. Msgr. Joseph P. Morrison, 4 May 1956. CVER 2/5.

[14] Letter of Godfrey Diekmann, o.s.b., and Michael Mathis, c.s.c., to John K. Ross-Duggan, 10 July 1956. CVER 2/5.

[15] Letter of John K. Ross-Duggan to Father Michael Ducey, o.s.b., 6 August 1956. CVER 2/5.

[16] Letter of John K. Ross-Duggan to John Agathen, 7 November 1956. CVER 2/5.

[17] Letter of Michael Ducey, o.s.b., to Monsignor Joseph Morrison, 6 October 1956. CVER 2/5.

[18] AAS 48 (1956) 725.

[19] Leonard, 150.

[20] Letter of John K. Ross-Duggan to John Agathen, 7 November 1956. CVER 2/5.

[21] William E. Wiethoff, "Popular Rhetorical Strategy in the American Catholic Debate Over Vernacular Reform, 1953–1968," unpublished Ph.D. dissertation, University of Michigan, 1974, 2.

[22] Wiethoff, 74.

[23] "Tentative Critique of Monsignor Romita's Articles Attacking the Assisi Congress and Any Use of the Vernacular Even in Non-Liturgical Devotions." CVER 2/5.

[24] Letter of Robert Sherry to Irwin St. John Tucker, 5 August 1958. CVER 1/19.

[25] Michael Ducey, o.s.b., "Vernacular Movement." CVER 2/5.

[26] Ducey, "Vernacular Movement."

[27] Godfrey Diekmann, o.s.b., "Assisi in Retrospect," Worship 31 (1957) 50.

[28] Diekmann, "Assisi in Retrospect," 51.

[29] Letter of Rt. Rev. Msgr. Robert J. Sherry to Ross-Duggan, 6 December 1956. CVER 2/5.

[30] Letter of John Agathen to Monsignor Morrison, 19 January 1957. CVER 2/5.

[31] Letter of Abbot Baldwin Dworschak, o.s.b., to Very Rev. Michael Ducey, o.s.b., 13 May 1957. CVER 1/16.

[32] "The Vernacular Society," Amen 12 and 13 (March 1958) 14.

[33] Letter of Edward T. Groark (Greenbelt, Maryland) to John Agathen, 27 December 1958. CVER 2/5.

[34] "New Directors Elected by Society," Amen 13 (Dec. 1958–Jan. 1959) 13.

[35] Theodore P. Vermilye, "Saving of Souls Main Argument for Vernacular," Amen 13 (Dec. 1958–Jan. 1959) 11.

[36] AAS 50 (1958) 630–63.

[37] "Commentary," Worship 32 (1958) 628.

[38] Report of interview with Very Rev. Fr. F. Antonelli, o.f.m., Sacred Congregation of Rites, Vatican City, 24 October 1957. CVER 3.

[39] John Agathen. Minutes of Special Meeting of the Executive Committee of the Vernacular Society, 28 October 1958. CVER 1/24.

[40] Memo of W. Michael Ducey, o.s.b., to Officers and Executive Committee, The Vernacular Society Inc., 28 November 1958. CVER 1/24.

[41] John Agathen. Minutes of Special Meeting of the Executive Committee of the Vernacular Society, 6 December 1958. CVER 1/24.

[42] See The Wanderer (19 Feb. 1959) 1.

[43] Rt. Rev. Msgr. Robert J. Sherry, "Your Part in the Mass: Wide Use of the Vernacular Authorized by New Instruction on Liturgy, Especially in Low Masses," Our Sunday Visitor (12 July 1959) 1.

[44] Rev. Joseph T. Nolan, "Vernacular in the Liturgy" (The Benedictine Abbey Press, Chicago, Ill., 1959) 1.

[45] Nolan, "Vernacular in the Liturgy," 7.

[46] Nolan, "Vernacular in the Liturgy," 8.

[47] Nolan, "Vernacular in the Liturgy," 7.

[48] Nolan, "Vernacular in the Liturgy," 9.

[49] Nolan, "Vernacular in the Liturgy," 13.

[50] Letter of George E. Wedemeyer (Wedemeyer Electronic Supply Company), Ann Arbor, to Most Rev. John F. Dearden, Archbishop of Detroit, 20 December 1960. CVER 2/17.

[51] Rev. Joseph L. Imesch (Secretary to the Archbishop) to George E. Wedemeyer, 28 December 1960. CVER 2/17.

[52] The proceedings were published in a volume edited by Johannes Hofinger, *Liturgy and the Missions: The Nijmegen Papers* (New York: P. J. Kennedy & Sons, 1960).

[53] See Augustine Cornides, O.S.B., "The International Study Week on Missions and Liturgy" *Worship* 33 (1959) 645–50. Prior to the Study Week and the published proceedings which he edited, Hoffinger's ideas on liturgy and missions were developed in his book *Worship: The Life of the Missions* (Notre Dame: University of Notre Dame Press, 1958).

[54] Clifford Howell, S.J., "White in Missions—and a man should keep his hat on!" in the London *Catholic Herald* (25 September 1959) 2.

[55] Letter of Rev. Eugene Hillman, C.S.SP. (Tanganyika Territory, East Africa), to John Agathen, 2 May 1959. CVER 1/22.

[56] Letter of Gordon Bodenwein (Acapulco, Mexico) to John Agathen, 9 March 1959. CVER 1/22. Letter of Arthur Perry (Buenos Aires, Argentina) to the Vernacular Society, 1 June 1960. CVER 1/9. Letter of Bill Wharton (Khartoum, Sudan) to John K. Ross-Duggan, 29 March 1960; letter of Frederick Serra, S.J., to John K. Ross-Duggan, 7 August 1961. CVER 2/20, letter of Rev. Ralph Underwood (Queensland, Australia) to John Agathen, January 1959. CVER 1/22.

[57] "Japanese Bishop Urges Fore-Mass All in Vernacular," *Amen* 15 (June 1960) 7.

[58] As quoted in "Episcopalians Win N.Y. Puerto Ricans by Use of Spanish," *Amen* 15 (June 1960) 4.

[59] Eugene McCarthy, letter to Vernacular Society, 7 January 1960. CVER 2/19.

[60] "1959–1962: Interviews." CVER 2/15.

[61] "New York Area Meeting of the Vernacular Society," *Amen* 16 (March 1961) 11.

[62] Dolores Cahill, "Catholic Women Acclaim Eastern Liturgy in English," *Chicago Sun Times* (Sat., 19 Oct. 1961) 1. CVER 1/10.

[63] Letter of Alfred J. Berger to Irwin St. John Tucker, 1 May 1959. CVER 3/1.

[64] Florence S. Berger, "Tape of the Month Club," *Worship* 36 (1962) 533–34.

[65] Letter of Thomas Cardinal Tien to John K. Ross-Duggan, published in *Amen* 12 (1 April 1957) 2.

[66] Letter of Archbishop Thomas Roberts, S.J. (Archbishop Emeritus of Bombay) to John K. Ross-Duggan, 8 September 1961. CVER 2/19.

[67] Letter of Ross-Duggan (Las Palmas) to Monsignor Hillenbrand (Winnetka, Ill.), 11 February 1959. CVER 2/18.

[68] Letter of John K. Ross-Duggan (Palma de Mallorca), 1959. CVER 2/16.

[69] Letter of Ross-Duggan (Palma de Mallorca), 1959. CVER 2/16.

[70] John Bennett Shaw, "Letter to the Editor," *Amen* 12 (1958) 14.

[71] John Cogley, "The Case for the Vernacular" *Amen* 12 (1958) 14.

[72] The Rt. Rev. Ignatius Esser, O.S.B., "Letter to the Editor," *Amen* 16 (1961) 3.

[73] Letter of João Konzen to John Agathen, 13 April 1958. CVER 1/19.

[74] Letter of James Lyke to the Vernacular Society, 8 December 1958. CVER 1/19.

[75] Letter of K. F. McCurtis to John K. Ross-Duggan, 10 November 1958. CVER 3/9.

[76] Letter of K. F. McCurtis to John K. Ross-Duggan, 22 October 1959. CVER 3/9.

[77] Quoted in the letter of the Rt. Rev. Robert J. Sherry to Irwin St. John Tucker, 28 May 1958. CVER 1/20.

[78] James Shea, "Journalism, Ministry Have Great Deal in Common, Convert Editor Believes," *The Catholic Telegraph-Register* (Fri., 20 Feb. 1959), p. A-12. CVER 1/21.

[79] He later explained: "My dropping the editorship of *Amen* at Pittsburgh was because I was prevented by Col. Ross-Duggan from making any report. . . . When he (Ross-Duggan) gave it up, he told Msgr. Sherry that he would keep his hands off thereafter. It was then $1200 in debt, the printer had refused to handle it any further; the subscription list was down, and it had been coming out very irregularly. In three years it had paid all debts—never missed an issue—subscriptions steadily increasing. He simply tried to grab it back. . . . So I quit and started 'The Briefery.' It was this publication that circulated the petitions to Vatican II which turned the tide." Letter of Irwin St. John Tucker to Rev. Thomas McEvoy (UND Archivist), 18 March 1968. CVER 1/21.

[80] The petition will be treated later in this chapter.

[81] Letter of John K. Ross-Duggan (Tenerife, Canary Islands) to Father Michael Ducey, O.S.B., 30 November 1956. CVER 2/5. The Vernacular Society Archives contain an abundance of similar letters revealing a certain possessiveness and paranoia about the running of the Society.

[82] Letter of Dr. William Storey to Father Crowley, 29 April 1961. CVER 1/28.

[83] Editor, *Amen* 1 (July 1961) 3–4.

[84] Editor, *Amen* 1 (July 1961) 4.

[85] Letter of Rev. Frank Troesch (Marine, Illinois) to John Agathen, 19 January 1961. CVER 1/10.

[86] Letter of John Agathen to Rev. Frank M. Troesch (Marine, Illinois), 30 January 1961. CVER 1/10.

[87] Letter of John Agathen to the Rt. Rev. Joseph H. Fischer, 18 December 1961. CVER 1/10.

[88] Letter of Agathen to Fischer, 18 Dec. 1961.

[89] Letter of William G. Poole (The St. Paul Seminary) to *Amen* (27 Feb. 1961).

[90] Dolores McCahill, "Professor To Renew Appeal For Use of English in Mass," in the *Chicago Sun Times* (19 Aug. 1961) 18.

[91] Joseph P. Evans, M.D., "The Vernacular Question and the Liturgical Apostolate," in *Bible Life and Worship: The Twenty-Second North American Liturgical Week (August 21–24, 1961)* (Washington: The Liturgical Conference, 1962) 16.

[92] Editor, "8000 at Liturgical Conference Sign Plea for an English Liturgy," in "The Briefery," vol. 1 (Sept. 1961) 1. CJPE 62. The text of the petition read:

"Responding with joy to the suggestion of the Secretariat for Christian Unity that the people of the Church indicate to the Second Vatican Council their hopes and wishes regarding the Sacred Liturgy, we, the undersigned, respectfully submit the following petition:

"That in English-speaking countries, specifically in the United States of America, permission be given to celebrate the liturgy in the English language, so that all people may understand what is being said or done."

[93] Quoted in Anne Russell, "Offer Mass in English, Catholic Doctor Pleads," *The Cincinnati Enquirer* (Thurs., 7 Dec. 1961) 21.

[94] Letter of the Rt. Rev. Edward J. McCarthy to Dr. John Willke, 5 September 1961. CVER 2/8.

[95] Letter of +Karl J. Alter, Archbishop of Cincinnati, to Dr. John Willke, 11 October 1961. CVER 2/8.

[96] Letter of Annibale Bugnini to Monsignor Robert J. Sherry, December 1961. CVER 2/8.

[97] Letter of Msgr. J. G. Willenbrands, Secretary, to Father John O'Brien, 7 July 1961. CJPE 62/10.

[98] J. C. Willke, "Petition for Vernacular," *Worship* 36 (1962) 52.

[99] "Petition for An English Liturgy," quoted in "The Briefery," vol. 1/4 (Sept. 1961) 2–3. CJPE 62/10.

[100] "We, the undersigned students of _____ College, cognizant that a full measure of participation in the public prayer of Christ's Mystical Body is the source from which is derived the spirituality which will enable us to witness to Christ in the world, respectfully request Your Excellency, the Moderator of the National Federation of Catholic College Students and as a member of the Preparatory Commission on the Discipline of the clergy and laity, to petition the Fathers of the Second Vatican Council that the Liturgy of the Church may be celebrated in the vernacular, so that all who by baptism and true faith are God's holy people may not only hear, but also understand the word of salvation which He speaks to mankind through the Eucharistic Sacrifice and the Sacraments." Quoted in "The Briefery" (Sept. 1961) 2–3.

[101] Letter of Ed Groark (Chairman, Board of Appeals and Review, U.S. Civil Service Commission) to John K. Ross-Duggan, 14 March 1962. CVER 2/20.

[102] John K. Ross-Duggan, "Memorandum to all those interested in a fuller understanding of the Mass," 12 June 1962, in "Edwin Wintermute Vernacular Society Correspondence (1957–1966)." CVER 3.

[103] No. 15. Cited in "Editor's Notes and Quotes," *Worship* 36 (1962) 57.

[104] No. 19. *Worship* (1962) 57.

[105] Wiethoff, 108.

[106] Letter of Gerard Sloyan to Godfrey Diekmann, 15 May 1957, as quoted in Kathleen Hughes, *The Monk's Tale*, 236.

[107] Francis Vandenbroucke, o.s.b., "At the Roots of Our Liturgical Malaise," *Theology Digest* 9 (Autumn 1961) 13.

[108] Theodore M. Hesburgh, c.s.c., interview with author, 22 November 1993.

[109] "Forum," *The Wanderer* (25 Feb. 1965) 8, as quoted in Wiethoff, 110.

[110] Letter of John Agathen to Ross-Duggan, 9 March 1961. CVER 1/10

[111] Letter of Rev. Joseph Nolan to Most Rev. James Griffiths (New York), 6 August 1921. CVER 1/10.

[112] Giuseppe Alberigo and Joseph Komonchak, *History of Vatican II* (Maryknoll, N.Y.: Orbis, 1995) vol. I, 219.

[113] Baccalaureate Address, Marquette University, 3 June 1961. Marquette University Archives.

[114] Letter of John Agathen to Ross-Duggan, June 1961. CVER 1/10.

[115] Letter of Irwin St. John Tucker to Joseph P. Evans, M.D., 25 July 1961. CJPE 62.

[116] Letter of Most Reverend Mark Carroll, Bishop of Wichita, to John K. Ross-Duggan, 4 June 1963. CVER 2/26.

[117] Pope John XXIII to Monsignor I. Anglés Pamies as quoted in Robert F. Hayburn, *Papal Legislation and Sacred Music 95 A.D. to 1977 A.D.* (Collegeville: The Liturgical Press, 1979) 315.

[118] Alberigo and Komonchak, *History of Vatican II*, vol. I, 224–25.

[119] National Catholic Welfare Council, "News Release: Liturgists, Seminary Educators See Broad Significance in Holy See's New Declaration on Latin," 5 March 1962. CVER 1/11.

[120] Frederick R. McManus, *"Veterum sapientia,"* *Worship* 36 (1962) 408.

[121] McManus, *"Veterum sapientia,"* 408.

[122] McManus, *"Veterum sapientia,"* 408.

[123] National Catholic Welfare Council, "News Release," 5 March 1962.

[124] Israel Hubbard, *"Veterum sapientia*: A Comment," in *The Christian Century* (18 July 1962) 886–87.

[125] "Statement from the Episcopal Patron of *Amen* Magazine and the President of the Vernacular Society," 15 March 1962. CVER 1/11.

[126] Letter of Bishop Mark Carroll to John K. Ross-Duggan, 15 March 1962. CVER 1/11.

[127] Letter of Joseph P. Evans, M.D., to the Most Rev. Mark K. Carroll, Bishop of Wichita, 28 February 1962. CVER 1/11.

[128] Letter of John K. Ross-Duggan to John Agathen, 2 April 1962. CVER 1/11.

[129] Letter of John K. Ross-Duggan to John Agathen, 11 March 1962. CVER 1/11.

[130] Lane Smith, "Use of English in Mass Debated in Church Week," *The Seattle Daily Times* (Thurs., 23 Aug. 1962) 2.

[131] Editor, "Religion: Liturgy" in *Time* (5 Oct. 1962) 84.

Chapter 4
Vernacular Worship and Ecumenical Exchange

4.1 INTRODUCTION

From the time of the Reformation until the Second Vatican Council, use of the vernacular clearly demarcated worship between Roman Catholic, Anglican, Orthodox, and Protestant Churches. To worship in the Catholic West meant to worship in Latin; vernacular was for those "others." In the first chapter we saw some historical exceptions to the rule, but in general, to pray in Latin was a tangible way in which the Church demonstrated her Catholicity.

There were, however, several interesting vernacular, ecumenical exchanges and even borrowing taking place in the interim, and we have significant evidence, as shall be seen in this chapter, that the vernacular question was fundamentally an ecumenical one.

4.2 LESSONS FROM THE REFORMATION

One of the hallmarks of the Reformation was its insistence on the vernacular. Even aside from vernacular usage within liturgical prayer, Martin Luther (+1546) published his major treatises in German precisely to assure wider readership among the masses.[1] Swiss reformer Ulrich Zwingli (+1531),[2] Luther's contemporary, insisted that his own works be published in Swiss-German, while second-generation reformer John Calvin (+1564) was published in his native French.[3] The results of such a paradigmatic shift to the vernacular had significant effects far beyond the borders of Reformation Germany, Switzerland, or France. Reformation scholar Alister McGrath is succinct on this point:

"The result was not merely an enhanced accessibility of the ideas and practices of the Reformation; the form of most modern western European languages were decisively shaped by the writings of the reformers, particularly through the publication of the Bible in the vernacular."[4]

A fundamental shift occurred in 1520 when Luther took the decision to leave his platform as an academician, arguing in Latin with the academic elite in favor of a new role as a pastoral reformer arguing and promoting his cause in German to a much wider public. The advantage of vernacular usage was seen even more clearly in Switzerland where vernacular public debates between Reformers and Roman Catholics were followed immediately by a plenary vote where assembled citizens would decide on whether or not to accept the Reformation.[5] Not surprisingly, vernacular usage was a non-negotiable when it came to preaching and liturgical reforms.

Luther is often viewed as the leader of vernacular reform in the sixteenth century, perhaps because his liturgical reforms are the best known. But Luther was hardly the first. Indeed, at the time Luther was engaged in his own liturgical revisions of the Roman Rite, there was already vernacular experimentation taking place elsewhere in Germany and Switzerland. In 1522, Wolfgang Wissenburger introduced German liturgies at Basel joined by Johann Schwebel who produced a similar vernacular translation at Pforzheim. Kaspar Kantz prepared his own German Mass in that same year at Nördlingen to be used by the Carmelite community where he served as prior. In 1523, Thomas Müntzer arrived in Alstedt as pastor of the main Church of Saint John in the New Town and almost immediately published his Evangelical German Mass, Matins, and Vespers set to plainsong, which he completed the following year. Commenting on the importance of worship in the vernacular, Münster wrote:

"This attribution to the Latin words of a power like the incantations of the magicians cannot be tolerated any longer, for the poor people leave the churches more ignorant than they entered them contrary to what God has declared in Isaiah 54, Jeremiah 31, and John 6, that all the elect should be instructed by God."[6]

Even as he recognized Müntzer's good intentions, Luther criticized the pastor's vernacular efforts for having been done in haste as reflected in the final product.[7]

Despite Luther's concerns about moving too quickly with makeshift vernacular translations, liturgical texts in German continued to be produced. In 1524, Diobald Schwartz prepared the Strasbourg German Mass, a conservative revision of the Roman Rite, and Martin Bucer produced his own vernacular liturgical rite called *Grund und Ursach*.[8] Bucer began guiding the revision of the Strasbourg liturgy in 1525 which underwent eighteen revisions over a period of fourteen years until 1539 when the definitive Strasbourg German Mass was published. And as the Strasbourg liturgy continued to be revised, other vernacular worship continued to emerge. In 1534, a German Mass which included a revision of the Roman Canon was prepared at Worms while vernacular liturgies were introduced in Reutlingen, Wertheim, Königsberg, and Strasbourg.[9]

It is plausible that the Bucerian liturgical structure had some influence on Luther's own reforms. Luther was less quick to respond than others with a rapidly composed vernacular worship, but rather pondered the pastoral situation carefully before making changes. He was above all dedicated to the promotion of "evangelical freedom," and a key element in that freedom was language with special attention to the ordinary and uneducated layperson. Thus, in Luther's liturgical reforms we see a fundamentally pastoral approach. Well ahead of his time, he also realized that producing quality liturgical texts required more than a literal translation from Latin into German. Some of his Reformation colleagues had done just that, and Luther recognized the limits of such an approach. In his short text *Against the Heavenly Prophets* written in 1524, he wrote:

"I would gladly have a German mass today. I am also occupied with it. But I would very much like it to have a true German character. For to translate the Latin text and retain the Latin tone or notes has my sanction, though it doesn't sound polished or well done. Both the text and notes, accent, melody, and manner of rendering ought to grow out of the true mother tongue and its inflection, otherwise all of it becomes an imitation in the manner of the apes."[10]

Finally in 1526, he published his vernacular version of the Mass, the *Deutsche Messe*[11] and it conservatively followed the structure and form of the Roman Rite, although he continued to allow for Mass to be celebrated in schools where those in the congregation would be able to grasp that which was being said.[12]

4.2.1 *The English Reformation*

Vernacular promotion played a major role within the English Reformation as well. Noted Oratorian liturgical scholar Louis Bouyer records an exchange between Thomas Cranmer (+1556), the chief architect of the *Book of Common Prayer* (hereafter *BCP*), and Stephen Gardiner on the issue when both were still Roman Catholic priests. Cranmer was reported to have said: "How sad it is that the people in the nave of this church do not understand anything about what is being celebrated in the sanctuary!"[13] Gardiner, who later became bishop of Winchester, responded by trying to persuade Cranmer that it was futile to attempt making the liturgy intelligible to the congregation:

"For in times past, when men came to church more diligently than some do now, the people in the church took small heed what the priest and the clerks did in the chancel, but only to stand up at the Gospel and kneel at the Sacring, or else every man was occupied himself severally in several prayer. And as for the priest's prayer, they could not all have heard and understood, although they would, and had given ear thereunto. For such an enterprise to bring that to pass is impossible, without the priest should turn his face to the people when he prayeth, and occupy many prayers to them to make them hold their peace. And therefore it was never meant that the people should *hear* the Matins or *hear* the Mass, but be present there and pray themselves in silence; with common credit to the priests and clerks, that although they hear not a distinct sound to know what they say, yet to judge that they for their part were and be well occupied, and in prayer; and so they should be."[14]

Archbishop Cranmer, for his part "held to the higher vision," in the words of Anglican liturgical pioneer Arthur G. Hebert, s.s.m. (+1963), giving the worship book of the Church of England a rich treasury based on ancient liturgical sources such as missals, pontificals, and Church offices and sound liturgical principles such as vernacular worship and active participation of the faithful.[15]

It was at Nuremberg in Lent of 1532 that Thomas Cranmer had his first experience of Lutheran worship in the vernacular. While it is not clear whether or not his thoughts turned immediately to the creation of a similar liturgical book in English, what is clear is that his Lutheran experience during that Nuremberg sojourn had a significant effect on his own desires for vernacular worship in England.[16] Two years earlier, George Joye had already published a vernacular edition of The Psalter from Martin Bucer's Latin version published in 1529. In that same year as Joye's vernacular publication, 1530, he published a second text, *Hortulus Animae*, which bore a common title used for devotional primers of the period. The difference was that unlike the other primers of the day Joye's text included vernacular versions of the Hours, Penitential Psalms, and some prayers taken from Luther's *Short Catechism* (published in 1529). Joye's two books were quickly condemned in England, but a certain fascination with things Lutheran remained, helped largely by Henry VIII's determined break with Roman Catholicism in the years 1532–34.[17]

Another text published in 1534, *A Primer in English,* received a six-year patent and enjoyed greater success than Joye's, despite the fact that he reprinted the entire *Hortulus Animae* adding almost as many original texts including a preface, expositions of the Creed, the Lord's Prayer, "Hail Mary," and the Ten Commandments. During the same period publishers Robert Redman, John Gough in England, and Nicholas le Roux in France produced their own translations into the vernacular and introduced their own original texts. Redman produced three editions in 1535, 1537, and 1538; Gough's edition appeared in 1536; le Roux's text appeared in 1536 and was revised in 1537. The texts of these three publishers became source material of subsequent primers. In the words of the late Anglican liturgiologist Geofrey Cuming: "Each of the three contributed as much to the Book of Common Prayer as the primers of the Joye group. Not surprisingly, in 1537 archbishop of York Edward Lee ordered the epistle and gospel to be proclaimed in English during liturgical celebrations.[18] Translation into English was indeed the keynote of the decade."[19] Another new primer written by bishop of Rochester John Hilsey, *The Manual of Prayers,* appeared in 1539. In 1545 came the definitive text, *The Primer Set Forth by the King's Majesty and his Clergy,* "for the avoiding of diversity of primer books that are now abroad, whereof are almost innumerable sorts . . . and to have one uniform order of all such books throughout all our dominions." The text was published in English, in Latin, and in a bilingual Latin-English edition. This was to be the definitive Primer and all other extant editions of the Primer were to be destroyed.[20]

Edward VI was enthroned in January 1547 and within six months decreed that the epistle and gospel were to be read in English. Vernacular experimentation began almost immediately in England. Easter Compline was prayed in the vernacular in the Chapter Royal. In May 1548, Morning Prayer, Mass, and Evening Prayer were being prayed in English at Saint Paul's, while at Westminster Abbey the Mass to commemorate the death of Henry VII was sung in English. Oxford beat Cambridge by three months (Oxford in June 1548; Cambridge in September) in the introduction of vernacular Evensong, while vernacular experiments in the celebration of marriage began in October. As church wardens were purchasing copies of the English

Psalter, individual parishes were producing their own translations of the Mass in English.[21] As yet, there was no officially approved text, thus the experimentation. The translation of the Apostles' Creed was taken from *The King's Primer* for a four-part vernacular setting of the Mass since there was no officially translated text available of the Nicene Creed.[22] That officially approved text came the following year, in 1549, with the publication of the *Book of Common Prayer and Administration of the Sacraments and Other Rites and Ceremonies of the Church, after the Use of the Church of England* with the second edition following only three years later in 1552.[23] Interestingly, all this vernacular experimentation was taking place almost simultaneously as Roman Catholic bishops were fiercely debating the possibility of vernacular liturgy down in Italy at the Council of Trent.

As we have already seen, when the reformers initiated the process of liturgical translation, it was to Latin sources that they turned as base texts for their own work. In particular, one finds what the late Episcopalian liturgical scholar Boone Porter referred to as the "Hispanic influence" in the *BCP:* the influence of the Quiñones Breviary on the Divine Office and the Spanish Mozarabic or Visagothic Rite on the baptismal rite in its earlier editions, and eucharistic rites and offices in later editions.[24] Thanks to the extensive work done by British physician and liturgical scholar John Wickham Legg (+1922), we have come to better understand the Quiñones foundations for the Offices in the First Prayer Book of Edward VI.

The popular and simplified breviary created by Spanish Franciscan Cardinal Francisco Quiñones (+1540) was first published in 1535 and went through several editions immediately. Before its suppression in the 1560s by Pius V, over one hundred editions of the breviary had been printed. As Cranmer experimented with developing Anglican Offices of Morning and Evening Prayer, which he called "Common Prayers . . . commonly called Divine Service," he chose to rely heavily on the revisions of Quiñones. His use of Quiñones work is clearly seen in the preface of the 1549 *BCP* which closely follows the preface found in the Quiñones text. This went largely unnoticed in sixteenth-century England. It was only the historian Edmund Bishop, succeeded by John Wickham Legg, who uncovered this rich relationship between the work of Quiñones and Cranmer.[25]

Cranmer largely followed the Quiñones structure and principles "to the radical extreme" according to H. Boone Porter, condensing the daily Offices into two services: Morning Prayer called "Matins" and

Evening Prayer called "Evensong," using greater amounts of Scripture in each office while curtailing the sanctoral cycle and hagiographic legends. In the final analysis, Cranmer did not base the actual contents of Matins and Evensong on the contents of the Quiñones text; rather, he merely imitated the concept and structure. For the contents, Cranmer relied on lay primers and books of Hours, as well as his own creativity in composing texts.[26]

As mentioned above, the Mozarabic influence on the older versions of the BCP can be found exclusively in the baptismal rite. In the Mozarabic baptismal rite, one finds four short "supplications" each followed by an "Amen," which assist the transition from the vows of the candidate or his or her sponsors to the blessing of the baptismal font. Modeled on that practice, the 1549 BCP contains eight similar "supplications" placed at the blessing of the font primarily for use once each month when the water in the font was changed. Despite the fact that Anglican scholar Jeremy Taylor (+1667) did commend the translation of Mozarabic prayers, it was only in the mid-nineteenth century that those "supplications" were recognized as coming either from a Gallican or Mozarabic source. Later editions of the BCP (including national editions like the American Book) show an expanded Mozarabic influence in the changeable parts of the Liturgy of the Hours and Eucharist—a hallmark of Gallican and Mozarabic Rites as opposed to the sober and unchangeable Roman Rite.[27]

Despite use of Latin sources and the BCP's Catholic roots, however, the staunchly Catholic Mary Tudor despised both the text and the mere concept of vernacular liturgy, even though the first edition of 1549 was far more Catholic than its successor three years later which has subsequently been described as more Zwinglian or Calvinistic.[28] Thus the "Prayer Book Rebellion" against its imposition found fertile ground in her reign. While the BCP appeared too radical for Mary and the more conservative contingent, it was criticized for being too traditional and Catholic by the other side; thus it failed to be accepted in either camp.[29] After the publication of the first edition of the BCP in 1549, Mary refused to allow the new Communion service to be celebrated in her private chapel but rather continued to prefer Mass said in the old way. Her discontent continued, and upon her own enthronement one of the first official acts of Queen Mary was to repeal Edward's liturgical legislation in favor of a return toward the more doctrinally conservative liturgy of Henry VIII all in an effort to restore the Catholic Liturgy in England. To this end, the doctrine of transubstantiation was again affirmed.[30] On the eighteenth of August Mary issued a proclamation calling for the restoration of the old Latin liturgy while allowing Anglicans to continue using its *BCP* until such time "as further order by common assent may be taken." The shift was symbolic of the Queen's desire for a complete (albeit gradual) restoration of Catholicism throughout the country.[31] Within a week on the twenty-fourth, feast of Saint Bartholomew, the celebration of Mass in Latin had returned to at least five or six parishes in the center of London. This is not to suggest that all were in full agreement. London, in fact, remained divided over the issue given its large Protestant constituency.[32]

Commenting on Mary's conservative liturgical legislation, Reformation historian Philip Hughes wrote:

"If Mary had had the powers of the King of France she would have annulled the whole of the religious legislation of the last two reigns on the day she took possession of her throne. But acts of Parliament can be repealed only by acts of Parliament. And when the Parliament elected in the fall of 1553 met, while there was no real difficulty about securing a majority for the restoration of the Mass, there were ominous signs that members were not so friendly to the proposal to 'bring back the pope.'"[33]

Mary had the distinction of being a Catholic Queen recognized by Pope Julius III (+1555) so much so that upon hearing the news of Mary's accession to the throne, the Pope immediately commissioned the renowned Cardinal Reginald Pole (+1558),[34] a relative of the Queen, as his personal legate to England with the task of doing everything possible to restore Roman Catholicism there. Ironically, Pole himself had just missed election as pope by one vote.[35] On his appointment as legate, he was still in minor orders and was ordained priest one day and consecrated a bishop the next, celebrating his first Mass on the day after Cranmer was burned alive.[36] Queen Mary had already decided that she wanted Pole to become the next archbishop of Canterbury.[37] To assist his efforts as legate, Pole was given wide-ranging powers in decision-making lest key opportunities for reconciliation be lost. On the thirtieth of November 1533, Cardinal Pole absolved the English nation of schism as five hundred members of Parliament knelt before him to receive his blessing and together the entire assembly sang the *Te Deum*—in Latin.[38] Hope was ripe for a lasting reunion between both churches. But by 1554 the political and ecclesial climate in England had changed dramatically and hopes for an imminent reunion with Rome were dashed. In April 1557, Pope Paul IV (+1559) recalled Pole to Rome, closing the door on further ecumenical efforts.[39]

In November 1558, Mary's Protestant stepsister Elizabeth acceded to the throne and quickly demonstrated the desire to restore Henry VIII's liturgy to the Church. Like her predecessor, Elizabeth also preferred the old liturgy and insisted that the Latin *Missale* be used in her private chapel.[40] A Latin edition of the *BCP* appeared in 1560, only two years after her coronation.[41] Interestingly, the Queen had the hobby of translating Latin collects into English in her spare time. By royal decree she called for a return to use of the English Litany and to the proclamation of the epistle and gospel in English during public worship, as well as the reading of the Creed, Lord's Prayer, and Ten Commandments in English. Elizabeth was hardly innovative in her penchant for collects. Even prior to the work of Cranmer's liturgy, Roman collects were being translated into the vernacular as early as the late fifteenth century.[42] Prayer Book revision continued into the seventeenth century and in 1662 a new edition of the *BCP* was published following the restoration of the monarchy.[43] Meanwhile, Pius IV had been elected Pope in 1559 and held a more pragmatic approach to what was called "the English Question." Attempts were again made at reunion, this time thanks to the help of Cardinal Charles Borromeo, then secretary of state, to bring Elizabeth back "to the bosom of the Church," but she refused the Vatican's desire to send an ambassador and all negotiations were off.[44]

If Mary and Elizabeth preferred those old Roman Catholic liturgical books, there was some textual borrowing taking place on the other side of the fence, as well. In England, for example, Roman Catholics continued to use the *BCP* in the time of Mary Tudor since Roman liturgical books had been burned. Meanwhile, much later across the Atlantic and in the privacy of his own chapel, Archbishop John Carroll preferred to use the *BCP* for his own personal devotions.[45] Anglican prayer book history is far more of a complicated story than has been presented here, but even a glimpse of how the vernacular issue unfolded in the creation of the *BCP* is helpful.

4.2.2. *The Reformation in Scandinavia*

An interesting example of ecumenical desires focused on the vernacular comes from Sweden in the late sixteenth century and the ecumenically minded King Johan III (+1592). The king had been steeped in patristic studies which embedded within him a strong sacramental piety and made him critical of the more Protestant tendencies evident within selected works of Luther, Melanchthon, and others. Johan acceded the throne in 1568 and was no stranger to Catholicism. His wife Katarina was Catholic, and he willingly provided Catholic chaplains for her spiritual needs; and he raised his son, Sigismund, in the Roman Catholic tradition. Thus, it should not surprise us that his own liturgical reforms would reflect something of that ecumenical spirit with which he lived and governed.[46]

In 1571, just three years into his reign, Johan promulgated a rather Roman order of worship that called for the use of Latin in the recitation of psalms and prayers and included the possibility of the veneration of the saints, the restoration of monastic life, confession, excommunication, and the doing of public penance. This reform was accepted by the archbishop of Uppsala, Laurentius Petri Gothus, who assisted in its implementation.[47] Only several years later, yet another form of worship would be introduced. Much to the shock and disapproval of Swedish clergy, an even more Roman liturgy was produced in his *Liturgia Svencanae Ecclesiae Catholicae et Orthodoxae Conformis* of 1576 which insisted that bishops should be anointed with oil at their consecrations and should properly be vested with mitre and pastoral staff in liturgical processions. Commonly called "the red book" because of the color of its binding, Johan's revised liturgy was simply too Catholic and formal for many of his subjects to take, and there was much consternation as a result, led by a group known as the "Anti-Liturgists." One might hold that their descendents are still among us today, but that would be another book! Actually, the "Anti-Liturgists" opposed the "Red Book" not so much because it was so liturgical but because it appeared as a deliberate attempt to bring the Swedish Church back to Rome. They were, in fact, convinced that the book had been written by Jesuits, an opinion sustained by the fact that, indeed, Johan had allowed a Jesuit Mission to be established in Sweden much to the opposition of many.[48]

What concerns us here, of course, is the role the vernacular played in Johan's efforts. As it turned out, the "Anti-Liturgists" were not completely off the mark. With the introduction of his new liturgy in 1576, King Johan petitioned the Roman Curia for a special dispensation to Sweden allowing vernacular liturgy along with several other requests, which would then facilitate the return of Sweden to Roman

Catholicism.[49] The Roman Curia responded in the negative, in that such permission might establish a precedent for other churches and regions seeking similar dispensations, and the liturgical uniformity which had finally been established at Trent might again be lost. That is not the end of the story, however.[50]

The Curia sent a papal legate, the Jesuit Laurentius Nicolai Norvegus, who was himself a newcomer to Catholicism, and had been involved with previous Jesuit Missions in Norway and Sweden. Johan received the Roman representative openly, apparently believing that amicable dialogue with the Jesuit would lead to an eventual granting of vernacular concessions along with his other requests. This is clear from Johan's essay *"Quae Rex Suetiae cupit ut a Serenissimo Domino Nostro obtineantur ut sine perturbationae Suetiae restituatur Religio Catholica"* published in March 1578, which included his strategy for the gradual reintroduction of Roman Catholicism into Sweden. Included in that essay was the same request to the Pope to allow Mass to be celebrated in Swedish. He was so optimistic about an ultimate reunion that he stopped taking Communion at Lutheran Eucharists after Easter 1577 when the Jesuit Antony Possevinus encouraged Johan to accept the teachings of Trent even without the concessions. Johan agreed by making his profession of faith and taking Communion in the Roman Catholic Church even as he kept the hope alive for vernacular liturgy, the chalice for the laity, and a married clergy. His hope was to be short-lived, however. Pope Gregory XIII responded in October 1578, again denying requests for vernacular concessions (along with many of Johan's other requests). Disillusioned at future prospects for re-union, Johan returned to his earlier practice of communicating at Lutheran masses by July 1579. In 1581, the Pope reconsidered on at least one of Johan's requests: offering the chalice to the laity, provided that France and Spain would agree; but Johan's enthusiasm had waned and the Swedish Mass, along with its Church, separated from Roman Catholicism.[51] After the death of Katarina in 1583, the Jesuits were expelled, and ten years later at the Synod of Upsala, the Augsburg Confession was permanently adopted as the Creed of Sweden.[52]

So it has remained, not only for the Church of Sweden, but also for the Church of England and numerous other Churches which for four hundred years enjoyed vernacular worship while Roman Catholics upheld their own tradition of Latin worship. In the middle of the twentieth century, however, the vernacular as an ecumenical issue reemerged.

4.2.3 The Seventeenth through the Nineteenth Centuries: Movements in the Church of England

By the year 1660, even though Latin continued to be the language of scholarship throughout Europe, it had become a dead language as far as everything else was concerned. Reformation historian Owen Chadwick contends that up until the seventeenth century there were at least some examples of Latin as a living language. In 1500, for example, Erasmus had used Latin as the chosen literary expression "of the highest contemporary prose." Not so in 1660 when the vernacular had become normative for all literature whether prose or poetry and so too for the Christian Churches that did not share membership in the Roman Catholic or Orthodox communions.[53]

In the seventeenth century, Presbyterians in England and Scotland had produced an English version of John Calvin's Genevan liturgy, but unlike the *BCP* the Presbyterian text was meant to serve as a guidebook of recipes for vernacular common prayer rather than a fixed liturgical text to be followed. This is clear in the 1644 *Westminster Directory* that replaced the *BCP* for English Presbyterians and provided outlines of liturgical rites with suggestions for the Reformed worship.[54]

In Germany during the eighteenth century, the liturgical language in the churches of the Reformation was influenced by a certain moralism due to the Enlightenment's emphasis on rationality. The turn toward pietism on the part of many Lutherans during this period was a reaction to this tendency.

The eighteenth and nineteenth centuries in English-speaking countries witnessed further ecumenical textual exchange between Anglicans, Methodists, and Presbyterians.[55] In the eighteenth century, John Wesley launched the Methodist Revival within the Church of England which focused on the importance of more personalized vernacular preaching and the centrality of the Eucharist reflecting a certain mark upon him left by his academic experience at Oxford. John's brother, Charles, also left a vernacular legacy through his composition of hymns, many of which found their way into Roman Catholic hymnals after Vatican II precisely because they were well-crafted texts that reflected a solid and very orthodox theology. Early Methodists developed what came to be called "The Preaching Service," which also included prayers of intercession following the sermon, as well as spontaneous prayers offered and the singing of hymns. In 1784, John Wesley produced his own revision and simplification of the *BCP*.[56]

The Anglo-Catholic Oxford Movement founded on 14 July 1833[57] defended the *BCP* and called for a close adherence to the rubrics within the Prayer Book which had gradually been ignored over the years. Essentially, the Oxford Movement based its efforts on a strong sacramentality with a return to the Church's apostolic foundations. It promoted the restoration of sacramental celebrations and regularized eucharistic celebrations, all in the vernacular, of course. Less than ten years later, the Camden Society (later the Ecclesiological Society) founded at Cambridge in 1839 added another important ritual dimension to the reform, especially through the regular publication of its periodical *The Ecclesiologist*.[58] Like their Oxford counterparts, the Cambridge group advocated dignified worship with a recovery of proper ceremonial and increased frequency in eucharistic celebrations. The Parish Communion within the Church of England added its own important *tessera* to the mosaic, particularly regarding the important dimension of worship's social dimension—what we now call the relationship between liturgy and social justice.[59] In all three of these movements within the Church of England, properly celebrated liturgy in the vernacular was central to the agenda.

4.3 THE VERNACULAR ISSUE IN THE TWENTIETH CENTURY: INSTRUMENT OF ECUMENICAL HOSPITALITY

As vernacular consciousness grew within the twentieth century both within Catholic and non-Catholic circles, one factor in the debate which emerged was the concern that non-Catholics were consistently excluded when attending Catholic worship services because of Latin's unintelligibility. At times this concern was expressed evangelically, suggesting that the vernacular would "bring the wayward children back to the fold," as had indirectly been suggested in the sixteenth century by Pope Julius III when he sent Reginald Pole to bring about the reunion of the two churches. At other times, the concern was expressed simply as a gesture of hospitality. Twentieth-century vernacular promotion revealed some interesting ecumenical exchanges and *Amen* played its own role in the process. Anglicans and Protestants were quick to react to diverse Roman Catholic initiatives regarding the vernacular and it was not long before numerous "letters to the editor" began arriving from many non-Catholics. One Lutheran pastor wrote a rather passionate and lengthy letter to Ross-Duggan in which he linked the vernacular issue with the reunion of the Christian churches. In these postconciliar years of the twenty-first century, the tone of the pastor's letter strikes us as being overly apologetic, not sufficiently appreciative of his own Reformation tradition, and offensive to our ecumenical ears. Nonetheless, the letter is instructive in how he poses the vernacular question in its wider ecumenical context. I quote the letter at length:

"In German we have a proverb: *Was der Bauer nicht kennt, das isst er nicht* (What the farmer isn't acquainted with he doesn't eat). This might readily be applied to the average Protestant attitude toward Catholicism. . . . Lutheran liturgics have drawn from the liturgical thesaurus of Catholicism; but because of the language barrier, many of the clergy and practically all of the laity fail to realize this . . . .

"If Lutherans today could behold the Mass in the Roman Church, even partly in English . . . I believe most sincerely that the Lutherans of today would stop and re-evaluate the Reformation. The immediate causes of the Reformation no longer exist, and therefore by all rights the Reformation itself should come to an end and the Church again should be one.

"To the average Protestant the Roman Church is that group which teaches saints, purgatory, the pope, and bingo. The tremendous salutary theological offerings to be found in her liturgy and ceremony are completely lost to the Protestant mind. He walks into a parish church, sees a man all dressed up, mumbling to himself in a language no one understands, and immediately he comes to the conclusion that the Roman Church knows not Christ.

"Your society is doing tremendous work. . . . A liturgical life such as one can find in Catholicism, when presented in the vernacular, can offer to the entire realm of Protestantism the media of worship and living which they seek but somehow cannot find. I can say this with conviction of experience since I have found this to be so in my own life.

"May I add my voice to the thousands there must be, and urge you for the love of God to persevere in the tremendous work you are doing? In a sense, you are the hope of the Protestant world. For you have within your sphere of desire that work which will make known to them the mysteries of God."[60]

More positively, one religious sister who worked with "borderline Catholics" addressed the vernacular issue in terms of ecumenical hospitality when non-Catholic spouses accompanied their partners to Sunday Mass. Those ecumenical guests were often left feeling lost, excluded, or disillusioned because of the Latin. In some cases the Catholic spouse left to join the church of the non-Catholic partner precisely because the worship there was more intelligible and the community more welcoming. In the words of one former Roman Catholic: "In that new church, I really learned what the love of Christ is."[61]

Similar concerns were voiced in a pamphlet entitled "Vernacular in the Liturgy" written by Wichita presbyter Joseph T. Nolan:

"The greatest number of Protestant Christians and Jews and non-believers that will ever happen to attend a Catholic Mass will do so at a wedding or a funeral. Should we lose this priceless opportunity to impress them with what Christ gave us, and what we have to share? This is not just the problem of dealing with the prejudiced and ignorant non-Catholic.

"President Eisenhower headed the dignitaries who attended the funeral Mass for Pius XII at St. Matthew's Cathedral. Perhaps you saw the picture of Clare Booth Luce assisting the President first with a leaflet missal and then with her own daily missal. Neither appeared to be having an easy time.

"I am convinced that all across the land, we are missing countless opportunities to reach our non-Catholic neighbors with the meaning of the Mass—weddings and funerals above all, but also the Mass attended by the non-Catholic husband or wife or neighbor or friend. Until we use the vernacular it is going to remain a mystifying ritual to the stranger who comes with good will."[62]

Ross-Duggan viewed the problem as one of ignorance on the part of Vatican officials who were unable to understand the complexity of Christian worship in such an ecumenically diverse countries as the United States and Canada, Australia and New Zealand, England, Ireland, Scotland, and Wales. In a letter sent to Cardinal Alfredo Ottaviani, Prefect of the Holy Office, he wrote of the Congregation of Rites' inexperience with English-speaking Catholicism and ignorance as to what was contained within Anglicanism or Protestantism. He framed his remarks in the larger context of ecumenism and the vernacular, lamenting the "leakage" from Roman Catholic parishes toward the Episcopal Church in the United States, precisely because they found greater pastoral care and a more accessible, intelligible liturgy celebrated in English.[63] In September 1959, at the beginning of the Congress for Liturgy and Missions held at the University of Niemegan, Holland, Ross-Duggan wrote to his old friend and fellow-vernacularist, Cardinal Gracias, archbishop of Bombay, who was one of the major speakers at that meeting. The Colonel was less diplomatic than he had been with Ottaviani in expressing his frustration:

"Can you imagine a Congregation of Rites headed up by four men who have no knowledge of English nor of English thinking? Protestantism is a closed, despised book to them. There are over 20 Protestant bishops and clergymen who subscribe to *Amen*. One wrote me the other day: 'In September you slap us across the face with a denunciation of any vernacular liturgy (Sept. 1958), and then the new Pope in February 1959, lovingly invites us to send observers to a council for ecumenical unity. Which voice is the correct one?' This situation applies to all lands, both settled and missionary."[64]

Along with the Protestant clergy to which Ross-Duggan referred, there were even more contacts with former Anglican and Protestant clergy who had subsequently joined the Roman Catholic Church. T. Whitton, who served as an Anglican priest for thirty-three years before becoming Roman Catholic, offers a typical example of the kinds of letters written by that constituency:

"When I was an Anglican, many of us desired Latin and used it when we could because it was Roman, and we imagined it would help toward reunion with the Holy See. I was converted to the vernacular after I became a Catholic when I was asked by the priest to take a class of adult Catholics who wished to understand the Mass. To see what they lost was a revelation."[65]

And there were plenty of regular lay folk, as well, who "swam the Tiber" toward Roman Catholicism and voiced their own lament at the continuation of Latin in the liturgy. One woman who described herself as an "ex-Anglican Catholic," wrote that "so many of those whom I have left behind would be encouraged to return to the true fold, were

they not met with the obscurity of a language they cannot understand." The writer also recognized that the problem was not limited
to former Anglicans and Protestants:

"So many of the less educated Catholics seem to content themselves
lazily with fixing their eyes on the altar and priest, and saying the
rosary. It is difficult enough to captivate one's wandering mind when
following in the Missal, but to leave the priest alone all the work
of offering prayers to the Almighty is surely a sad lack of corporate
worship."[66]

Noted ecumenist George Tavard expressed similar concerns in addressing 3,500 delegates at the thirtieth biennial convention of the National Council of Catholic Women held in Las Vegas. Tavard spoke on
the reunion of the Christian churches and whether or not the Roman
Catholic Church was ready for such a reunion in light of the recently
announced ecumenical council. He responded in the negative:

"Our administrative centralization, our scholastic rigidity, our liturgical matter-of-factness which leaves so little room for personal imagina-
tion—our unity itself, symbolized by an outmoded liturgical language
which no longer has the quasi-universality it once had—may not con-
stitute the best incentive for effort on their part (non-Catholics) to
understand the apostolic government of the church, the theological
implications of the Gospel, the spiritual wealth of the sacramental life,
or rich variety of Catholic unity."[67]

Tavard's concerns were echoed by many ordinary Catholics, as well
as evidenced both in numerous private letters sent to Ross-Duggan
along with published "letters to the editor" that appeared in *Amen*. A
Catholic woman living in an ecumenical marriage who described her
husband as "a sometime Baptist," expressed her frustration that her
spouse, who often accompanied her to church on major feasts and
special occasions with their Catholic son, was excluded, like so many
others in similar situations. She noted the contrast in Protestant
churches with a clear emphasis on congregational participation and
hymn singing unlike the Catholic experience where one "just simply
sits out the service while we say our silent prayers."[68]

One Catholic pastor from Georgia called Latin "the greatest handicap" in attempts at evangelization and efforts to make newcomers to

Catholicism feel at home, i.e., "when they taste and see how sweet the Lord is in the Catholic Church." What they encounter, in fact, is that the Lord is "unspeakably complicated, unintelligible, lacking in clarity and response."[69] Planning ahead, an elderly vernacularist and former Episcopal priest had already told his non-Catholic friends not to attend his funeral, but rather to pray for him at home, "since I have seen and heard how many are choked off by a service they cannot understand."[70] That unintelligibility vanished for one woman who attended her first graveside service in English and heard the comforting words "I am the Resurrection and the Life" in her own tongue. She was especially comforted because of the presence of numerous non-Catholic family members who were finally included, at least enough to know that "we did believe in the resurrection!"[71]

Another southerner wrote of his own frustration with the continuation of Latin in the Mass, calling it the "iron curtain" that keeps the Catholic tradition clouded and cloaked from non-Catholics who might wish to enter in and experience it. He concluded: "Being a native Catholic of North Carolina, I feel that we are doomed to be a small minority."[72]

In January 1961, one Roman Catholic priest actually wrote to Pope John XXIII to express his concern at how Latin continued to exclude large numbers of Protestants from Roman Catholic worship. Bishop Mark Carroll of Wichita sent a copy of the letter along to Ross-Duggan, mentioning that it had been answered "promptly and courteously" by the secretary of state, Cardinal Tardini. Carroll called the letter "a classic":

"In the United States of America, the entrance of many million Protestants into the Church is blocked by the rigid, monolithic wall of the Latin language. This frustrating, psychological barrier makes our most sacred acts of public worship seem to be inhuman, ultra-mysterious, esoteric, and utterly incomprehensible. . . . It also robs our faithful people of their rightful place in the divine liturgy.

"After so many urgings and admonitions from the Holy See to 'take an active part,' our people at worship remain cold and inert. The use of strange tongues excludes them from genuine, active, intelligent, lay priestly participation. Nor can they explain to outsiders what they fail to understand themselves.

"Dear Holy Father, this problem weighs so heavily upon my conscience that I humbly beg you to take direct personal action to restore the Sacred Liturgy into the *native language of our faithful people . . .* " [73]

At the end of that same year, Catholic physician and vernacularist Jack Willke made a similar point in an interview he gave to *The Cincinnati Enquirer.* The following questions were posed: "Do you think that we could more easily attract converts if we had English? Might not the Orthodox churches come closer to reunion with us again if we used the language of the people as most of them do?"[74] To both questions Willke gave a resounding "yes." Catholic journals of opinion ran similar articles about the difficulty which "converts" experienced in following the Mass in Latin.[75]

Students at Saint Anselm's College in Manchester, New Hampshire, who were involved in the National Federation of Catholic Students, organized an education–petition program concerning the vernacular. The educational phase of the program consisted of speakers, a panel, and the publication/distribution of a pamphlet entitled "The Chinese Wall." Latin, wrote the students, was that "veritable Chinese Wall":

"There exists today in our Catholic churches a barrier between the altar and the pew. People at Mass rarely hear what the priest is saying, much less understand the language he is using. Practical unity and intercommunication between priest and people is disrupted by a veritable Chinese wall: Latin."[76]

Not surprisingly, concern was also voiced for non-Catholics and newcomers to the Catholic Church who were consistently excluded because of that "veritable Chinese wall." Once students had been educated on the vernacular issue, they were then asked to sign the vernacular petition sent to the Episcopal Moderator of the National Federation who was a member of the Preparatory Commission on the Discipline of the Clergy and Laity at the Second Vatican Council. From Saint Anselm's, the plan was adopted as a pilot project of the Federation's New England region that included twenty-one colleges. From New England, the program was then launched nationally at the Chicago National Convention in September 1961 giving the vernacular cause attention on one hundred and sixty campuses around the United States—a total of ninety thousand students. Vernacular Society officers assisted the organizers.[77]

Another New Englander, Russell Young, strategized a plan to gain the support of Cardinal Cushing of Boston for the vernacular cause. Cushing was eager to get Cardinal Augustin Bea, president of the Vatican's Secretariat for the Promotion of Christian Unity, to Boston for what he called a "unity tour." On the schedule was a visit to the prestigious Groton School which had a large number of Anglican students. Since Young had been asked by Cushing to host the visit, he chose to use that opportunity to raise the vernacular issue when the three met privately, thereby offering pro-vernacularist Cardinal Bea the opportunity to instruct Cushing on how the vernacular cause was fundamental in the search for Christian unity. Young wrote to Ross-Duggan that he also intended to talk with Bea about the "Anglican Confraternity of Unity" and its desire for admission into the Roman Catholic Church with the request to continue celebrating Mass in the Anglican Rite using the *BCP*.[78] Meanwhile, as Boston was preparing to welcome ecumenist and vernacularist Augustin Cardinal Bea, s.j., the notably anti-vernacular apostolic delegate to the United States, Archbishop Vangozzi, had refused to transmit a papal blessing to the magazine *Christian Art* "because too many non-Catholics write for it."[79]

4.4 LESSONS FROM TWENTIETH-CENTURY ANGLICAN WORSHIP

As has already been mentioned the Vernacular Society drew a sizable number of former Anglicans who had been steeped in vernacular worship from their birth and recognized the tremendous potential for vernacular worship in Roman Catholicism. Several of them, like Irwin St. John Tucker, had been Episcopal priests prior to becoming Roman Catholic. They knew instinctively the great dignity and beauty inherent within properly celebrated worship in the vernacular, at once transcendent and yet also accessible. Numerous letters on this subject appeared in the pages *Amen*. The following letter is representative:

"When I was an Anglican, I frequently attended so-called 'Masses' at St. Clement's Church, 20th and Cherry Streets, Philadelphia, where the full ceremonial of the Roman Rite is faithfully and beautifully carried out in English. There is nothing Episcopalian about *this* Episcopal church! I wish that some of our priests could get permission from their bishops to attend passively a 'solemn mass' at St. Clement's. Then I am sure that any thoughts about the use of English making worship less impressive as compared with Latin would be eradicated."[80]

Cardinal Augustin Bea

Serafini

Martin Luther (right), John
Wesley (below right), Thomas
Cranmer (below left).

Alcuin Photo Library

Two years later, Society officer John Agathen wrote of his own experience observing vernacular worship at the Episcopal Church of the Ascension in Chicago. He noted that despite the liturgy celebrated in the vernacular in a small church, it was still impossible to understand everything being said by the celebrant with his back to the people. Thus, he concludes that "if and when" the vernacular is introduced "or restored as Father Reinhold insists on putting it," an adequate sound system will be essential along with "a movement toward the greater use of altars which face the people."

Agathen was surprised at the close proximity of the Eucharist at Ascension to the Roman Rite. The lengthy account of what he witnessed merits citation:

"When the old Gregorian melodies start ringing in your ears and you momentarily suspend the verdict of your senses, it is just as if you had gone off to an unfamiliar church of your own communion for Sunday Mass. Until the vernacular wakes you up with a start. . . . Their Introit, Gradual, Offertory, and Communion Proper came from the Roman Missal . . . and incidentally, these parts were all sung by the congregation . . . though they do have a small choir whose only function seems to be that of leading the congregation. The Creed—our Nicene Creed—verbatim and straight out of the Prayer Book at that— was sung by the congregation with everyone kneeling while 'And Was Incarnate by the Holy Ghost' was sung. The Canon was said audibly (to remind everyone that there was, after all, a Reformation???). A noteworthy deviation from our practise was the common singing of the Lord's Prayer by celebrant, ministers, and congregation—or was this once the custom with us?

"The theme of the sermon was taken from the life of St. Luke and concerned with the Church's mission of spiritual healing. My ears are not delicately attuned to all the gentlest reverberations of heresy, but it sounded to me as if it could have come from any good Roman pulpit . . .

"While they have gone about as far as possible in principle with congregational participation, there was not a 100% response from the people, since some of the elderly particularly remained passive, either because they did not care to put forth the effort or were too unfamiliar with the music. It takes quite a bit of familiarity with the liturgy, of

148

course, to do the proper as well as the ordinary. But the anomaly of finding Catholic principles and practices in the matter of worship carried out to such a degree by others is inescapable when the situation is contrasted, for instance, with our own showplace (Old St. Mary's) where the principle seems to be the more intricate the music and the more expertly it is performed, the more God is worshipped, even though the people do not understand a word of it and may even be dozing in their seats.

"I was very interested in hearing chant in the vernacular. . . . I am without training in liturgical music and I realize my opinion isn't worth a tinker's damn but it sounded pretty good to me. As a vernacularist intelligibility has priority for me over perfection and I like it fine.

"One final deviation: after a very unhurried service . . . the congregation remained to the last parishioner for the singing of the closing hymn (all four stanzas!). . . . Then I knew I was in the wrong place!

"And oh, yes! The padre recognized me as a stranger as I came out and insisted on knowing who I was, but I didn't tell him I was an eavesdropping Roman."[81]

For his part, Colonel Ross-Duggan noted the liturgical renewal taking place within the Episcopal Church and recognized that Roman Catholic vernacularists had much to learn from their separated brothers and sisters. He maintained extensive contact with Episcopalian clergy and laity alike, a number of whom subscribed to *Amen*. In 1954, prompted by his ecumenical contacts, he decided to give regular coverage in *Amen* to Episcopalian liturgical advances happening within the United States, both to spread the good word in a wider ecumenical context but also to further prod Catholics in advancing the liturgical renewal.[82]

When Irwin St. John Tucker reflected back on his Anglican past, the two things he missed most as a Roman Catholic were congregational singing of "liturgically proper" hymns and people's participation "in the stately dignity of public prayer in their own language."[83] And Tucker was not alone in his liturgical nostalgia. Eucharistic celebrations within Anglicanism continued to be lauded in the pages of *Amen* as examples of what could be done within Roman Catholicism. One article written from Acapulco, Mexico, argued that despite the beauty and transcendence within what he called a "High-church Anglican rite," its chief success comes from the fact that the rite is celebrated in the vernacular:

"The officiant is not carrying out some secret, silent and occult ceremony, some obscure and uncomprehended pantomime all by himself with snatches of singing by a choir of mixed voices thrown in. These congregations are not mere onlookers, nor is their only means of participation private reading of individual prayerbooks. They all take part in everything."[84]

A similar point was made by John Wicklein writing in the *New York Times* who reported on the success of the Episcopal Diocese of New York in attracting new members from among Puerto Rican immigrants living on Manhattan's Lower East Side. Already in 1960, those Episcopalian immigrant communities were celebrating the Sunday Eucharist in both Spanish and English, creating an environment of hospitality and familiarity for newcomers. One Puerto Rican interviewed in Wicklein's article said: "Many Spanish-speaking people come into the Episcopal Church from the Roman Catholic Church because the Mass is in the language of the people and we understand it."[85]

When Anglican worship was offered to Roman Catholics as an example to be followed, there were, of course, opponents who condemned both the *BCP* and Anglicanism itself, denying the validity of Anglican orders and dismissing the doctrinal authority of its worship. Responding to such criticisms, Jesuit (later Cardinal) Roberto Tucci, s.j., wrote in the Italian Jesuit review *La Civiltà Cattolica:*

"The Church of England exercises a providential restraining function on doctrinal disintegration within Protestantism. An eventual rapprochement between Anglicanism and Catholicism might depend on its success of those people who work for the aim of giving back to the Church of England its old physiognomy."[86]

But even among those who were supportive of adopting that Anglican liturgical book for Roman Catholic worship at least some recognized the complexity of such a task and were more realistic about the prospect. Dr. Willis Nutting of the University of Notre Dame had been an Anglican priest prior to becoming Roman Catholic and an active member of the Vernacular Society. He wrote:

"I have had enough experience with English as a prayer language to be an ardent apostle of the vernacular in liturgy, and also to see that it is not a cure-all. . . . We must not expect too much. People who mumble Latin can mumble English just as well and I have little hope that the realization that they should be understood will shame them into being more distinct. You should hear some English vicars! The idea of rushing through the service, of hitting only the high spots, is not automatically removed when our prayers or readings are shifted into English."

He then proceeded to address the care with which liturgical texts should be translated:

"There is English and English. It is not sufficient to have parts of the Liturgy in English. It must be in the *right* English. Chesterton said somewhere that the use of the word "sweet" in our English prayers has probably alienated more people from the Church than have the lives of bad Catholics. A Chesterton exaggeration, of course, but the sentimentality of some of our translated prayers is nauseating.

"Greatness must characterize not only the individual words of the vernacular liturgy, but also the ways the words are put together. There must be a dignity and beauty in the sound of the sentences and the paragraphs—a dignity and beauty that will make people love to recite them, thus forming a pattern from which these people will go on to form their own prayer language.

"In the translation of liturgical prayers from Latin there is a great temptation to follow the Latin order so closely that the requirements of a beautiful English word order are violated. . . . If our vernacular liturgy is to be fully effective, we must be willing to work to make every passage in it as perfect as possible."[87]

4.4.1 *The* Book of Common Prayer

Concern for expertise and care in translating liturgical texts was voiced by other former Anglicans as well, Irwin St. John Tucker being one of the most vocal. Tucker saw the vernacular issue as a "bridge" to Anglicans and felt that we were neglecting our "apostolate" to them in continuing to uphold Latin as *the* liturgical language. Conversely, Anglican liturgists like U.S. Episcopalian pioneer William Palmer Ladd

(+1941) recognized the vernacular issue as a "bridge" to Roman Catholics, arguing that the *BCP* served to stimulate lobbying on behalf of Roman Catholics in North America for vernacular in the liturgy.[88] Ladd was consistently searching for ecumenical links within Christian worship, especially regarding the Eucharist, and had founded the interdenominational Liturgical League in New Haven in the 1930s when he served as dean of the Berkeley Divinity School, to assist precisely in that purpose.

However one interpreted or traveled the vernacular bridge, Irwin Tucker, for his part, recognized the kind of care and beauty of which Willis Nutting spoke in one classic Anglican text: the *BCP*, and proposed that in advocating a vernacular liturgy, Roman Catholics would do well to seriously consider adopting that liturgical book as a base text. Tucker developed his proposal in an article, "The *Book of Common Prayer:* It's Catholic—Let's Claim It!" which appeared in *Amen*. He based his own proposal on the thesis of Louis Bouyer in the classic text *Liturgical Piety*[89] where Bouyer argued that the *BCP* is fundamentally a Catholic document. Tucker concurred with Bouyer's statement and concluded that it logically followed that such a Catholic text, beautifully crafted in Shakespearean English, should be worthy of usage in Roman Catholic vernacular worship. A second reason for the proposal was more pragmatic: with such a classic vernacular liturgical text in our midst, why "re-invent the wheel" and engage in the tedious process of translating liturgical texts from the Latin *editio typica*?

Tucker also insisted on using the American form of the *BCP* rather than the English version, consistent with his promotion of an "American Rite" within Roman Catholic worship and also because, unlike the British version, the American edition had undergone constant revision over the years.[90] He defended his position in "The Briefery":

"Why the American Form? The Church of England, being a department of the State, cannot change its official worship without permission of Parliament, frequently dominated by hostile elements. The American Episcopal Church, freed at the Revolution from political chains, has for nearly 200 years been steadily revising its book through triennial General Convention after experimental use by the whole continental membership. Revisions are steadily in a Catholic direction.

"The original English liturgy was made up chiefly of direct translations from Latin, condensing into one handy volume the Missal, Breviary, Manual, Pontifical, and Ritual. Scholars of English literature universally express admiration for the excellence of its literary forms. Liturgists emphasize the powerful, effective simplicity of its dignified yet appealing rites. It affords a first-class example of what can be done in building a People's liturgy, in which there is full, intelligent, popular participation.

"I am therefore suggesting that it be studied with sympathy by Catholics interested in liturgical reform, in unity, and in missions. Refusal to study it results in ignorance of one of the great formative elements in the psychology of the English-speaking people in general, but in particular of the founders of the American Republic, who were powerfully influenced by it. Most of the American denominations have been strongly affected by it. If these denominations are to be won to the cause of Christian unity, their mentality must be understood. Without knowledge of the psychological impact of this English prayer book, this is a difficult task.

"Return of the *'Angolorum gentes'*—the English races—to the unity of faith of the Universal Church is one of the prime areas of the Church at this era. When they return, they will bring this treasure with them, not as starving prodigals slinking home in rags and want, but as travelers returning from a far country in spiritual garb of surpassing beauty."

Tucker then offered readers an "official" copy of the *BCP* (American edition) "for study only" by completing the form included with his newsletter and sending one U.S. dollar.

Letters of support came streaming in from Tucker's colleagues in the Society. Ed Groark who was chief vernacular lobbyist among Roman Catholic members of the U.S. House of Representatives wrote from Washington, D.C.:

"I absolutely agree with Mr. Tucker's views that we ought to give the fullest consideration to Anglican translations. They are generally excellent, and why in the world, at a time when we are trying to get the churches together, should we come out with (separate) translations of the Gloria, Sanctus, etc. that seem to have no other point than to be different from what the Episcopalians and the Lutherans are using?"[91] Groark then proposed that, following the example of the Episcopalians who had favorably impressed many Roman Catholics with a recent long-playing recording produced by Columbia Records entitled "The Music of the Liturgy in English," the Vernacular Society produce a similar recording called "The Mass in English" using simple psalm tones to demonstrate the feasibility of vernacular worship. The purpose would be to provide Roman Catholics with an opportunity to see how much more meaningful the Mass would be if they could celebrate it in English.[92]

Meanwhile, others continued to join Tucker in promoting the *BCP* for Roman Catholic usage. John M. Todd, who served as assistant editor of the *Downside Review* (published by the English Benedictines of Downside Abbey, near Bath), added his own voice of support: "There lies by our side, ready made, part of the remedy which the Church (Roman Catholic) may eventually need."[93] Despite numerous supporters for the plan, however, there were also plenty of opponents, even within the Vernacular Society itself. The Society's archives reveal extensive discussion on the matter both among Society officers and its wider constituency as evidenced in numerous articles and "letters to the editor" that appeared in *Amen*.[94] Michael Ducey, O.S.B., of Weston Priory, Vermont, had strong reservations about Tucker's article, since the *BCP*, despite its literary elegance, had been condemned by Pius V in the sixteenth century and remained on the "condemned books list" for Roman Catholics. Such a radical proposal on the part of vernacularists could well destroy the very goal they were trying to achieve once the Vatican heard any favorable mention at all of that classic Anglican liturgical text.[95]

Even aside from adopting the *BCP*, some saw the entire vernacular proposal in itself as an attempt to make the Roman Catholic Church more Protestant.[96] One woman cancelled her subscription to *Amen* because of the "disturbing" "letters to the editor" coming from "converts" who were attempting to push Roman Catholics closer toward Protestantism using vernacular worship as the primary instrument. The normally gracious and polite John Agathen sent an unusually strong response to the writer:

"Undoubtedly, there have been disturbing and uncomfortable letters and even articles published in *Amen*, particularly during the last few years, but it is doubtful whether anything can be accomplished in any undertaking or movement if one confines oneself simply to the comfortable.

"The vernacular movement is only one aspect of the general under-taking of liturgical reform and renewal now under way in the Church but to many of those engaged in it, (the vernacular) seems to be at the heart of the whole problem. Reforms are never brought about by wishful thinking and the folding of hands. To assume this is to ignore history of both Church and State.

"As for the 'Dorothy' letter to which you make specific reference, it was written by Mrs. Dorothy Fremont Grant, a convert from Anglican-ism, and if you were bothered by it, I suppose that was the point of it. The letter . . . was only one of the more typical which we receive, mostly from converts. . . . After all, can you honestly say with com-plete assurance that these letters, so disturbing and bothersome at times, are *not* the Spirit blowing where it listeth? The Spirit is not only soothing and comfortable but mighty disturbing as well. And to as-sume that we can learn nothing from these sources is not the most humble approach either."[97]

It was, in fact, former Anglicans themselves who remained the most optimistic about greater ecumenical cooperation regarding the sharing of liturgical texts, even proposing the creation of an Anglican Rite within Roman Catholicism. When Pope John XXIII announced the Ecumenical Council, which would include Anglican observers, one former Anglican wondered if it might not be possible for Anglicans to maintain their own liturgy and traditions, "all in communion with the Roman See." He continued: "The married priesthood, the vernacular, the Prayer Book services (somewhat modified, of course), the choice of vestments, the same hymnaries and all the rest could surely be kept without any compromise of faith."[98]

4.5 THE VERNACULAR AS AN INSTRUMENT IN THE SEARCH FOR CHRISTIAN UNITY

At the beginning of the Second Vatican Council, Ross-Duggan wrote to Pope John XXIII and included a complete set of the published is-sues of *Amen* bound in the papal colors, along with his letter. He had already presented similar volumes to some of the more influential cardinals of the Church like Tisserant, Alfredo Ottaviani, Montini, Lercaro, Suenens, Döpfner, Gilroy, Cushing, and Brown. The cardinals' volumes were bound, of course, in scarlet. In the letter to the Pope that accompanied his gift (copies sent both in Italian and English), the

Colonel gave clear emphasis to the significance of ecumenical factor in vernacular discussions:

"Since I have much Protestant blood in my family I am deeply devoted to ecumenical unity. Will it surprise you to know that Anglican bishops and priests, Lutheran and other Protestant ministers sent subscriptions for *Amen* freely? Therefore, you may appreciate my great disappointment when the Congregation of Rites on Sept. 3, 1958, issued an *Instruction* forbidding use of the mother-tongue in the liturgy of the Catholic Church. This was not only a great disappointment to the millions of Catholic clergy and laity throughout the world, but I fear will be a detriment to the spiritual success of the Ecumenical Council which you have announced.

"The Orthodox and Protestant churches fear that 'Latinization' will be the immediate result of any ecumenical union. It is very unfortunate in my view, that this *Instruction* of the Congregation of Rites appeared shortly before the beginning of your pontificate.

"At least, may I ask that you will take an interest in the use of the mother tongue in the liturgy and place the subject of vernacular language on the agenda of the forthcoming Ecumenical Council, and particularly the use of the vernacular in the Mass of the Catechumens."[99]

Similar concerns were voiced in the United Kingdom where ecumenical families were quite common, and the Vernacular Society of Great Britain did much lobbying on behalf of that constituency. The Lady Millicent Taylour was a Catholic born into a Protestant-Catholic environment and recognized the great potential of the vernacular to bring ecumenical families closer together. She collaborated with several other British vernacularists in preparing an "open letter" to the bishops of England, Wales, and Scotland:

"From my point of view as a laywoman of experience in England and Ireland, this is of paramount importance both for the spiritual benefit of practising Catholics to enable them to increase their understanding of the Liturgy and therefore of their faith, and for non-Catholics who come to our services, to enable them to begin to comprehend the Liturgy. . . . Further, I consider it to be of very great importance that funerals, at which non-Catholics are so frequently present, should be conducted in the vernacular."[100]

4.5.1 The Vernacular and the Secretariat for the Promotion of Christian Unity

In preparation for the upcoming ecumenical council, the Subcommission on Liturgical Questions of the Vatican's Secretariat for the Promotion of Christian Unity met in February 1961 and drafted a text requesting "the widest use possible of the vernacular" both in the celebration of the Eucharist and the sacraments; that text was then amended prior to the April Plenary Session to read "a wider use of the vernacular," perhaps in response to the strong feelings in some Roman circles about retaining Latin. When the Secretariat for Christian Unity held its own April meeting, its president, Cardinal Augustin Bea, s.j., opened the session with a very uncompromising statement: "We must strongly oppose the idea that Latin is a sign of unity." Bea's statement was ultimately reflected in the text the Secretariat for Christian Unity eventually sent to the Liturgical Commission:

"That the Council, when it presents the principles of liturgical renewal, carefully refrain from any expressions which might suggest that the Catholic liturgy is identified with the Latin Roman liturgy and that the Latin language is a necessary bond of Catholic unity."[101]

Soon afterwards, John A. O'Brien on behalf of the Vernacular Society, wrote Cardinal Bea to represent the Society's conviction that the vernacular was a fundamental issue in the search for Christian unity. Along with the letter, he enclosed his article published in *America*, which upheld the same position, along with the exchange of letters which followed. Bea's response was sent by the secretary, (later Cardinal) Jan Willebrands:

"Dear Father O'Brien,

"His Eminence Cardinal Bea has asked me to answer your kind letter of June 16th, and to thank you for letting us all share those informative letters from both Catholics and non-Catholics in the United States who have commented on your provocative article in *America*, 'English in the Liturgy.' It is so important that we catch the laymen's viewpoints, as well as those of liturgical scholars. Needless to say, the problem of the vernacular is immensely important to our Secretariat for Promoting Christian Unity. We doubly welcome, therefore, your sending us the material.

"Realizing this request may take some of your valuable time I neverthe-less boldly suggest that you forward the like matter, and whatever other information on the vernacular—especially from the layman's side—you can muster, to the Secretary of the Liturgical Commission prepar-ing for the Second Vatican Council. I am sure he can use this wisely.

R.mo. P. Annibale Bugnini, C.M.
Segretario, Commissione della Sacra Liturgia
Piazza Pio XII, Roma.

"Wishing you the best for continued good work in your apostolate, I am

"Yours sincerely in Christ,
(Mons.) J.G.M. Willebrands
Secretary"[102]

Willebrands' letter was widely disseminated among members of the Vernacular Society and their friends and letters were sent to Bugnini in the thousands, coming from all parts of the English world and from Catholics and non-Catholics alike. John D. Davis, a presbyter of the Archdiocese of Louisville, Kentucky, was one of those who wrote Bugnini defending the vernacular in terms of its role in the Mystical Body of Christ:

"The grandeur of the Church is not the Latin language. The grandeur of the Church is the Church—the Mystical Body—the countless men and women and children of every nation and clime of the earth . . . joined to Christ their head and his Vicar on earth . . . in common be-lief and worship. The grandeur of the Church is the grandeur of the countless numbers outside the Church. . . . The unity of the mystical body (is not) dependent on the use of Latin any more than the unity of the human race is dependent on a common tongue. The unity is there despite a variety of tongues and God seems to wish it so."[103]

Following the heated debate at the April Plenary Session of the Sec-retariat over increased vernacular usage, the first draft of the liturgy schema, completed by the Liturgical Commission in August 1961, called for introduction of the vernacular particularly in the instructive parts of the rites. Regarding the Breviary, the commission's statement on the vernacular was even stronger. It upheld the idea that Latin was indeed a sign of unity, but it also acknowledged that the study of Latin was declining everywhere, and it was impossible to reverse this reality. Moreover, the statement noted that the issue of liturgical language was, in fact, a cultural rather than religious question, and it was not pastorally or spiritually beneficial to insist that priests who did not understand Latin should be forced to use it in their private prayer. Finally, the commission affirmed a position that had long been held by members of the Vernacular Society: that an increase in vernacular usage would assist the reunion of Christians. The revised schema of November 1961, retained the same general principle and specific applications as had been proposed in the August draft.[104]

Curious about how work was proceeding, Ross-Duggan contacted Liturgical Commission member Balthasar Fischer who responded from Trier:

"You know that our thoughts, wishes, and prayers go in the same direction as yours. Unfortunately, we are not entitled to speak about the procedures of the Liturgical Commission of the Council. . . . What may be said is this: the climate of the Commission is better than we would have thought and we are rather optimistic. But the decisions are up to the Fathers of the coming Council and laypeople have the responsibility to talk as much as possible to bishops about their preoccupations, in your case about the real situation of the Vernacular problem in the English-speaking world. That will do a lot of good."[105]

4.6 THE WICHITA CONFERENCE OF "ASSOCIATED PARISHES"

As the Secretariat for the Promotion of Christian Unity deliberated over the vernacular in its wider ecumenical context and as the Liturgical Commission worked on drafting the liturgy schema, the Episcopal Church in the United States[106] was engaging in practical ecumenism as it pursued its own process of liturgical renewal. The Episcopalian movement "Associated Parishes for Liturgy and Mission" was founded in 1946 by twelve Episcopal priests who dedicated themselves to forging a closer relationship between liturgy and human society, not unlike the concerns voiced back in 1935 by English Anglican liturgist A. G. Hebert. Within three years of the founding of "Associated Parishes," the Church of England founded its own "Parish and People Movement" in 1949 which had some elements in common with "Associated

Parishes" and continued in vigor until 1970. While "Associated Parishes" did not itself engage in revising the *BCP*, it served as a catalyst for subsequent Prayer Book revision.[107]

"Associated Parishes" generated interest and enthusiasm for its agenda through annual conventions held around the United States. Of particular interest to our topic of the vernacular was its convention held from the fifth through the seventh of November 1962 in Wichita, Kansas, on the topic of "Liturgy and Mission," with over nine hundred and fifty people attending from forty-six states. Frank S. Cellier who edited the conference papers, called the gathering "an outstanding milestone in the liturgical thinking of the Church," signifying "the Church's desire to reassume the ancient kerygmatic obligation which it owes more than ever to the world of the later twentieth century."[108] Topics ranged from "Liturgy and Work" to "the Church's Mission to the artist, to a scientific culture, and to urban society." Aside from major speakers like Episcopal liturgical pioneer Massey Shephard Jr., who would later assist at the Second Vatican Council as an ecumenical observer, and Bishop James A. Pike of the Episcopal Diocese of California, Catholic liturgical leader and vernacularist Rev. Joseph Nolan gave a major address at the gathering entitled "The Liturgical Movement in the Roman Catholic Church" which, not surprisingly, focused largely on the vernacular. Bishop Mark Carroll called Nolan: "The Episcopalians want you to give a talk at their conference, and you have my permission to do so." It turns out that Godfrey Diekmann, o.s.b., had been scheduled to speak but was unable to do so; thus Diekmann recommended Joe Nolan because he was local. Aside from Nolan, there were several other Catholics in attendance: Mark Carroll was there himself in his capacity as Roman Catholic bishop of Wichita. He was accompanied by Monsignor Joseph Fischer who was an early member of the Vernacular Society and served as head of the Diocesan Liturgical Commission. And Jesuit liturgical pioneer Gerald Ellard (+1963) was there, as well.[109] Had there been a different bishop of Wichita there might well have been no Roman Catholic representation at all, but Carroll was courageous and open as he looked toward the future. Years later, Joseph Nolan reflected back on the leadership and ministry of his former bishop: "Carroll did all the right things without even knowing why." He was a man of integrity and principle who trusted his instincts and was not afraid to take risks.[110] It was a historic meeting in that it was the first to which Roman Catholics had been invited as official participants or major speakers.[111]

In Nolan's plenary address at Wichita, he suggested that Roman Catholics in North America adopt the Episcopal Hymnal for their own worship since there was nothing like it in Catholic parishes. Participants rose to their feet and applauded for three minutes. In fact, the *1940 Hymnal* represented the fruit of the liturgical movement with its strong emphasis on the full and active participation of the faithful in the liturgical celebration, offering musical settings to be sung by the congregation (and not the choir) both for the Eucharist and the Liturgy of the Hours, with a rich collection of hymns comprising both ancient and modern tunes and texts.[112] Nolan had won his audience over, and an open and frank discussion on his proposal and the vernacular issue itself ensued.[113] The idea of a common lectionary had already been proposed by several other speakers where the same lessons would be read in churches of major Christians denominations on Sundays. Nolan responded: "Why not? We not only share the Bible but a common belief in the efficacy of God's word."[114]

In the general discussion which followed Nolan's talk, several Episcopalians asked Nolan if he considered Latin as much of a "handicap" to liturgical participation as Anglicans and Protestants thought it to be. Nolan's recounted the exchange to the officers of the Vernacular Society:

"I answered that we found it a considerable handicap, and that brought many questions on the vernacular. I mentioned . . . the necessity of good translations and good speaking, and finally suggested that if we perhaps had over-valued Latin in some ways and retained it too long, perhaps some of them felt the same way about their use of Elizabethan English. This was well-received, as apparently many of our Episcopalian brethren would not object to updating the Prayer Book."[115]

Almost forty years later Nolan remarked: "Today, there is still a lack of skill in language in our own worship forms. It is too bad that we didn't adopt the Episcopal Hymnal!"[116]

4.7 CONCLUSION

The Wichita conference was prophetic, for in these postconciliar years one of the greatest fruits of our ecumenical liturgical collaboration has been the formation of common liturgical commissions. In 1968, the Commission on Worship and the Consultation on Church Union joined together to form the Consultation on Common Texts (CCT). One Lutheran participant in the Consultation summarized its task: "the group endeavored to arrive at agreed-on versions of liturgical elements in general use in Christian church services: the Our Father, the creeds, the canticles, the chants of the Mass."[117] The International Consultation on English Texts (ICET) followed with its publication *Texts We Have in Common* (1970). ICET was ultimately replaced by the English Language Liturgical Consultation (ELLC) in 1982, leading to their 1988 publication of *Praying Together*.[118] And that same ecumenical cooperation has led to a certain borrowing of liturgical texts (collects, eucharistic prayers, etc.) among the churches as they have revised their own liturgical books in the past twenty years.

The newly published liturgical book of the Church of England, *Common Worship*,[119] for example, contains a variation on the Roman Catholic translation of the Second Eucharistic Prayer[120] prepared by the International Commission on English in the Liturgy (ICEL) and based on the ancient text found in *The Apostolic Tradition*. Moreover, its "Eucharistic Prayer G"[121] is a slightly edited version of ICEL's "Eucharistic Prayer A" which had been proposed as an original text for the new Sacramentary and ultimately rejected. The Church of England's Liturgical Commission slightly revised the prayer to best be prayed by Anglicans in the United Kingdom.[122] Likewise, when the ICEL Collect Prayers for Years A, B, C were not able to be published or used by Roman Catholics, they were published by Anglicans in Britain.[123] The Common Lectionary Project[124] where the mainline Christian churches would share the same lessons offers yet one more example of such ecumenical liturgical collaboration.[125] As Anglican liturgist and Canon *Emeritus* of Westminster Abbey Donald Gray stated during his address at the Rome's Pontifical Liturgical Institute in 1997:

"Sadly, we are still very divided at the altar, perpetuating the scandal of baptized Christians of different traditions unable to stand or kneel together and stretch out hands side by side to receive that same Lord and Savior, whom we worship and serve, in his real and sacramental presence in the holy eucharist. We could all be sitting under the same pericopes from the word of God; we could all be being fed by the same scriptures. Yet we could be fully united around the scriptures. *The Revised Common Lectionary* would provide that."[126]

Gray, who has been a major figure in the English Language Liturgical Commission, proceeded to explain the commission's discussion on a proposed "common eucharistic prayer" that might be reverenced and shared by all the churches.[127]

We have made great ecumenical progress in these postconciliar years as we continue to seek a common vernacular language in which to worship, but much remains to be done. At the threshold of the Second Vatican Council, Massey Shepherd reflected on the ecumenical liturgical collaboration that had consumed so much time and energy on the part of so many scholars over a number of years earlier in the last century. Such joint efforts, wrote Shepherd, led to an

"exact scholarship . . . not bounded by ecclesiastical commitments. There is a community of scholars that transcends confessional loyalties. . . . It is impossible to estimate what the Liturgical Movement owes to the pure and disinterested research of liturgiologists."[128]

Thanks to the cooperation of those ecumenical pioneers and liturgiologists, all of whom returned to the same patristic texts and discovered the same liturgical foundation at its source, the road was paved liturgically for the ecumenical council.[129] And thanks to the initiative of Cardinal Augustin Bea and the Secretariat for the Promotion of Christian Unity, ecumenical concerns played a significant role in promoting the vernacular at the Second Vatican Council. It is to that council and its treatment of the vernacular question that we now turn.

NOTES FOR CHAPTER 4

[1] For an extensive treatment of Luther's vernacular promotion, see Herman A. P. Schmidt, s.j., *Liturgie et langue vulgaire: Le Problème de la langue liturgique chez les premiers Réformateurs et au Concile de Trent* (Rome: Analecta Gregoriana, 1950) 23–58.

[2] On Zwingli's treatment of the vernacular see Herman Schmidt, *Liturgie et langue vulgaire*, 58–62.

[3] On Calvin's defense of the vernacular see Herman Schmidt, *Liturgie et langue vulgaire*, 63–71.

[4] Alister McGrath, *Reformation Thought: An Introduction*. 3rd ed. (Oxford: Blackwell Publishers, 1999) 235–36. For a good summary of the vernacular issue as central to the Reformation, see Herman Schmidt, *Liturgie et Langue Vulgaire*, 71–79.

[5] McGrath, 236.

[6] *The Collected Works of Thomas Müntzer*, trans. and ed. Peter Matheson (Edinburgh, 1988) 168, as quoted by Bryan D. Spinks, "Evaluating Liturgical Continuity and Change at the Reformation: A Case Study of Thomas Müntzer, Martin Luther, and Thomas Cranmer," in R. N. Swanson, *Continuity and Change in Christian Worship*, Studies in Church History 35 (Suffolk, England: The Boydell Press, 1999) 156.

[7] James F. White, *Protestant Worship: Traditions in Progress* (Louisville, Ky.: Westminster/John Knox Press, 1989) 43. For more information on Münster's liturgical

reforms see Bryan D. Spinks, "Evaluating Liturgical Continuity and Change at the Reformation: A Case Study of Thomas Müntzer, Martin Luther, and Thomas Cranmer," in R. N. Swanson, *Continuity and Change in Christian Worship* (Suffolk, England: The Boydell Press, 1999) 151–71.

[8] Frank C. Senn, *Christian Liturgy: Catholic and Evangelical* (Minneapolis: Fortress Press, 1997) 281.

[9] Senn, 281–82.

[10] *Luther's Works* 40, ed. Jaroslav Pelikan and Helmut T. Lehmann (St. Louis: Concordia Publishing House; Philadelphia: Fortress Press, 1955–86) 141, as quoted in Senn, 283.

[11] See Frank C. Senn, "Luther's German Mass: A Sixteenth Century Folk Service," *Journal of Church Music* 18 (1976) 2–6.

[12] White, 42–43.

[13] As quoted in Louis Bouyer, *Liturgical Piety* (Notre Dame: University of Notre Dame Press, 1955) 2.

[14] Written in 1547. From no. 125 in *The Letters of Stephen Gardiner,* ed. J. A. Muller (Cambridge, 1933) 355ff., as quoted in A. G. Hebert, *Liturgy and Society: The Function of the Church in the Modern World* (London: Faber and Faber Ltd., 1935) 172–73.

[15] Hebert, 173–74.

[16] Geofrey J. Cuming, *A History of Anglican Liturgy* (London: The Macmillan Press Ltd., 1982) 32–33.

[17] Cuming, 30.

[18] Cuming, 30.

[19] Cuming, 31.

[20] Cuming, 38.

[21] Cuming, 39.

[22] Cuming, 39–40.

[23] Cuming, 45–86. See also G. J. Cuming, *The Godly Order: Texts and Studies Relating to the Book of Common Prayer,* Alcuin Club Collections 65 (London, 1983).

[24] H. Boone Porter, "Hispanic Influences on Worship in the English Tongue," in *Time and Community*, ed. J. Neil Alexander (Washington, D.C.: The Pastoral Press, 1990) 171–84.

[25] H. Boone Porter, 172–73.

[26] H. Boone Porter, 173. See Geoffrey J. Cuming, *A History of Anglican Liturgy* (London: The Macmillan Press Ltd., 1982) 33–35; 47–52. On the Quiñones Breviary, see Robert F. Taft, *Liturgy of the Hours in East and West* (Collegeville: The Liturgical Press, 1986) 319.

[27] H. Boone Porter, 175–77.

[28] James D. Crichton, *Lights in the Darkness: Fire-Runners of the Liturgical Movement* (Blackrock, Co. Dublin, 1996) 87.

[29] Owen Chadwick, *The Reformation* (London: Penguin Books, 1964, 1969, 1972, 1990) 120.

[30] Cuming, 87.

[31] Eamon Duffy, *The Voices of Morebath: Reformation & Rebellion in an English Village* (New Haven: Yale University Press, 2001) 154.

[32] Eamon Duffy, *The Stripping of the Altars: Traditional Religion in England 1400–1580* (New Haven: Yale University Press, 1992) 528.

[33] Philip Hughes, *A Popular History of the Reformation* (Garden City, N.Y.: Hanover House, 1957) 298.

[34] See the excellent biography by Thomas Mayer, *Reginald Pole, Prince and Prophet* (Cambridge: Cambridge University Press, 2000).

[35] Richard P. Mc Brien, *Lives of the Popes* (San Francisco: Harper, 1997) 283.

[36] Bernard and Margaret Pawley, *Rome and Canterbury Through the Centuries* (London: Mowbray, 1974, 1981) 9.

[37] Bernard and Margaret Pawley, 9.

[38] Owen Chadwick, *The Reformation* (London: Penguin Books, 1964, 1969, 1972, 1990) 125.

[39] Chadwick, 298–301.

[40] Chadwick, 307.

[41] Cuming, 90. Her Catholic tendencies were to be short-lived, however. She soon called for the suppression of all Roman Catholic ceremonial and decreed that altars and sacred images should be destroyed. Eamon Duffy, *The Voices of Morebath,* 170.

[42] See James A. Devereux, "Reformed Doctrine in the Collects of the First Book of Common Prayer," in *Harvard Theological Review* LVIII (1965) 49–68. The author is indebted to Alan Detscher, James Devereux, s.j., Kenneth Larson, and John R. Page for this information. E-mail of John R. Page to the author, 12 March 2002.

[43] Crighton, 87.

[44] Bernard and Margaret Pawley, *Rome and Canterbury Through the Ages,* 20.

[45] The author is grateful to John R. Page for this information.

[46] Frank C. Senn, *Christian Worship: Catholic and Evangelical* (Minneapolis: Fortress Press, 1997) 414.

[47] Chadwick, 372.

[48] Senn, 423–24.

[49] The other dispensations requested included Communion from the cup, a married clergy, and the possibility for Catholic Queen Katarina to receive Holy Communion at Lutheran Eucharists.

[50] Senn, 424.

[51] Senn, 424–26.

[52] Chadwick, 372.

[53] Chadwick, 298–99.

[54] John Fenwick and Bryan Spinks, *Worship in Transition: The Liturgical Movement in the Twentieth Century* (New York: Continuum, 1995) 81–82.

[55] See Cuming, 128–64.

[56] Fenwick and Spinks, 38–39. See also Adrian Burdon, *The Preaching Service: The Glory of the Methodists* (Alcuin Club) (Bramcote: Grove Books, 1991).

[57] See Christopher Dawson, *The Spirit of the Oxford Movement* (London: The Saint Austin Press, 1933, 1945, 2001).

[58] Fenwick and Spinks, 39. See also James F. White, *The Cambridge Movement: The Ecclesiologists and Gothic Revival* (Cambridge: Cambridge University Press, 1962, 1979).

[59] See Donald Gray, *Earth and Altar: The Evolution of the Parish Communion in the Church of England to 1945* (Norwich: Alcuin Club, 1986).

[60] Letter from "A Lutheran Pastor" to John K. Ross-Duggan (undated), printed in *Amen* 8–9 (Feb. 1954) 3.

[61] Sister Hildegarde, "Letter to the Editor," *Amen* 9 (July 1954) 3.

[62] "Vernacular in the Liturgy" (Chicago: Benedictine Abbey Press, 1959) 11–12. CVER 5. Nolan, currently professor of theology at Boston College, was ordained in 1953 and became involved with the Vernacular Society through the influence of Boston liturgical pioneer William Leonard, s.j. Nolan recalls thinking "we'll never give up the Latin." But then a letter arrived from India to the Vernacular Society saying, "You people arguing for Latin don't know anything. We have people who can't read or write, can't afford missals etc." Rev. Joseph T. Nolan, interview with the author, Boston College, Thursday, 22 July 1999.

[63] Letter of John K. Ross-Duggan to His Eminence Alfredo Cardinal Ottaviani, Congregation of the Holy Office, 5 November 1959. CVER 2/18.

[64] Letter of John K. Ross-Duggan to His Eminence, Cardinal Gracias, 9 September 1959. CVER 2/18.

[65] T. Whitton, "Letter to the Editor," *Amen* 15/4 (1960) 12.

[66] Constance Gillespie-Taylor, "Letter to the Editor," *Amen* 15/4 (1960) 12.

[67] George Tavard, "Address to the 30th Biennial Convention of the National Council of Catholic Women at Las Vegas, Nevada," as recorded in *Amen* 16 (March 1961) 4.

[68] Letter of Gertrude M. Hoyt to Father Hans A. Reinhold, *Amen* 10 (July 1955) 2.

[69] Letter of J. H. McCown, s.j., Macon, Georgia, to the Vernacular Society, 11 April 1956. CVER 1/16.

[70] T. Whitton, *Amen* 15/4 (1960) 12.

[71] "A Sad Heart," *Amen* 11 (Dec. 1956) 2.

[72] Thomas D. Bradely, Salisbury, North Carolina, "Letter to the Editor," *Amen* 14 (June 1959) 2.

[73] Letter of Rev. Joseph G. Bartos to His Holiness, Pope John XXIII, 15 January 1961. CVER 1/10.

[74] Anne Russell, "Offer Mass in English, Catholic Doctor Pleads," *The Cincinnati Enquirer* (Thurs., 7 December 1961) 21.

[75] See, for example, Joseph A. Brieg's article "English in the Dialogue Mass: Letters to a Columnist Stir Up Some Pointed Comments on the Dialogue Mass," that appeared in the fifteenth December 1962 issue of *America*.

[76] Letter of Daniel T. Harley (St. Anselm's College, Manchester, N.H.) to Rev. Michael Ducey, o.s.b., 20 January 1962. CJPE 62/13.

[77] Letter of Daniel T. Harley (St. Anselm's College, Manchester, N.H.) to Rev. Michael Ducey, o.s.b., 20 January 1962. CJPE 62/13.

[78] Letter of Russell S. Young (Groton School, Groton, Mass.) to John K. Ross-Duggan, 9 January 1963. CVER 2/21.

[79] Letter of Irwin St. John Tucker to John K. Ross-Duggan, 13 May 1963. CVER 2/18.

[80] Letter of Mr. D.H.P. to Editor of *Amen* (May–June 1951) 15.

[81] Letter of John Agathen to Monsignor Joseph Morrison, 5 November 1953. CVER 1/28.

[82] Letter of Ross-Duggan to Mr. Phil Gundermann, Park Forest, Illinois, 8 September 1954. CVER 1/2.

[83] Irwin St. John Tucker, "The Book of Common Prayer: It's Catholic—Let's Claim It," *Amen* 11/3–4 (1956) 11.

[84] Gordon Bodenwein, "High Church Anglican Rites Show Value of the Vernacular," *Amen* 14 (June 1959) 2.

[85] "Episcopalians Win N.Y. Puerto Ricans By Use of Spanish," *Amen* 15/2 (1960) 4. The issue of hospitality and welcome continues to be an important reason why believers leave one church to join another. In the 1990s, for example, Rome's Episcopal Church of St. Paul's "Within the Walls" attracted a fair number of Latin Americans because it was virtually the only parish in Rome offering significant pastoral outreach in Spanish to Latin Americans. As this book goes to press there continues to be a vibrant Sunday Eucharist celebrated weekly in Spanish with over 150 Latin Americans participating. Rome offers no comparable Roman Catholic equivalent. Catholic Masses are celebrated in Spanish in several places but without the dynamism, music, and welcome found at St. Paul's.

[86] As quoted in Irwin St. John Tucker, "The Briefery" (undated). CVER 5.

[87] Willis D. Nutting, Ph.D., "On the Verge of the Vernacular," *Amen* 11 (December 1956) 4–5.

[88] William Palmer Ladd, *Prayer Book Interleaves: Some Reflections on How the Book of Common Prayer Might Be Made More Influential In Our English-Speaking World* (New York: Oxford, 1942; 2nd ed., Greenwich, Conn.: Seabury, 1957) 64, 155, 157, as quoted in Michael Moriarty, *The Liturgical Revolution: Prayer Book Revision and Associated Parishes: A Generation of Change in the Episcopal Church* (New York: The Church Hymnal Corporation, 1996) 37. Ladd was both mentor and friend to that other major liturgical figure in the Episcopal Church, Massey Shepherd (+1990), and we see similar concerns for the social dimension of Christian worship, ecumenism, and intelligent participation. Moriarty, 27.

[89] *Liturgical Piety* (Notre Dame, Ind.: University of Notre Dame Press, 1955).

[90] The proposal of an "American Rite" within Roman Catholicism was supported by other members of the Vernacular Society as well, evidenced in the circular letter of the Society's president, Joseph Evans, M.D., "To the Officers of the Vernacular Society," 15 February 1963. CVER 2/7.

[91] Letter of Edward Groark to John Agathen, 8 June 1960. CVER 1/9.

[92] Groark. CVER 1/9.

[93] Quoted in Irwin St. John Tucker, "The Briefery" (not dated). CVER 5.

[94] Irwin St. John Tucker, "The Book of Common Prayer: It's Catholic—Let's Claim It" *Amen* 11 (Nov.–Dec. 1956) 11.

[95] Letter of Michael Ducey, O.S.B., to John K. Ross-Duggan, 27 July 1956. CVER 2/5.

[96] Letter of Rev. Frank M. Troesch (Marine, Illinois) to John Agathen, 19 January 1961. CVER 1/10.

[97] Letter of John Agathen to Miss Bernadette Regan, 25 April 1961. CVER 1/10.

[98] D. H. Williams, "Letter to the Editor," *Amen* 14 (June 1959) 1.

[99] Letter of John-K. Ross-Duggan sent to His Holiness Pope John XXIII, 1960 (day/month not given). CVER 2/25.

[100] The Lady Millicent Taylour, "An Open Letter Addressed to the Most Reverend Archbishops and the Right Reverend Bishops of the Hierarchy of England and Wales and the Hierarchy of Scotland," 15 September 1963. CVER 4.

[101] As quoted in Alberigo and Komonchak, *History of Vatican II*, vol. I, 221.

[102] Letter of Jan G. M. Willebrands to John A. O'Brien, 7 July 1961. CVER 5.

[103] Letter of John D. Davis to The Most Reverend Annibale Bugnini, c.m., 28 August 1962. CVER 2/26.

[104] Alberigo and Komonchak, *History of Vatican II*, vol. I, 221.

[105] Balthasar Fischer to Ross-Duggan, 12 August 1961. CVER 2/20.

[106] For a summary of the Episcopal Church, see David L. Holmes, *A Brief History of the Episcopal Church* (Valley Forge, Pa.: Trinity Press International, 1993).

[107] Michael Moriarty, *The Liturgical Revolution*, 38.

[108] Frank S. Cellier, ed., *Liturgy Is Mission* (New York: Seabury, 1964) 30–31, as quoted in Moriarty, 81.

[109] Rev. Joseph T. Nolan, interview with the author. Boston College, Chestnut Hill, Mass., Thursday, 22 July 1999.

[110] Rev. Joseph T. Nolan, interview with the author, 22 July 1999, Boston College, Chestnut Hill, Mass.

[111] Moriarty, 81.

[112] Moriarty, 29.

[113] Moriarty, 29.

[114] Circular letter of Joseph Evans, M.D., to the Officers of the Vernacular Society, 15 February 1963. CVER 2/7.

[115] Evans. CVER 2/7. Catholic speakers continued to be invited to the annual Episcopal liturgical conferences and numbers of Catholic participants continued to increase. Three years after Wichita, when "Associated Parishes" held their conference at the Waldorf-Astoria Hotel in New York City, there were over forty-five Roman Catholics participating, and Jack Mannion, president of the Liturgical Conference in Washington, D.C., was one of the major speakers. Letter of Robert Bennett to John K. Ross-Duggan, 7 May 1965. CVER 2/18.

[116] Rev. Joseph T. Nolan, interview with author.

[117] Herbert F. Lindemann, *The New Mood in Lutheran Worship* (Minneapolis: Augsburg Publishing House, 1971) 32–33, as quoted in Timothy C. J. Quill, *The Impact of the Liturgical Movement on American Lutheranism* (London: The Scarecrow Press Inc., 1997) 111.

[118] *Praying Together: A Revision of "Prayers We have in Common" (ICET 1975). Agreed Liturgical texts prepared by the English Language Liturgical Commission* (Norwich, England: The Canterbury Press, 1988).

[119] *Common Worship: Services and Prayers for the Church of England* (London: Church House Publishing, 2000).

[120] "Eucharistic Prayer B," 188–90.

[121] 201–03.

[122] The author is indebted to Canon Donald Gray, Canon *Emeritus* of Westminster Abbey, for this reference given during his lecture "Common Words and *Common Worship*: Liturgical Renewal in the Church of England" at the *Centro Pro Unione*, Rome, 21 March 2002.

[123] *Opening Prayers: Scripture-related collects for Years A, B & C from The Sacramentary: The ICEL Collects* (Norwich, England, 1997).

[124] See Consultation on Common Texts, *The Revised Common Lectionary* (Nashville: Abingdon Press, 1993).

[125] See Frederick R. McManus, "Ecumenical Liturgical Convergence: Sunday Lectionary," in *Studia Liturgica* 26/2 (1996) 168–77.

[126] Donald Gray, "Ecumenical Liturgical Cooperation—Past, Present, and Future," in *Studia Liturgica* 28/2 (1998) 232–43.

[127] Gray, 242–43.

[128] Massey H. Shepherd Jr., "The History of the Liturgical Renewal," in *The Liturgical Renewal of the Church*, ed. Massey H. Shepherd Jr. (New York: Oxford, 1960) 27, as quoted in Moriarty, *Liturgical Revolution*, 35.

[129] See Arthur M. Allchin, "The Liturgical Movement and Christian Unity," in *Studia Liturgica* 1 (1962) 61–68.

Chapter 5

Vatican II and the Vindication
of the Vernacular Society: 1962–1965

5.1 INTRODUCTION

With the departure of many clergy from the Vernacular Society because of *Veterum sapientia,* another round of soul-searching emerged as members wondered whether the Society itself should disband. John Agathen was among the most persuasive advocates for disbanding. He expressed frustration both with the Society's lack of realism and its "ineffectiveness," misreading the way in which "the wind was blowing." Moreover, he questioned the viability of continuing the Society without the clergy:

"The liturgy is the special custody of ecclesiastical authority and a layman's group established to concern itself exclusively with the subject is an anomaly to me. The Vernacular Society made sense because it was composed of a group of clergy (even an Episcopal patron!) and laymen earnestly desirous of bringing about a reform of the liturgy, and in that respect it represented a real breakthrough to me. I always felt that a layman had a definite place in it. . . . But the clergy now are expressly forbidden to do any writing on the subject of the vernacular. . . . In other words, it amounts to writing for the clergy on the latter's own specialty."[1]

President Joseph Evans was more optimistic, calling for a strong representation of the vernacularist position to Roman authorities:

"Those who have been opposed to the use of the vernacular hailed it (The Apostolic Constitution) as the death knell of the vernacular movement; those who have been in favor of a wider use of the vernacular have pointed out that the Constitution really was aimed at the use of Latin as the official medium for communication and for instruction of seminarians. There has been some expectation that a clarification might be given in the near future. . . . I therefore believe that we should make a courteous but firm presentation of the position of the Vernacular Society to the responsible authorities in Rome."[2]

But clergy involvement was "easier said than done." With the advent of *Veterum sapientia* Bishop Mark Carroll had removed his own episcopal sponsorship of *Amen* "under obedience." Nonetheless, he encouraged its continued publication "under lay auspices" and without official, ecclesiastical approval, much in the way that *Commonweal* was published. Despite doubts of officers like Agathen, the majority of board members and Society members themselves opted to continue fighting for the cause rather than disband. Meanwhile, at the age of seventy-five, Colonel Ross-Duggan advised members to hold firm to their vernacular convictions and not succumb to the temptation to amalgamate with the Liturgical Conference:

"I have close relations with Father Frederick McManus, President of the Liturgical Conference and, with the majority of all my contacts, he urges me to carry on, emphasizing that action at this time is essential for information and persuasion. May I pray that you will devote yourself to the specific work of the Vernacular Society which is still in being? Do not give your vernacular efforts to the Liturgical Conference because they include both pro and con vernacularists; and therefore no concentrated decision or action is possible. My friends in the Liturgical Conference agree with this, although, of course, those favorable to our cause, e.g., Father Godfrey Diekmann, o.s.b., Father C. J. McNaspy, s.j. . . . and others will continue to help us; but we also have much opposition in the ranks of the Liturgical Conference."[3]

It is curious that the pro-Latin document *Veterum sapientia* and the convocation of the Second Vatican Council fall so closely together. Ironically, the Liturgical Preparatory Commission of the council had already been meeting to discuss the vernacular question, and many saw the new document as an admonition to those progressives who were advocating the use of local languages in worship. Annibale Bugnini who served as secretary of that Preparatory Commission called this period after the publication of *Veterum sapientia* the *"Via purgativa"* for what would become the Constitution on the Sacred Liturgy.[4] Indeed, most vernacularists would have found the possibility of an all-vernacular liturgy hard to imagine following such a restrictive document, and yet only months later, decisions made at the Second Vatican Council would have global ramifications for the cause.

Just how much influence did the Vernacular Society have within the council itself? In other words, would the fathers of the council have come to the same conclusions about the importance of vernacular worship even if the Vernacular Society and initiatives like the vernacular petition never existed? Perhaps, although it would seem unlikely that one could completely rule out any Vernacular Society influence on council delegates, given the extent of international contacts and lobbying present as evidenced in chapters 2 and 3.

5.2 *THE* BURNING ISSUE IN THE LITURGICAL RENEWAL

The two *periti* singled out by Annibale Bugnini as pleading that "the door be opened to the mother tongues" in the subcommittee work of the Preparatory Commission hailed from the United States: Godfrey Diekmann, o.s.b., and Frederick McManus, and both had extensive contact with the Vernacular Society; Godfrey Diekmann had been a charter member.[5] For Diekmann in particular, the vernacular was *the* burning issue within the liturgical renewal; it was the very heart of the liturgical movement and the symbol of what "full and active liturgical participation" meant.[6] Just prior to the opening of the council those convictions brought Diekmann some professional challenges when Bishop William J. McDonald, rector of The Catholic University in Washington, D.C., disinvited him teaching there in the summer of 1962. The rector claimed that he had received complaints about Diekmann's criticizing *Veterum sapientia* in class. When Diekmann wrote to Gerard Sloyan, then dean of the Department of Religious Education at Catholic University, seeking counsel on whether a trip down to Washington might smooth out the situation, Sloyan reassured the accused:

"Avoid a confrontation with our William. His ignorance of fact is massive, and his use for what passes as data with him is alarming. First, it is neither your orthodoxy nor good name that is in question. It is simply that he has heard someone speak strongly against you. His list of scholars who have been represented to him as *non gratae* is as long as your arm—anyone who has done anything pastorally or theologically productive in other words."[7]

Despite Diekmann's unfortunate exchange with the administration at Catholic University, he was greatly respected by the majority of bishops in the United States and would soon gain the admiration and respect of many bishops and advisors attending the Vatican Council in the Rome. Frederick McManus was equally revered by the U.S. hierarchy. Together with Archbishop Paul Hallinan of Atlanta, he founded the "Bishops' Commission on the Liturgical Apostolate" (later the Bishops' Committee on the Liturgy). McManus had already come to know Father Annibale Bugnini in 1953 while doing research for his dissertation on the Congregation of Rites. They met again in Assisi at the international liturgical congress of 1956 and then again at the Eucharistic Congress of 1960.[8] For its part, the Vernacular Society continued to wax and wane as it discerned a future path. What follows, then, is a closer look at the Society's function during the years of the council and its evolution in this final stage of its existence.

5.3 THE PREPARATORY LITURGICAL COMMISSION

Of the thirteen subcommissions working within the Liturgical Commission itself, the sub-commission *De lingua latina* would deal with the controversial subject of liturgical language. As we shall see, that topic brought about a significant amount of tension and debate within the Preparatory Commission itself and in its relationship to other curial commissions; indeed, it was one of the most complicated and thorny issues of all liturgical topics discussed. At least some saw the issue of language as raising a question of the relationship between the doctrinal and the pastoral, while others saw the push for more vernacular as the very symbol of what such a pastoral council stood for in its desire to "open the windows" and communicate with the modern world.[9]

Even among the large number of members on the Preparatory Commission who were on the side of the vernacular, there were tensions over just how far to go. Godfrey Diekmann recounts one particular meeting of the Liturgical Commission:

"Vernacular—on the presidential prayers in vernacular: Grimshaw, Hallinan, McManus and I are the only ones who fought. . . . Even Wagner spoke up for keeping the collect in Latin! 'It would be beautiful to have this island of Latinity in the Foremass, as it would be to have an island of vernacular in the Canon.' We argued violently. . . . I was so mad I could spit. Wagner, Martimort, not *honest*. There, priest whispers collect in Latin, and commentator reads it aloud in *German*."[10]

In November 1960, the Preparatory Commission established the subcommission *De lingua latina* whose task was laid out in the form of three questions: (1) whether the liturgy was to continue being celebrated completely in Latin; (2) whether a limited use of the vernacular should be permitted, and if so, which parts of the liturgy and how much; and (3) greater attention to Latin instruction for the clergy so that they might better appreciate the texts they were praying in public. The subcommittee was led by Monsignor Pietro Borella and assisted by five others, including Bernard Botte and Frederick McManus. Borella himself was in favor of greater use of the vernacular but was concerned that asking for too much too soon might jeopardize the petition; thus he argued for a gradual process of vernacularization "so as to provoke not a revolution but an evolution."[11]

When the Latin subcommission held its first meeting on the fifteenth of November 1960, Pietro Borella suggested that the matter of Latin usage in the liturgy could be handled easily enough since several Roman Congregations had already spoken out on the matter, thereby revealing the opinion of the Holy See. Borella's colleagues on the subcommission reacted strongly against such a quick solution, arguing that a more systematic approach would be needed with firm principles that would then govern the issue of liturgical language for the whole Church. Bernard Botte was charged with the task of preparing a historical report on the topic of liturgical language that concluded with a measured exposition of the reasons both in favor of and against greater use of the vernacular.[12]

Not surprisingly, one of the strongest opponents to greater vernacular privileges within the Preparatory Commission was Monsignor Anglés Pamies, president of the Pontifical Institute of Sacred Music, whom we encountered in the third chapter. Pamies served as relator of the subcommission on Sacred Music. Understandably, he was a great defender of Gregorian chant and saw an increased use of the vernacular as equivalent to a decrease in the promotion of chant. Between November 1960 and April 1961, when the full Preparatory Commission met, Pamies spread the word in the Roman Curia that the Liturgical Commission was attempting to undermine the Church's ancient Latin tradition and would push for radical vernacular concessions at the council itself. Anglés Pamies' influence was so strong that Annibale Bugnini issued a statement on the fourth of March 1961 defending the commission against those charges.

As plans were underway for the Plenary Session of the Preparatory Commission scheduled for April 12–24, 1961, the Secretariat of the Liturgical Commission made a strategic decision to remove the topic of Latin from the agenda, given the heated climate at the time, suggesting instead that it be treated under the particular headings of the other subcommissions. At Bugnini's request, Benedictine Cipriano Vagaggini composed a text as a compromise offer to both camps, namely, that the vernacular be allowed in the more instructive parts of the liturgy while continuing the use of Latin throughout the rest of the Mass. Some of the more conservative members of the commission reacted against the proposal to strike Latin from the agenda since they perceived the commission's Secretariat as being too "pro-vernacular." They insisted, instead, that the topic be discussed publicly and as a separate item with all members of the commission present. Cardinal Cicognani, Prefect of the Congregation of Rites and president of the Preparatory Commission, agreed, and he prepared his own statement on the matter. Annibale Bugnini, the commission's secretary, recalled the event:

"For more than two hours on the appointed day, the *periti*, one from each country, pleaded—some of them in sorrowful tones, including Father Godfrey Diekmann, an American Benedictine, and Professor Frederick McManus of the Catholic University in Washington, D.C.— that the door be opened to the mother tongues. It was an evening of deep emotion; all were shaken, being deeply moved by what had been said and heard. Finally, the Cardinal spoke. He had collected from the Book of Leviticus all the passages describing the Ark, the temple, and the liturgical services, in order to bring out the beauty of the liturgy and the need of being faithful to tradition. His exposition was itself given in a rather unusual mixture of Latin, Italian, and Spanish, and was thus the most eloquent proof of the position taken by the commission that the vernaculars should be used."[13]

5.3.1 Melkite Vernacular Privileges

In February 1961, the Commission for the Oriental Churches approved a text *De usu linguarum vernacularum*, which was then presented to the Preparatory Commission in January 1962. The vernacular issue reached the Oriental Commission because for the three previous years, Melkite Catholics in the United States had been engaged in a debate with the Holy Office over vernacular usage in their own liturgies. The issue is an interesting one. In December 1959, the anti-vernacular apostolic delegate, Archbishop Vagnozzi, told Melkite bishops in the United States that all Eastern-rite priests in their dioceses were to stop celebrating the Liturgy in English; the delegate was acting on orders given directly by the Holy See.[14] The reason for the prohibition was simple:

"They must avoid causing confusion by introducing the vernacular language into the mass, for, in so doing, they offer to promoters of the abandonment of the Latin language in the Sacred Liturgy an opportunity to cite as an example and a precedent what the Oriental priests are doing in their midst."[15]

Upon further inquiry, it was discovered that those Vatican orders had not come from the Oriental Congregation at all, but rather from the Holy Office. His Beatitude Maximos IV, Melkite Patriarch of Antioch, went directly to Pope John XXIII himself on the fifth of February 1960. Less than two months later, on the thirty-first of March, the Holy Office issued a statement formally allowing use of the vernacular in the Melkite Rite, with the exception of the anaphora. This new document was rather offensive in its ignorance of the Byzantine liturgy; nonetheless, it was accepted by Maximos IV as at least a provisional step until a complete vernacular liturgy for Melkite Catholics could be ratified by the upcoming council.[16] Not surprisingly, among the first to support these Melkite developments to fellow vernacularists was none other than Ross-Duggan. Almost immediately, a number of Melkite clergy and laity in the United States were added to the Vernacular Society's mailing list.

Prompted by the exchange between Melkite Catholics and the Holy See, the Commission for Oriental Churches appealed to the Preparatory Commission to promote the restoration of the ancient practice that allowed Eastern churches to employ whatever local languages were pastorally suitable. Three of the four formal respondents to this schema reacted with a certain level of concern, "lest the Latins say 'if these and those, why not we also?'"[17] The Commission on the Missions made its own voice heard in its schema *De sacramentis ac de s. liturgia* which the Preparatory Commission discussed in late March 1962:

"From Scripture we know that all languages are ordered towards the praise of Christ. Such praise is expressed especially in the liturgy, where the law of intelligibility of liturgical language for all gathered was stated by the Apostle. A diversity of customs and of rites has always existed in the Church, showing most clearly the riches of the Church's unity."[18]

Despite its strong appeal to Scripture and ancient tradition, however, this particular document requested only "some use of the vernacular and some adaptation of rites to the genius of peoples and to local conditions."[19] Just weeks before the promulgation of the liturgy constitution *Sacrosanctum Concilium,* Maximos IV wrote to Ross-Duggan expressing his satisfaction with how the Melkite request for vernacular privileges had turned out and praying that all Catholics would be granted the possibility of greater participation in the liturgy.[20]

5.3.2 *The Vernacular Question and Vatican Diplomacy*

The commission's problems, however, were far from over. In December, Pope John XXIII sent his famous letter to Anglés on the occasion of the fiftieth anniversary of the Pontifical Institute of Sacred Music where the Pope lauded the Institute for its defense and cultivation of liturgical Latin. Then, only two months later, came the apostolic constitution *Veterum sapientia* on the teaching of Latin in seminaries.[21] As for the Pope's letter to Anglés, Bugnini opted for a benign interpretation, cautioning against giving the letter too much juridical weight. Nonetheless, for political purposes, Bugnini urged that a clarification be added into the schema where liturgical languages was treated: "The use of Latin into the western liturgy must absolutely be preserved." This was added while retaining the call for greater vernacular usage in the text.[22] Following the second blow to the vernacular cause that came with *Veterum sapientia,* the liturgy schema which was sent to the Preparatory Commission included Bugnini's addendum about the absolute preservation of liturgical Latin while also allowing for greater vernacular usage in the Eucharist, other sacraments, and recitation of the Breviary.[23]

When the text finally came before the full Preparatory Commission there was a new Prefect of the Congregation of Rites. Cardinal Gaetano Cicognani died on the fifth of February 1962 and was replaced by Cardinal Arcadio M. Larraona, c.m.f., a Spanish-born conservative canonist who was known to be anti-vernacular from the beginning. Prior to this nomination, he had spent most of his life teaching canon law and working as Under-Secretary and then Secretary of the Congregation for Religious with extremely limited pastoral experience. Larraona was appointed to head up the Preparatory Liturgical Commission on the twenty-second of February 1962—the same day in which *Veterum sapientia* was published. When Larraona assumed his responsibilities as president of the commission, he appointed Fernando Antonelli, o.f.m., as secretary, deliberately ignoring Annibale Bugnini who had done all of the commission's foundational work and was the chief author of the schema itself. Undaunted, Bugnini maintain his own political contacts to guarantee that his efforts on behalf of liturgical renewal would not be obliterated by Larraona. And he succeeded.[24]

Larraona consistently appealed to *Veterum sapientia* when discussions about greater vernacular privileges in the liturgy arose, and to the document's prohibition of any further discussion on liturgical vernacular. Vernacular discussions continued nonetheless with Cardinals Léger and Montini as two of the strongest defenders of the vernacular against Larraona. Léger argued that the text "must absolutely be preserved" be modified to "should be preserved." Montini, for his part, appealed to the reference in *Veterum sapientia* to the use of ancient liturgical languages. On the other side of the issue, Cardinal Ottaviani defended Larraona especially regarding the push to allow recitation of the Breviary in the vernacular:

"What most horrifies me is the new wound being inflicted on Latin in the liturgy. The possibility is being insinuated that priests are saying the Breviary in the vernacular. The reason would be that many do not understand Latin. I am astonished that anyone could be ordained a priest without knowing Latin well. And I especially regret that a remedy should be suggested that is not in accord with the latest pontifical document, *Veterum sapientia*, and that consecrates by its concessions ignorance of the liturgical, scholastic, theological language of the Church itself."[25]

Ironically, during the Second Vatican Council itself it became clear that a sizeable number of the bishops were missing a significant portion of the discussions taking place since they were unable to understand the Latin. And when they made public statements in the aula, they had to employ a Latinist to translate the statement from their own vernacular language into Latin, which they would then stumble through aloud, so council officials opted for simultaneous translations into the major languages as the only reasonable solution. Translated or not, only about ten to fifteen U.S. bishops made interventions in the aula. As a group, the U.S. delegation was known to be reserved and timid as compared with their European counterparts. The one exception was pro-vernacularist Cardinal Joseph Ritter of Saint Louis. Years later, Frederick McManus remarked: "Ritter was so outspoken that the Europeans thought he was a German!"[26]

Noted ecclesiologist Joseph Komonchak makes an important observation on the controversy over Latin:

"On an organizational level, it illustrates the complex relations that existed not only among the various preparatory commissions and between the various Curial congregations but also between the Pope and the preparation of the Council and between the Curia and the Council itself. Substantively, a review of the controversies that preceded *Veterum sapientia* and of the commentaries on it, both favorable and critical, reveals how many important issues were considered to be at stake in the question of the Church's language."[27]

What was at stake in the language debate, according to Komonchak, was the very ecclesiological tension that continues today between universal and local church—between the universal primacy of the pope and the authority of diocesan bishops including a theology of the local church where the gospel and, indeed liturgy itself, is inculturated in the particular local context.[28]

After numerous discussions and debates, the liturgy schema was finally approved with the others on the thirteenth of July 1962, and the volume of these preparatory documents was sent to all the council fathers.[29] Upon completion of the schema, Bugnini remarked:

"The members and consultors of the preparatory liturgical commission were in possession of the schema they had approved and could gauge the changes that had been made: the *declarationes*, so useful in helping non-specialists to understand the text, had been completely eliminated; the decentralization so ardently sought was 'watered down' (local authorities could only make suggestions to the Holy See); nothing was said of communion under both kinds for the laity; concelebration was limited to a few occasions; no reference was made to the use of the vernacular by priests celebrating the Divine Office. The title page carried the statement: 'The sole purpose of this Constitution is to provide general norms and the fundamental principles governing general liturgical reform. The practical application to particular cases is to be left to the Holy See.'"[30]

This was a first step toward the kind of progress the Vernacular Society was hoping for, but it was only the beginning. Joseph Evans remained skeptical that the U.S. delegation would be sufficiently vocal on the vernacular issue once it was introduced into the council for discussion. And if the U.S. bishops failed to take the lead, then an ultimate victory for the vernacular was anything but certain. Evans wrote to Clarence Issenmann, bishop of Columbus, Ohio, to express his concern:

"My personal concern is that the American bishops, for reasons that I am not sure I wholly understand, may not press for the vernacular in proportion to the influence they should exert. Living as I do in the midst of a secular society, it seems to me that there is tremendous need for a revivification of the liturgy, and in act of all Christian thinking. Anyone would be dull indeed to think that the vernacular is in any sense a panacea, but in any event it would make the Church more comprehensible to the man in the street, and after all Our Lord did indicate that there were those not of this fold in whom He was interested. The need for a resurgence is desperate indeed, it seems to me."[31]

5.4 THE SECOND VATICAN COUNCIL'S FIRST SESSION AND THE VERNACULAR DEBATE

Joseph Evans' concerns about American episcopal reticence were quickly put to rest. The vernacular issue surfaced quite early in the council itself, led largely by the Americans despite the presence of several key vernacular opponents in their midst like Cardinal Francis J. Spellman of New York and Cardinal James F. McIntyre, a former auxiliary bishop and chancellor in New York prior to becoming archbishop of Los Angeles. Spellman held the interesting position of being opposed to the vernacular in the Mass but in favor of its usage in the Breviary because his own knowledge of Latin was weak.[32] Predictably, pro-vernacularists were labeled as the "progressives" while those who upheld the continuation of liturgical Latin were called the "conservatives." In general, the delegates from the United States were perceived as moderates although their voting on the vernacular issue usually came down on the side of the progressives. This was largely because the reasoning for a move toward greater use of vernacular in the liturgy was more logical and pastorally valuable.[33]

During the council sessions, several officials of the Vernacular Society found their way to Rome for short periods of time to learn of vernacular developments and even do some private lobbying on the side. Predictably, Ross-Duggan was there for much of the council having obtained a press pass under the auspices of *Amen*. Pro-vernacularist *periti*

Godfrey Diekmann and Frederick McManus were helpful in providing access for those vernacularists who did visit. Joseph Evans wrote to Godfrey Diekmann to express his gratitude for access granted:

"The particular purpose of my letter . . . is to thank you warmly for giving me the name of Father Yzermans, who was most gracious and helpful and who really proved the key to my making many good contacts during the four days I was there. I had good visits with Father McManus. Father Yzermans took me to a press conference and to one of the seminars and assisted me in several other ways. I twice had lunch with him and with Bishop Bartholme. The latter, I think, has become a changed man and I think you and others who have been working so hard for liturgical reform may be richly rewarded if only the voting can be accomplished before the adjournment. I suspect the Curia will be doing its best to stall decisions."[34]

Upon returning home to Chicago, Evans found a letter waiting for him from H. A. Reinhold. Consistent with the more prudent members of the Society, Reinhold was concerned that vernacularists cease their activism and opt for silence and discretion lest they irritate the bishops and jeopardize "the cause." The letter reads:

"I don't think it would be too wise to publish *Amen* for the time of the Council. If one thing is resented by the hierarchy, it is pressuring. The Vernacular Society has had its days when it was necessary to express popular desire for the vernacular. But since then it has become an almost universal battle cry of the faithful and some of the clergy. Don't misunderstand me. I'm for the vernacular, as much as one can expect and hope for. I only feel this is not the time to be noisy about it."[35]

Evans responded by recounting his brief experience at the council:

"There was a grand fresh breeze blowing there, and it would appear that very real concessions are going to be made in the way of liturgical reform and wider use of the vernacular. I had an evening with Father Frederick McManus and saw him on two other occasions during the four days I was there. He was cautiously optimistic. It would be my guess that the work of you pioneers in the liturgical movement is seed that will flower in your own lifetimes."[36]

Meanwhile, as news spread of conciliar developments on the vernacular front, Ross-Duggan, Joseph Evans, and other Vernacular Society officials received increasing numbers of letters from Roman Catholics, Anglicans, and Protestants in the United States and Great Britain, expressing their satisfaction at vernacular advances.[37]

5.4.1 The Vernacular Debate Unfolds

On Monday, the twenty-second of October 1962, in the Fourth General Congregation of the council, Cardinal Arcadio Larraona, Second Chair of the Preparatory Liturgical Commission initiated a discussion on the liturgy *schema,* describing how the Church must listen to the signs of the times by adapting the liturgy to the pastoral needs of peoples and nations. Bugnini's successor as secretary, Ferdinando Antonelli, o.f.m., then summarized the *schema*'s eight chapters for those present.[38] Antonelli was assisted by Italian liturgists Carlo Braga and Rinaldo Falsini. A debate on the *schema* then ensued led by Cardinal Frings of Cologne, followed by Cardinals Ruffini of Palermo, Lercaro of Bologna, Montini (later Paul VI) of Milan, Spellman of New York, Döpfner of Munich, Tatsuo of Tokyo, and Silva Henriques of Santiago, Chile. These bishops represented some of the most significant dioceses in the world and spoke from the perspective of tremendous experience. Each of these bishops had, to varying degrees, experimented with liturgical changes and pastoral accommodations to the needs of their people whose reality of daily life was radically different from the pre-Vatican II liturgical experience largely shaped by a monastic spirituality within an agricultural society.[39] Cardinal Lauréan Rugambwa of Bukoba, Tanganyika, and Bishop Devoto of Goya, Argentina, both spoke in favor of the vernacular on behalf of four colleagues each.[40]

Frings, Lercaro, Montini, Döpfner, and Doi argued that the liturgy schema responded well to the needs of contemporary worshipers and was in harmony with John XXIII's desire that the council read the signs of the times and respond pastorally with very concrete aspects of the Church's mission in the world. Of course, there was no better example of a contemporary pastoral response than a shift toward vernacular liturgy. A debate over collegiality was initiated by Cardinals Frings and Döpfner who noted that the original text of the schema had been altered internally (within the Roman Curia) "by unknown hands" from the time it had been approved by the Central Commission to the time it was distributed to the bishops. Changes included an insertion which cautioned that the liturgy schema gave only general principles while application of those principles would need to be approved directly by the Holy See. The two cardinals were concerned that such an insertion could easily rob the council of its effect, leaving liturgical reforms to the whim of Vatican officials as was the case throughout the Tridentine period. The majority of bishops, in fact, desired national or regional liturgical commissions to be established who would have legislative powers regarding proposed liturgical changes. The Vatican could serve in coordinating a central commission that would occasionally gather together representatives from these different regional commissions both to share information and foster unity among the diverse groups. Of course, such a move (which was in agreement with the first chapter of the liturgy schema) would significantly lessen the power of the Sacred Congregation of Rites, which had previously been the only legislative body in charge of the Church's liturgical life. Thus, the discussion on the liturgy opened the door for the very important discussion on collegiality, the role of bishops' conferences in their relationship with the Holy See, and the authority of diocesan bishops to lead and govern their own local churches.[41]

Discussion on the vernacular was introduced by Cardinals Ruffini and Spellman, commenting on the schema's preface and its assertion that local languages should be used both in the celebration of Mass and other sacraments. Spellman argued that Latin should be retained for the celebration of the Eucharist for the purpose of maintaining unity and uniformity, but vernacular languages might be used for the other sacraments.[42] Moreover, he warned against an "exaggerated 'historicism' and a zeal for novelties," where liturgical experimentation, even when approved by the hierarchy, can bring about "confusion, astonishment, and injury," when the faithful "see the unchangeable Church changing her rites."[43]

Apostolic delegate to the United States, Archbishop Vagnozzi, complained that the document was not well organized and too general in its definitions. He suggested that the text be reworked in light of the 1947 encyclical *Mediator Dei*. Archbishop Dante, who served both as the Papal Master of Ceremonies and Secretary of the Congregation of Rites, also criticized the schema as being too radical. He favored a document that would simply offer a few basic principles. Moreover, while bishops' conferences could recommend liturgical changes to the Holy See, only the Vatican should determine what changes are granted. He defended the continued use of Latin both in the Mass and the recitation of the Breviary and lamented the fact that the schema mentioned nothing about the veneration of relics.[44]

5.4.2 Debemus Levare Linguam Latinam

Discussion on the liturgy schema continued the next day, October twenty-third, in the Fifth General Congregation at which Cardinal Spellman presided. Making his first intervention on the schema, Cardinal Ottaviani suggested that the schema be given over to his Theological Commission for revision, since the text lacked theological precision. He questioned the appropriateness of employing terms like "paschal mystery" regarding the liturgy and expressed his disagreement with the idea that the liturgy should be the principal means of educating the faithful.

Cardinal Joseph Ritter of St. Louis then spoke in favor of the schema as it stood, making only some general remarks about its implementation, contending that "the very nature of the liturgy and the Church strongly persuades and even demonstrates the need for reform."[45] Bishops D'Avack and Fares of Italy, Goicoechea of Spain, and others then spoke out against the document. Next, Cardinal Francis Spellman spoke through a narrator, since the council participants were having a rather difficult time understanding his Latin pronunciation. What followed then was a discussion on the schema's first chapter initiated by Cardinal Ruffini, who sided with Archbishop Vagnozzi in arguing that the document should be reconsidered in light of *Mediator Dei* and that the Holy See was to be the sole legislative body regarding liturgical changes. Thus, episcopal conferences were to have no authority on their own. As for use of the vernacular, Ruffini warned that the such a concession would be dangerous to the unity of the Church.[46]

The intervention of Cardinal Feltin of Paris was more pragmatic and pastoral. Arguing in favor of the vernacular, he focused his remarks in consideration of the outsider who enters the Church during Mass and witnesses what looks more like magic than a lived, intelligible reality. The corporate worship of God should be accessible, argued the archbishop, immediately obvious both to Catholics and non-Catholics, believers and unbelievers alike. If the words spoken fail to convey meaning because they are unable to be understood, then they fail in their primary purpose since the purpose of language is to communicate.[47]

Cardinal McIntyre, archbishop of Los Angeles, followed with an unequivocal defense of Latin in the Mass. Afterwards, Archbishop

Hallinan heard comments from a number of bishops that McIntyre's intervention had "advanced the cause of the vernacular in the liturgy by twenty years."[48] Cardinal Godfrey, archbishop of Westminster, supported McIntyre's intervention, stating: *"Debemus levare linguam Latinam,"* with the desire of conveying to his colleagues the importance of upholding Latin for the whole Church. The Italian press, however, failed to grasp the import of the cardinal's message and mistranslated his statement. In Italian, the word *"levare"* means "lift up" but it can also mean "remove," thus the next morning, much to Godfrey's surprise, the daily newspaper *Il Tempo* quoted the cardinal as saying that Latin should be abolished![49]

The last bishop to speak on October twenty-third was Ross-Duggan's old friend, Maximos IV, Melkite Patriarch of Antioch. Disobeying the rule that Latin was to be the only official language at the council, the colorful eighty-four-year-old patriarch made his intervention in French, much to the relief of many bishops who had their own problems both in speaking and understanding Latin.[50] He argued that Latin was not the language of the East and, therefore, his own speaking in Latin would have made little sense. He also called for a change in conciliar procedure so that vernacular speeches might be allowed with simultaneous translation. Regarding the liturgy, he contended that it would be strange for a presider to pray in a language different from that of the liturgical assembly, and since most liturgical assemblies were largely unable to pray in Latin, the vernacular was the only solution. A living Church has no reason to sustain a dead language, and since the Holy Spirit guides the Church and its worship, a living language of worship was essential.[51] He proceeded to argue that vernacular decisions should be left to episcopal conferences or regions. He continued: "Episcopal conferences should not be called just to propose, but to decide something."[52]

Discussion on the vernacular continued in the next ten congregations exhibiting very clear lines of demarcation between those who were strong proponents of a vernacular shift and those who were determined to uphold the continued use of liturgical Latin. The conservatives were led by Cardinal Ottaviani with the professional theological support of Irish Dominican Cardinal Browne. There were a large number of Italians and Spaniards in this group representing, interestingly, two countries where the preconciliar liturgical movement registered little success. The majority of bishops in the conservative camp had very little pastoral experience and spoke more from the perspective of theory than praxis.

5.4.3 Vernacular in the Service of Cultural Adaptation

Cardinal Tisserant, Prefect of the Vatican Library, was the first to address the vernacular question at the Sixth General Congregation on Wednesday, 24 October, arguing that Latin was not the only liturgical language since Hebrew and Greek had been used by the early Christians and that the Congregation of Rites had already approved both the Slavic languages and Chinese for liturgical usage. Tisserant was eloquent in his interventions and had a good grasp of history, which greatly helped his promotion of the vernacular during the council. Cardinal Gracias of Bombay, who was no stranger to the liturgical movement and had a close association with Ross-Duggan, stated that from the time he was ordained bishop he had been calling for the renewal and cultural adaptation of the liturgy. And even as he acknowledged the challenges brought on by many different languages spoken in the same region or country, he nonetheless remained convinced that the vernacular was essential for the intelligibility of worship. He concluded that decisions on the vernacular should be left to episcopal conferences. The African bishops expressed their own reservations about the use of Latin and their dissatisfaction with the expression "western liturgy." Such a term was too closely associated with Western Europe and did not reflect the cultural diversity of other parts of the world that also celebrated the Roman Rite.[53]

Cardinal Bacci, a member of the Curia, spoke in favor of Latin as the bond of unity par excellence, reminding his colleagues that in the nineteenth century Father Rosmini was condemned for claiming that the use of liturgical Latin erected a barrier between the clergy and faithful. Like Francis Spellman, Bacci was not opposed to the laity using vernacular missals while the priest celebrated in Latin, and he was in support of the proposal for at least some vernacular in the celebration of certain sacraments.[54]

Cardinal Meyer of Chicago spoke out clearly in favor of the vernacular, leaving such decisions to diocesan bishops in consultation with the Holy See, rather than to episcopal conferences.[55] The Papal Sacristan, Bishop Van Lierde, addressed the formative/instructive side of liturgy and spoke out in favor of vernacular usage so as to assist the pedagogical aspect of worship. Dublin's Archbishop McQuaid defended the continued use of Latin at Mass but allowed for a shift toward the vernacular in the celebration of certain sacraments. On the involvement of episcopal conferences, he sided with Cardinal Meyer, arguing in favor of vernacular decisions to be made by individual bishops. Archbishop Descuffi of Smyrna emphasized the pastoral value of the vernacular in the liturgy since liturgy was for the benefit of those present rather than the opposite. He dismissed the idea that vernacular permissions should be limited to mission territories since in the contemporary world every country had become a mission country. Brazilian Archbishop Gonçalves de Amaral argued in favor of Latin since the paschal mystery did not need to be articulated or explained in local languages. For his part, Archbishop Ramanantoanina of Madagascar defended cultural adaptation of the liturgy that included the adaptation of language especially in places like Africa and the South Pacific.[56]

At this point, Archbishop Parente, who served as Cardinal Ottaviani's Assessor of the Holy Office, strongly criticized the schema for its weak theological foundations, expressing his frustration at the way in which members of the Roman Curia were being labeled as arch-conservatives: "At the Holy Office we are all martyrs. We have already yielded on many points, yet this is the thanks we get! If any changes are to be sanctioned by the Council, they must be made with the greatest prudence."[57] Parente was supported by Archbishop Dino Staffa, Secretary of the Congregation of Seminaries and Universities (later the Congregation for Catholic Education). Archbishop Seper of Zagreb was the last to speak at that session, adding his voice to those of other pro-vernacular bishops. As Christians were increasingly a minority in the modern world, Seper contended, there was no reason to make the living out of their faith any more difficult by insisting on use of a language no one could understand.

The first to make an intervention on Friday, the twenty-sixth of October, was Cardinal Siri of Genoa who relied on the recent document *Veterum sapientia* in his defense of Latin and sided with Parente and other conservative members of the Roman Curia, calling for the submission of the schema to the Theological Commission for revision. Episcopal conferences were certainly free to suggest certain things to the Holy See or make particular requests, but they should not be permitted to make decisions for their respective countries on such issues as vernacular privileges. Such activity would risk too many abuses and promote confusion, threatening the unity of the Church.[58] Dutch Bishop Bekkers' remarks followed, defending both the vernacular as an important means to increasing full and active liturgical participation and bishops' rights to make decisions for their own dioceses as successors to the apostles. Bekkers acknowledged that the liturgy schema could be critiqued for its imperfections; nonetheless, it provided the necessary base for a true liturgical renewal which the Church needed. Auxiliary Bishop Ancel of Lyons sided with Bekkers, stating that unity and uniformity were not the same and that Church unity need not be impeded simply because there was a diversity of liturgical rites and languages. Ancel praised the schema for embodying the kind of pastoral emphasis the Pope had desired for the council itself. Flemish Bishop Calewaert of Ghent offered a moderate position between the two camps, suggesting that Latin could be retained for the principal parts of the Mass (exceptions might be required for mission territories) while the vernacular could be used for the more instructive and dialogical parts of the Mass and for the other sacraments. This compromise solution appealed to a number of bishops, as it seemed to be a happy medium between the staunch conservatives of the Roman Curia and the pro-vernacularists.[59]

One of the strongest and uncompromising appeals on behalf of the vernacular was launched by Argentinian Bishop Rau of Mar del Plata, who argued for the total abolition of Latin since it impeded the prayer life of believers. He challenged those who wanted to suggest that the Church was itself a culture—a concept obviously contradicted by the Incarnation—and insisted that since the Church did not possess its own culture, it made little sense to suggest that it could have its own language. Rau was not subtle as he concluded his intervention: "I will be faithful unto death to the Roman Church, but not to the Latin language!"[60] Taiwanese Bishop Lokuang reminded his hearers of the mistakes made by the Roman Curia over the Chinese rites controversy of the seventeenth and eighteenth centuries that had condemned cultural concessions made by Jesuit missionaries as a necessary tool in evangelization. Moreover, he noted that in the contemporary Chinese experience, the Communists had brought the vernacular issue to the fore since, "If our people do not pray in their own language, they are accused of subservience to a foreign nationalism. . ."[61] Eastern German Bishop Spülbeck would later make the same point as Bishop Lokuang regarding the Communists. The Polish bishops added their own words of vernacular support, stating that the introduction of Polish into the Mass, which had taken place fifteen years prior to the Vatican Council, had been a tremendous gift for the Polish Church, and, indeed, saved the faith in their country.

The first intervention in the Seventh General Congregation on Saturday, the twenty-seventh of October, came from Bishop Kobayashi of Japan, who emphasized the importance of the vernacular within Japanese cultural experience as opposed to Latin, which was easily rejected as Western and therefore foreign to Japanese tradition. Since Christianity was universal, it was a grave error to link such a universal religion with a limited, Western language such as Latin. Kobayashi raised a very interesting question on the issue: "Is our unity with the Holy See so feeble that it has to be maintained by a rigid uniformity?"[62] The gathered assembly of bishops broke into applause. Discussion on the subject continued throughout the day until Australian Bishop Muldoon moved that the bishops vote on the preface and first chapter of the schema since they had engaged in more than enough discussion on the matter. He was not alone in his fatigue since the entire *aula* broke into sustained applause at the suggestion that they vote and move on. Observant of the protocol regarding the council sessions, Cardinal Ruffini, who happened to be presiding on that day, insisted that since the council's procedural policy lacked any rules of closure, it was impossible to exclude others who still wished to speak on the matter. Nonetheless, on the following Monday, the twenty-ninth of October, the council did indeed move on to the next chapter of the schema.[63]

5.4.4 Hallinan's Ecumenical Plea for Vernacular Worship

One of the best interventions in favor of the vernacular came during the Eleventh General Congregation and was made by Archbishop Paul Hallinan of Atlanta who had been a strong supporter of the Vernacular Society. He began by acknowledging that he spoke for many—although not all—U.S. bishops in making his vernacular plea. And appropriately for the United States, which unlike some other countries had an expansive ecumenical mixture of churches and Christian communities, Hallinan's plea was deliberately ecumenical:

"The liturgy of the Church must be public, but this can have real meaning for our people only if they understand enough to be part of it. They must be united to God not alone as in private prayer, but together with the whole Church in our head who is Christ. . . . In a particular manner this is desired by the bishops of those regions in which there are few Catholics. For example, in my own Archdiocese of Atlanta, scarcely two percent of the population is Catholic. The more we can do to render the Mass understandable to all, not just to those equipped by learning or formed by habit, the more we can open new avenues to the minds and hearts of Christians who are not Catholic. The Church is the loving mother of *all*."[64]

At least in part, Hallinan wanted it to be known to the Council that McIntyre and Spellman were hardly representative of the episcopate in the United States on the vernacular issue.[65] One can only wonder what thoughts were on the mind of pro-Latin apostolic delegate Archbishop Vagnozzi as Hallinan forcefully held his pro-vernacular stance and lobbied for "the cause" among his colleagues in the U.S. Episcopate. Several years prior to the council, Vagnozzi had once been a houseguest of Hallinan's in Atlanta and was favorably impressed by their encounter. Thus, when he needed to appoint a U.S. bishop to the Liturgical Commission, he chose Hallinan, expecting him to maintain the status quo and not cause trouble. In the end, Hallinan did anything but maintain the status quo and was probably the leading vernacular figure among the U.S. bishops at the council.[66]

Bishop Aloysius Willinger, c.ss.r., made his own very articulate intervention on the subject, agreeing with Hallinan:

"The introduction of the vernacular into the sacred liturgy of the Mass will implement the present yearning for and insistence on the participation of the laity in the liturgical function, contribute to the interest, understanding, and fervor of the faithful, center their minds and hearts on the essence and dignity of the mystery of the grand sacrifice that is to follow, and even appeal to the religious sense of our separated brethren."[67]

Like Bugnini and others in the progressive camp, Archbishop Hallinan was aware that Larraona and the conservatives were deliberately attempting to delay the work of the liturgical commission, fearful that a vote on the schema during one of the general congregations would surely mean an instant victory for the progressives. Ever the activist, Hallinan decided on a two-part strategy. Firstly, he would propose a procedural change in the commission itself allowing members to vote immediately on each proposed revision, forwarding the results to the general secretary of the council, rather than wait unnecessarily for each individual chapter of the schema to be completed. Secondly, he would bypass Larraona and take his case to the Vatican Secretary of State, Cardinal Amleto Cicognani, who was both a former apostolic delegate in the United States and brother of the former Prefect of the Congregation of Rites who had worked so closely with Bugnini.[68]

5.4.5 The Pope Addresses the Council in the Vernacular

Perhaps the greatest boon to vernacular promotion during the council came on Sunday, the fourth of November, the feast of St. Charles Borromeo, during a solemn Mass celebrated in the Vatican Basilica by Borromeo's successor as archbishop of Milan, Cardinal Montini. The Mass also served as a commemoration of the fourth anniversary of John XXIII's coronation. The event was already unusual in that it was one of the few times in which the Ambrosian Rite had ever been celebrated in St. Peter's, but it was even more distinctive in the language used as the Pope addressed the gathered assembly. After John XXIII praised Latin as the language "in which the prelates of the universal Church communicate with the center of Catholicism," he then shifted to Italian for the rest of his talk, since it was better understood by all those present—bishops included. The pontiff concluded his remarks:

"It is perfectly natural that new times and new circumstances should suggest different forms and methods for transmitting externally the one and same doctrine, and of clothing it in a new dress. Yet the living substance is always the purity of the evangelical and apostolic truth, in perfect conformity with the teaching of holy Church, who often applies to herself the maxim: 'Only one art, but a thousand forms.'"[69]

It was extraordinary to consider that this was the same Pope who had issued the document *Veterum sapientia* only nine months prior. Nonetheless, the Pope had "broken the ice," addressing the Second Vatican Council in Italian.

5.4.6 Vernacular Lobbying behind the Scenes

On the following day, James McIntyre of Los Angeles made yet another impassioned plea for Latin:

"The Latin language . . . gave rise to wonderful effects. Its severity overcame nationalities. In politics it was neutral. With great constancy its efficiency perdured into our epoch. Once adopted, Latin became truly universal, especially among educated and literary men. Having a mathematical rather than vulgar structure, Latin attained a continuous primacy and perdured through the centuries. It is very outstanding in intellectual, literary and scientific matters."[70]

Meanwhile, during that same week Paul Hallinan followed through on his vernacular strategy. On the seventh of November, exactly one month before the conciliar bishops would approve the first chapter of the schema, he had a discussion with the secretary of state as they walked in the Vatican Gardens, expressing his frustrations with Larraona and his concerns about attempts to block the very *aggiornamento* John XXIII had called for. He also gave the cardinal a copy of his proposal about changing the voting procedure in the commission. Cicognani responded positively and was supportive both of Hallinan and of attempts to push the vernacular issue forward. He said: "You are right in pushing for a vote on the liturgy. I try to push but I can only do so much. The curia is not all bad—only out of touch. We need bishops here."[71] Amleto Cicognani was also well aware of the problems with Larraona. He asked Hallinan quite directly: "Can you understand him? I can't." The Cardinal then proceeded to criticize Antonelli as "too conservative" but had nothing but praise for Bugnini, calling him an "excellent man" who had done "good work" for the commission.[72]

As Hallinan and Cicognani were meeting, the proposal was being presented to Larraona for his consideration by Archbishop Francis Grimshaw. Predictably, Larraona expressed his displeasure at the idea and was less than favorable to the results. Hallinan's plan was to have the proposal presented at the meeting of the commission rather than to the cardinal himself. Attempting an alternative strategy, Hallinan gained the support of thirteen members of the commission who agreed to sign a petition endorsing his original proposal. It was then presented to the commission that afternoon as they met, and the group voted unanimously to approve it and then proceeded to put into practice the new procedural rules. Larraona responded by canceling the next day's meeting as yet a further attempt to stall the process, arguing that there was no rush to send the votes to the council's general secretary since the entire assembly of conciliar bishops would not vote on the schema until the entire text had been revised by the commission.[73]

Further frustrated by Larraona's efforts to sabotage the progressives' agenda, Hallinan wrote to the Cardinal Secretary of State both expressing his discontent with Larraona's behavior at the meeting and calling into question the way in which the Prefect had interpreted the council's procedural rules.[74] Hallinan was not alone in his frustration. He began hearing from other episcopal conferences—especially France and Germany—that they too were angered by Larraona's tactics, that the Cardinal Secretary of State had visited the Pope about Larraona's attempts to impede the work of the Liturgical Commission, and that

Cardinal Montini of Milan was ready to intervene. Hallinan was further encouraged with a telephone call from Archbishop Krol, who informed him that the council's general secretary, Archbishop Pericle Felici, had admonished Larraona to move forward with the work of the commission more expeditiously.[75]

5.4.7 Discussion on the Liturgy Schema Concluded

In the General Congregation of the thirteenth of November, Cardinal Bernard Alfrink of Utrecht called for a motion on whether or not to conclude the discussion on the remaining chapters of the schema and the response was overwhelmingly positive. On the following day at the suggestion of Cardinal Tisserant, the conciliar bishops voted by a wide margin of 2,162 to 46 that the entire schema be sent to the Liturgical Commission. Byzantine Bishop Nicholas Elko of Pittsburgh, Pennsylvania, whose U.S. diocese had already known the experience of vernacular worship since 1959, was seated near the contingent of French Latin Rite bishops. When it came time to vote, they asked him, "Why are you voting for the vernacular? You already have it." Elko responded: "I am interested in the whole Church and I know how much the vernacular has done for increasing the fervor of Catholics."[76]

Following the vote, it became clear that it would be impossible to have the complete schema ready before the end of the council's first session since it was only several weeks away. What did seem feasible, however, was to have the first chapter approved with at least something concrete to show for their efforts. Significantly, it was precisely the first chapter that treated the vernacular.

5.4.8 The Vernacular Vote Is Cast

Assisted by Archbishop John Krol, Paul Hallinan took the lead in drafting a petition that he hoped the majority of U.S. bishops would endorse.[77] The mimeographed petition read:

"We the undersigned Bishops of the United States of America request that Chapter One of the *Schema de Sacra Liturgia* be brought to the General Congregation for the necessary vote, so that (if approved) the final text can be submitted to His Holiness, Pope John XXIII, before the session closes.

"Chapter One contains most of the principles on the renewal of the Sacred Liturgy; subsequent chapters can be deferred to subsequent sessions. The almost unanimous approval of the *Schema in genere* and the *Proemium* leads us to believe that the Fathers of the Council desire to vote on this fundamental chapter."[78]

When the U.S. bishops held their usual Monday meeting at the North American College on the twenty-sixth of November, Bishops Tracy and Connare circulated the petition, encouraging their colleagues to sign. McIntyre of Los Angeles and Joseph Hurley of St. Augustine refused to sign, but one hundred and thirty-two bishops did endorse the petition, and on the following day it was to be submitted to the presidency of the council by Cardinal Spellman. Whether or not Spellman ever did submit the petition is another matter.[79]

However one interprets the reasons, the Liturgical Commission suddenly reenergized itself and began to work expeditiously. Bishops like Hallinan and Krol were especially perplexed at such a shift since Larraona had been resistant for so long. Some wondered whether the council presidency itself had begun pressuring Larraona to speed things up. Whatever happened, the commission's secretary, Ferdinando Antonelli, surprised everyone by distributing texts of the first nine articles of the first chapter. Hallinan described the effect as "electric" and commission members immediately gave their approval. When the bishops arrived at the twenty-fourth article which treated the vernacular question, a bit of drama ensued when Papal Master of Ceremonies Archbishop Dante apparently began to scream only to be quieted by Larraona himself who reminded his colleague that an ecumenical council was higher then the Sacred Congregation of Rites as far as those decisions went.[80]

On the twenty-eighth of November, all the council bishops received a printed copy of the nine articles from Chapter One which the Liturgical Commission had just approved two days before. On the thirtieth of November, all nine articles were approved by an overwhelming majority. Returning to St. Peter's on Monday morning for the next General Congregation, Hallinan presumed that the remaining articles (16–31) would be distributed to the fathers upon their arrival. Instead, the speeches and discussions continued with no mention of voting on the remaining articles. He became convinced that Larraona and Antonelli had yet again succeeded in impeding the entire process of renewal. He even wondered if Cardinal Spellman had ever submitted the U.S. bishops' petition to the council's presidency. There were only four days left in the council's First Session, and Hallinan warned his colleagues that if those remaining articles were not distributed and brought to the floor for a vote in the following two days, then they would return home defeated by Vagnozzi, Dante, and colleagues, with nothing to show for their efforts.[81]

The remaining articles finally appeared on the following morning, and the council fathers applauded as the texts were distributed. On the fifth and sixth of December, during the Thirty-Fourth and Thirty-Fifth General Congregations, Bishop Karel Calewaert of Ghent carefully explained the revisions and the bishops approved thirteen amendments to the first chapter. It was the vigil of the major vote not only for Chapter One itself, but for a radical shift in favor of the vernacular, as well. On the seventh of December 1962, during the Thirty-Sixth General Congregation, the council fathers approved the entire first chapter of the liturgy schema, thereby voting in favor of the use of national languages in the liturgy. Of the 2,118 fathers who were present, a total of 1,922 voted in favor, 180 voted in favor but with some reservations, 11 were opposed, and 5 void.[82]

The vernacular question was the most discussed in the entire debate on the liturgy. Eighty-one speakers were heard on the subject and their opinions took up more than one hundred pages. The vote reflected three tendencies manifested in the discussions: a minority wanted no concessions to the vernacular at all; a majority wanted permission to say everything in the vernacular; a third group argued for the *via media*, maintaining the basic principle of Latin but also opening the door to some vernacular usage. At the end of the day, wider use of the vernacular won the victory largely because the reasons mentioned by vernacular proponents were more cogent.

5.5 END OF THE FIRST SESSION AND REACTIONS TO THE VERNACULAR VOTE

Jesuit liturgical pioneer Gerald Ellard noted a significant change in the U.S. bishops upon their return home after the vernacular vote:

"The fact that many of the bishops, after returning from the Council have made many generous statements to the press, indicates to my mind that the climate for the vernacular is now rapidly improving. Bishop John Wright was conspicuous in his opposition to vernacular formerly; now he says publicly that the consideration of pastoral care should take precedence over the general question of cultural unity. So I think, until the Council has resumed its work and gone farther into this topic in greater detail, we can presume that many bishops are taking a wider view than they had done formerly."[83]

Evans concurred:

"If I read the signs aright, the great majority of our bishops have come back changed people. I think . . . that one can count Cardinal Ritter and Cardinal Cushing on the side of the vernacular, and I am assured by priests here in whose judgment I have confidence, that Cardinal Meyer returned convinced of its pastoral value. It would seem to me a likely working argument that the bishops, if properly approached, will be glad to have the help of the Vernacular Society in implementation. It is my judgment , for what it is worth, that the bishops no longer need to be convinced, and that as a group they will be appreciative of intelligent cooperation at the parish level. In fact, I can see that there might be a role in the education not only of the laity, but of pastors who have not awakened."[84]

Thus, in writing to Ross-Duggan, Evans argued that the Vernacular Society should continue to exist as a body despite its goal of liturgy in the vernacular apparently having been accomplished. Privately, however, Evans continued to muse on what role the Vernacular Society really did play in influencing the Second Vatican Council. On the same day in which he wrote to Ross-Duggan, 22 January 1963, he also wrote to Bishop Mark Carroll who had been one of the earliest episcopal supporters of the vernacular: "I find it extremely difficult to assess the role which the Vernacular Society has played in helping the vernacular cause. There are some who feel that it may have actually hindered progress, but I find this difficult to believe."[85]

Whoever deserved the credit for the vernacular progress made, U.S. bishops returned home ready to talk openly to the press, as Gerald Ellard noted. The press, in turn, used its own influence to cast its vote for vernacular liturgy. There was no doubt about where the editors of *Look* Magazine stood on the subject:

"The Latin spoken in Roman Catholic churches is now a dead language that neither Christ nor the apostles ever knew, yet its use has given a uniformity throughout the world. Though it sounds the same everywhere . . . nowhere on earth do most worshippers comprehend it. Liturgically, form has taken precedence over sense. . . . If Pope

John XXIII gives his approval as expected, much of the Mass may soon be heard here with its noble Latin cadences translated into . . . stately English. This change in the Church may be the first of many."[86]

Journalists, however, would be hard-pressed to top Professor A. H. Armstrong's bold statement sent to the bishops of England, Wales, and Scotland in September 1963. What was intended to be a letter of gratitude to the bishops for their support of the vernacular at the council's First Session reads more like a thesis that could easily have been posted along with Martin Luther's ninety-five at Wittenburg. The fact that Armstrong was the Gladstone Professor of Greek at the University of Liverpool, made his pro-vernacular testimony all the more intriguing. He wrote:

"The decision of the Council that the vernacular is in principle admissible to the Liturgy is most welcome both for historical and pastoral reasons, and should be implemented, by introducing as much vernacular into the Liturgy as quickly as possible, in the English-speaking world.

"*Historical Reasons for This:* The claim that Latin is in any peculiar and exclusive sense 'the language of the Church' is not historically well founded (and is intensely irritating to Eastern Christians in and out of communion with Rome, as it ignores their own immemorial traditions). Latin is not the original language of a single book of inspired Scripture. It was not used by Our Lord, Our Lady or any of the Apostles. It was not the language of SS Peter and Paul, or of the Roman Church till the 3rd or 4th century A.D. when it was substituted for Greek because it was the current vernacular. If we really want to be faithful to the tradition of the Apostles and martyrs of Rome, we who use the Roman Rite should translate the Liturgy as quickly as possible into our several vernaculars. No saint mentioned in our Canon would have thought otherwise.

"*Pastoral Reasons:* As a Professor of Greek and former Senior Lecturer in Latin I can say with confidence that Latin is to-day useless as a medium of international communication and unnatural and hampering to true devotion as a medium of prayer. I cannot follow Mass without a missal except in a small chapel where the priest faces the congregation and speaks with unusual slowness and clarity. It seems to me urgently necessary, if we really care about the devotion of our own people and the conversion of England, to introduce a vernacular Liturgy as quickly as possible, and therefore for the Bishops of the English-Speaking world to set about the necessary preparations as soon as possible, and especially, with the help of competent scholars, pastoral liturgists, and good writers of English, to prepare a really first-class English translation, which will need a great deal of care and thought to achieve."[87]

Meanwhile, back in the United States the hot topic in the media was vernacular liturgy, and with optimism for full vernacular privileges to be granted, Gerald Ellard cautioned vernacularists to "lay fallow" lest too much agitation push council participants in the opposite direction. The vote at the end of the council's First Session reflected openness on the part of numerous delegates to rethink their opinions after hearing the presentations made by others in favor of the vernacular. Thus were some bishops who had been adamantly opposed to the vernacular, like John Wright of Pittsburgh, gradually influenced by their colleagues at the council to recognizing its pastoral value, as noted above.[88] Vernacular Society officer William Storey, now retired professor of liturgical studies at the University of Notre Dame, had numerous debates with Bishop Wright about the vernacular prior to the bishop's departure for the council. Departing for Rome, Wright told Storey that a vernacular liturgy would not come about for a thousand years. Returning from the council, Bill Storey joined the Pittsburgh clergy at the airport awaiting the bishop's plane. When he arrived, Wright greeted each one waiting on the tarmac. Arriving at the Vernacular Society official, Storey quipped "a thousand years, Bishop?" Wright blushed, turned, and walked away.[89]

5.6 ON THE FUTURE OF THE VERNACULAR SOCIETY

Despite Evans' earlier enthusiasm for the continuation of the Vernacular Society assisting in the work of vernacular implementation, subsequent correspondence with Society officials and several bishops reveal further ambivalence on the issue. Thus, he reopened the discussion with vernacularists about disbanding the Vernacular Society, polling officers and ultimately the Society itself about its future. He wrote:

"There are those who feel that there are sound arguments against continuing the Vernacular Society. One of them is that the cause has

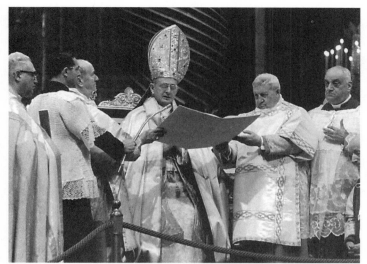

Giordani

Promulgation of 5 Documents, October 1965

Msgr. Annibale Bugnini, Cardinal
Gaetano Cicognani, Fr. Godfrey
Diekmann, O.S.B., 1960

Giordani

ICEL members in audience with Pope John Paul II, 10 June 1996 (Rome).

L'Osservatore Romano

Five founding members of ICEL, 1963 (Rome). L to R: Fr. Godfrey Diekmann, O.S.B., Cardinal Cordeiros (Pakistan), Cardinal Gordon Gray (Scotland), Archbishop Dennis Hurley, O.M.I. (South Africa), Msgr. Frederick McManus (U.S.A.).

ICEL meeting, 25 October–4 November 1982 (Rome). L to R: Msgr. John Fitzsimmons (Scotland), Archbishop Dennis Hurley, O.M.I. (South Africa), John Page (ICEL secretary), Fr. Godfrey Diekmann, O.S.B., Kathleen Hughes, R.S.C.J., Christopher Willcock, S.J. (Australia).

Archbishop Paul Hallinan

already been won, which may in fact be too optimistic a conclusion. Secondly, it is argued that the implementation is a professional matter, and that some of the bishops at least have been critical of what they regard as an intrusion by the Vernacular Society in their domain. Thirdly, it is thought by some that *Amen* is little read by the hierarchy, even though it may reach episcopal desks.

"The arguments for continuing the Vernacular Society are several. First, no official word is yet available concerning the action of the Council. Further efforts of an educational nature are in order to prepare pastors and people to implement the presumably forthcoming instructions of the bishops. Finally, there may be a role for the clergy to play in pressing the action of more conservative sections in North America."[90]

Evans then proposed three possible solutions: The first was to disband the Society completely, which he described as "inappropriate" since there had not yet been a formal word from the Vatican on the issue and also because there were valid reasons for continuing the organization. The second possibility was to hold the Society's activities in abeyance until official word arrived from Rome. The third choice was to continue with whatever energy and enthusiasm could be mustered, depending largely on the amount of help they could receive with organizing the regular publication of *Amen* since this was the main organ of their cause.[91]

One month later Evans wrote another circular letter to the Society's officers:

"There are some among my advisors who feel that the Society has actually impeded the work of the vernacular movement, but the greater majority are satisfied. . . . The universal opinion of those who feel that the Society should move ahead is that great care should be employed in the further approach to the hierarchy."[92]

He concluded with quotes from two board members which he used to demonstrate how he believed the Society should proceed:

"The first is from Julian Pleasants who has written: ' . . . Maybe we shouldn't want the hierarchy to hurry up with a definitive form of the "American Rite," but rather to permit wide experimentation and evaluation. During this time, the Vernacular Society could play an important role, as an expression of the results of this experimentation not only in language, but in symbols, and in manner of presentation.'

"The second is from Willis Nutting: 'It seems to me that the most important job right now is to exert very gentle influence on our American bishops, so that when the permission comes from Rome they may be willing to take full advantage of it. By antagonizing them we could ruin things for a long time to come. It might be far better for the high officers of the Society to be from the clergy, so that the bishops would never get the idea that the push for the vernacular is an anti-clerical movement. *Amen* is almost necessary as an instrument, I think, but there could be also a concerted private movement of writing to bishops. If each of us could write to the bishops he knows (and who will be favorably disposed to him) perhaps some minds could be opened farther than they are.'"[93]

Godfrey Diekmann argued for the continuation of the Society but cautioned against taking "any aggressive action" until the council's decision on the vernacular had been made public. Moreover, he also cautioned against allowing Ross-Duggan to serve either as the Society's president or quasi-official spokesman as he had been doing during the council since that would be doing "a great disservice to the vernacular cause." Diekmann was explicit:

"There is just too great an accumulation of distrust and annoyance against him on the part of the American hierarchy. And if there is one thing that the Council has made clear, it is that the question of the vernacular will be decided very largely by the local hierarchies."[94]

Perhaps because John O'Brien had worked less closely with Ross-Duggan, he was more benign in his treatment of the Colonel:

"There is no doubt in my mind that the recent decision on the part of the Bishops at the Ecumenical Council is due at least in part to your untiring efforts for the vernacular. Whatever may have been the direct result of your efforts only God can tell. Among one of the indirect and minor results is the promotion of the idea that vernacular IS possible and that it is NOT heresy. You have for many years been the mouthpiece of all those who hoped for better days."[95]

O'Brien continued by criticizing Society members who were ready to terminate their work and go home since their assistance would be essential to effective implementation of the vernacular on the local level.[96] Godfrey Diekmann recognized that the Vernacular Society would only be effective if it was linked with the wider network of the U.S. hierarchy, and so he encouraged Joseph Evans to gain the support of Archbishop Hallinan who was both prudent and bold as a vernacularist. With Hallinan's help, wider collaboration could then be forged with the U.S. bishops so that the vernacularists' continued efforts might bear fruit:

"It is useless to think of the Society going it alone. The cause is infinitely more important than any personalities involved. Any plan of action must necessarily involve the good will of the hierarchy. And so far as I can see now, Hallinan is the key man in the objective."[97]

Evans followed Diekmann's instructions but also consulted several other members of the hierarchy, Archbishop (later Cardinal) Krol of Philadelphia and Cardinal Meyer of Chicago among them. Meyer expressed his conviction that the Vernacular Society served no useful purpose while most lay women and men consulted believed that the Society continued to have an important role to play in expressing gratitude to the bishops for what has been granted and encouraging implementation on the parish level. Diekmann's wisdom can be seen in the closing lines of Evans' letter "To the Officers of the Vernacular Society":

"The universal opinion of those who feel that the Society should move ahead is that great care should be employed in the further approach to the hierarchy. It is quite clear that the Council's action will leave to local groupings of the hierarchy the degree of latitude and the choice of techniques for furthering the use of vernacular languages."[98]

Despite the vernacular progress registered at the council, internal disputes continued within the Vernacular Society, largely initiated by the Colonel. The latest round of attacks was directed at Joseph Evans, whom he accused of not having his heart in the matter of vernacular reform and ready to concede the Society to control by the clergy. Evans had written to the Colonel that "the clergy ought to be expected within the Vernacular Society itself to carry the official responsibility."[99] Several months later, Ross-Duggan gave Dr. Evans a candid evaluation of his vernacular leadership:

"I think you should realise that you are inclined to the 'conservative' as opposed to the 'progressives' or 'pastoralists.' In addition to hearing Fr. Hans Küng, I wish you could hear Cardinal Bea and other far-sighted leaders. . . . I pray that you make the effort to pull things together into a triumph instead of a miserable defeat."[100]

While encouraging continued lobbying at the council, social activist Daniel Berrigan, s.j., wrote a rather poetic defense of an approach that would make no distinction between clergy and laity in the vernacular movement:

"Why is it necessary to distinguish priest from layman in the movement toward life, as though God were a God of the dead, or as though life were ever in man's history, hostile to life? Please read my published opening speech of the liturgical week and take heart (also my books).

"I greet all of you in the Lord. It is clear that if we proceed, purified of fear and fanaticism (neither of which has ever produced life) we will win the body of Christ to the Mind of Christ, which latter is simply a passionate and serviceable will to be present to human life—to speak, to listen, to be available, to love, and finally, to serve."[101]

5.7 THE FOUNDING OF THE INTERNATIONAL COMMISSION ON ENGLISH IN THE LITURGY

Just weeks before the promulgation of the Liturgy Constitution, The United States' Press Panel issued a release on the eighteenth of October 1963, announcing that a meeting had been held on the previous evening with bishops representing ten English-speaking nations. The meeting was hosted by Francis Grimshaw, the archbishop of Birmingham, England, and took place at the Venerable English College near Piazza Farnese in Rome. The purpose of the gathering was to discuss plans for "a liturgical English vernacular text to be used in the Catholic Mass and Sacraments." This historic meeting marked the founding of the International Commission on English in the Liturgy (ICEL).

The press release continued:

"American representatives were Archbishop Paul Hallinan of Atlanta, GA, and Auxiliary Bishop James Griffiths of New York. Archbishop Dennis E. Hurley of Durban, South Africa; Guilford C. Young of

Hobart, Tasmania, Australia. The United States bishops were named by Archbishop Patrick O'Boyle, Chairman of the Administrative Board of the NCWC (National Catholic Welfare Council).

"The objective of the Committee is to lay the foundation for a long-range liturgical text to serve the Church in the English-speaking world. Liturgy experts will meet regularly with the group in Rome, and plans are being made to include Biblical scholars, musicologists, and stylists to ensure an English text true to the needs of public worship, as well as musical and literary requirements. The goal is a text that will win wide acceptance in those parts of the world where English is spoken.

"'The first steps are being taken,' said Archbishop Hallinan, 'toward a revitalization of the words of sacred worship. The Vatican Council has already pointed the way in two respects: it has called for a vigorous examination of the liturgy to ensure full participation of the laity; and it has authorized a generous use of vernacular languages.'

"The long-range plan—a liturgy in English to suit the present needs of people in the United States and other lands—will not slow down the avowed intention of the Council Fathers to use the vernacular as soon as possible, it was pointed out. According to the Council decrees now awaiting promulgation, each national body of bishops may (upon promulgation) implement them immediately. This will be done by the enactment of legislation to suit a whole region, and the authorization of suitable translations.

"'Many of these translations are already available,' Archbishop Hallinan said. 'As soon as the national conference of bishops authorizes "enabling legislation" for this area, a suitable selection of these translations can be approved for the Mass and the Sacraments. Meanwhile, the new committee and its specialists will be working on a common text that will suit all English-speaking nations. It is reasonably estimated that this common text will be ready by the time the post-conciliar commission has completed its revision of the liturgical rites.

"'By proceeding on both levels, it was pointed out by the committee members, the liturgy can be "vernacularized" for immediate use, and progress can meanwhile be made on the desired common text.'"[102]

5.8 THE LITURGY CONSTITUTION APPROVED

Less then two months later on the fourth of December 1963, the council fathers approved the liturgy constitution *Sacrosanctum Concilium* with an overwhelming majority of 2,147 to 4.[103] Even prior to the official promulgation of that document, vernacularists were already reveling in the news of imminent vernacular concessions to be granted. Ross-Duggan (along with Estelle and Reinhold Kissner) wrote to vernacularists announcing that their prayers and labors had borne fruit:

"The principle of the vernacular languages has been approved by the highest Council of the Church. We need not apologize for past misunderstandings; they were not entirely our fault anyway. We should now stand ready to serve with renewed vigor, under the guidance of the Holy Spirit, and in the sure knowledge that as members of Christ's mystical body we are doing God's will."[104]

Writing in *America* shortly after the announcement, Boston College professor and liturgical pioneer William Leonard, s.j., wrote:

"Perhaps we should not dwell so much on the labor of the undertaking as on the magnificent prospects that open before us. Think, for instance, of a Sunday congregation that will hear the word of God copiously and in its mother tongue; that will sing its praises, weep for its sins and beg for its necessities consciously and together . . . "[105]

The English-language weekly *Time* ran its own announcement of the victory in an article entitled "Roman Catholics: Praying it in English," noting that more vernacular privileges were granted than had been expected, but "the quality of the language . . . will be considerably below what Episcopalians have in their stately *Book of Common Prayer*."[106] The article continued:

"A few conservative bishops may try to stall off the switch to English as long as possible, but most U.S. dioceses will probably make the change on the First Sunday of Advent (Nov. 29), the beginning of the ecclesiastical year. Sweeping as the revisions seem, they are only the beginning."[107]

Despite the great victory for the vernacular and the renewal of the liturgy itself, Ross-Duggan continued his private lobbying in Rome and the Vatican until the very end of the council—with or without the approval of people like Joseph Evans or Godfrey Diekmann.[108] In his spare time, the Colonel traveled throughout western Europe to renew old liturgical acquaintances and thank Church leaders for having supported "the cause."[109] In 1963 and 1964, he visited Cardinal Lercaro in Bologna, Cardinal Döpfner in Munich, Cardinal Frings in Cologne, and Cardinal König in Vienna. His list of visits also included liturgical scholars and theologians: Joseph Jungmann, s.j., at Innsbruck; Johannes Wagner and Balthasar Fisher at Trier; Theodor Bolger, o.s.b., at Maria Laach; Anselm Schwab, o.s.b., at Salzburg; and Hans Küng at Tübingen. And to those whom he couldn't visit he expressed his gratitude in writing: to Cardinal Gilroy in Sydney, Cardinal Leger of Montreal, and Archbishop Romolo Carboni, apostolic delegate in Peru. Just before the conclusion of the council, French Dominican theologian Yves Congar sent a handwritten letter to Ross-Duggan congratulating him for his vernacular efforts and apparently sensing something of a kindred spirit in their mutual desire for reform within the Church.[110] Cardinal Ritter of St. Louis followed with a postcard on which was written "Regards and congratulations."[111] Founder of the Bishops' Committee on the Liturgy and *peritus* at the council, Frederick McManus, offered his own reflection: "Whatever the difficulties of the vernacular in its present form, there certainly is tremendous progress and I am sure that we are all extremely happy. It is really unbelievable that so much has happened in such a short period of time."[112]

Almost twenty years of lobbying on behalf of the vernacular finally bore fruit with the Second Vatican Council's granting of vernacular concessions to the universal Church, and this news was not lost on the media. In fact, a survey of Catholic journalists voted the topic of English in the Liturgy the "top religious story" of 1964.[113] The implementation of a vernacular liturgy, however, was to be done in stages rather than all at once, so as to avoid confusion.

Pope Paul VI was concerned that norms be established prior to the end of the council, which would guide the bishops in a limited amount of conciliar liturgical implementation as they returned to their respective dioceses. Thus, a working committee was formed with Cardinal Lercaro as chair and Archbishop Annibale Bugnini as secretary. The committee included familiar names like Josef Jungmann, Frederick McManus, Cipriano Vagaggini, and Johannes Wagner, and together, the group worked diligently to produce a workable document that they completed in only three months. On the twenty-ninth of January 1964, *L'Osservatore*

Romano published the *motu proprio Sacram Liturgiam* (dated for the feast of the Conversion of Saint Paul, 25 January), the fifth anniversary of John XXIII's convocation of that same council. The *motu proprio* was restrictive, allowing for only a limited use of what the council had promised, but as Bugnini notes, the concern was to facilitate a gradual implementation, rather than allowing for too much too soon.[114]

Despite its limits, the document was well received, at least until bishops, parish priests, and liturgists began to debate about how best to interpret the text and proceed with implementation of the liturgical reforms. One of the greatest criticisms came from bishops who re-sented the fact that their own episcopal conferences were not allowed to approve vernacular translations of liturgical texts. These criticisms were especially strong among the bishops' conferences of Austria, France, Germany, Italy, and Spain. At least some of those bishops per-ceived a lack of trust on the part of the Roman Curia and interpreted that restriction as a curial attempt to control or even block *Sacrosanc-tum Concilium*. Bishop Franz Zauner of Linz, Austria, was among the most vocal:

"We bishops and Council Fathers are distressed that so soon after the official approval of the Constitution, the Curia and parties within it are still insisting on centralization and resisting decentralization by every means at their disposal. Approval of biblical and liturgical texts in the vernacular has always been a prerogative of the bishops. . . . In the future, we bishops cannot be confident that this right will not be changed by the Curia, even though it has been clearly defined by the Council."[115]

5.9 THE *CONSILIUM* AND THE TASK OF IMPLEMENTING A VERNACULAR LITURGY

Only several weeks prior to the publication of *Sacram Liturgiam*, Annibale Bugnini received a letter from the Vatican Secretariat of State dated thirteenth January 1964, naming him secretary of the newly formed "Council for the Implementation of the Constitution on the Sacred Liturgy." That same letter named Cardinals Giacomo Lercaro, archbishop of Bologna, Paolo Giobbe, and Arcardio Larraona as mem-bers of that council. Paul VI would call the core group the "constituent assembly"—a type of preparatory commission for the much larger *Consilium* which would necessarily include a collection of theological and liturgical experts, bishops, etc. The official announcement of the formation of the new *Consilium* was included in *Sacram Liturgiam* along with the norms for liturgical implementation mentioned above.[116]

In several meetings between January and February of 1964, the "constituent assembly" of the *Consilium* discussed potential membership for the implementory council, reaching unanimous approval. That list of candidates was presented to the Pope who ratified their unanimous choice of candidates, and the list was published in *L'Osservatore Romano* on the fifth of March 1964. The first meeting of the full *Consilium* was set for March eleventh, and the first study group was established on the revision of the Psalter. It was considered expedient that the Psalter study group be formed immediately, given the complexity of the task, and the best biblical scholars in Rome were employed. Having accomplished its assigned task, the "constituent assembly" then disbanded as it awaited the first meeting of the *Consilium*.[117]

The *Consilium* was formed with forty-two members and was later expanded to fifty-one. As concrete plans for its establishment intensified, Bugnini began looking for a proper space to locate the office. Most of the other conciliar commissions were housed in the offices of the appropriate Congregation related to the work of that particular group. Not so with the *Consilium*. When Bugnini asked Cardinal Cicognani where he might locate his group, the response was direct: "Wherever you wish, but not at the Congregation of Rites." Thus, Bugnini settled for cramped quarters in the *Ospizio Santa Marta* which were made available to those commissions having no other available space.[118]

As one would imagine, some episcopal conferences had been more prepared than others regarding the implementation of vernacular liturgical texts. Such an uneven situation presented significant challenges to those in Rome responsible for overseeing that implementation. Even among members of the *Consilium* discussions were not always harmonious, and the vernacular issue was often at the heart of the debate. In general, there was a concern to make the shift toward vernacular liturgy gradual rather than an abrupt and total abolition of Latin. This was the desire of the *Consilium* in a letter dated March 25, 1964, and sent to the papal delegates in each country. Such a position was in keeping with the Liturgy Constitution of Vatican II, which never called for the complete abolition in the first place, but rather encouraged a "peaceful coexistence of Latin and the vernaculars."[119] While such an argument was proposed in favor of "prudence," the real issue was the fear that "too much was being taken away from Latin."[120] In any event, the *Consilium* upheld the "principal of gradualness" regarding the introduction of vernacular into the Roman liturgy.

One month after the *Consilium*'s letter to the papal delegates, Paul VI approved the *Consilium*'s criteria for the establishment of norms to determine which parts of the Mass and other liturgical celebrations could be translated into the vernacular. The *Consilium* next had to deal with the task of confirming the many decisions of episcopal conferences to approve vernacular liturgical texts. The very first *confirmatio* to be signed was to approve usage of the Sango language for biblical texts in the Republic of Central Africa. The date was the twenty-fifth of April 1964, and the decree was signed by the Cardinal President of the Commission.

As the *Consilium* continued its work on the various confirmations requested from episcopal conferences, members of that commission were also working on the definitive text *Inter Oecumenici*, i.e., the "Instruction on the Proper Implementation of the Constitution on the Sacred Liturgy" which was published on the twenty-sixth of September 1964 and destined to take effect on the seventh of March of 1965—the first Sunday of Lent—a date which Bugnini called "a milestone in the history of liturgical reform." He continues: "It was the first tangible fruit of a Council that was still in full swing and the beginning of a process in which the liturgy was brought closer to the assemblies taking part in it and, at the same time, acquired a new look after centuries of inviolable uniformity."[121] Nothing made that "tangible fruit" more striking than the shift from Latin to the vernacular, and the *Consilium* continued focusing its attention on that particular aspect of the reform, along with the Missal itself and the issue of concelebration.

Requests for the *confirmatio* continued arriving from around the world so that by the thirteenth of April 1965, eighty-seven episcopal conferences had requested the necessary approbation of vernacular liturgical texts, one hundred eighty-seven vernacular texts had already received the *confirmatio*, and two hundred vernacular languages had been allowed. Meanwhile, in the absence of official translations, provisional texts already approved for temporary use were allowed to continue until officially translated texts were composed. The goal, of course, was to have a unified liturgical text for each episcopal conference.[122]

Once the United States Episcopal Conference received the necessary *confirmatio* of its own request for vernacular liturgical texts, the Secretariat of the Bishops' Committee on the Liturgical Apostolate issued a press release to communicate the news:

"Rome, October 20, 1965. A wider use of English in the Mass has been decided upon by the Bishops of the United States and confirmed by the Holy See in a document dated October 15. The effective date for this new permission has not been set, but it will allow English to be used in almost all the parts of the Mass which are recited aloud or sung.

"These new concessions were contained in a response from the Commission for Implementation of the Constitution on the Liturgy, acting on behalf of Pope Paul VI. They came in answer to decisions taken this past summer by American Bishops, who balloted by mail and reached almost unanimous agreement. The decrees were sent to Rome on September 3 by Cardinal Francis Spellman of New York, President of the U.S. Conference of Bishops.

"The publishers of altar missals of the United States will begin typesetting at once for an official English-Latin missal supplement. It is expected that the production of the supplements, for use by the celebrant of the Mass, will take at least four months."[123]

Following the annual November meeting of the U.S. Catholic bishops, another press release was issued from the Liturgy Secretariat in Washington, D.C., on the fourth of December 1965—the second anniversary of the promulgation of *Sacrosanctum Concilium*:

"The increased use of English at Mass in the United States will begin on next Passion Sunday, March 27, according to a formal decision of the Conference of Bishops. This effective date for the concessions which were made public in October was voted upon by the American bishops at their annual meeting this year in Rome and was announced by the Bishops' Commission on the Liturgical Apostolate.

"To avoid confusion, a single date was chosen for the entire country, and all the new vernacular permissions for Mass will go into effect at the same time. The delay is caused by the need to publish and distribute throughout the country official liturgical books for the use of the celebrant at Mass.

"This marks the second stage of permissions to use the vernacular language at Mass in the United States. The principal texts affected are the prefaces of the Canon of the Mass and the prayers said by the priest and responded to by the people—the collect, prayer over the gifts, and prayer after Communion. The result will be to permit English to be used for almost all the parts of the Mass which are recited aloud or sung.

"The Conference of Bishops also approved musical settings for the English prayers of the priest when these are to be sung, as well as settings for the Lord's prayer sung by priest and people together. These musical settings, like the newly approved English translations, are provisional."[124]

The United States was the first country to succeed in publishing a vernacular edition of the altar missal, the *Roman Missal—Missale Romanum* which was published by the Catholic Book Publishing Company in New York. While the United States enjoyed the privilege of being the first country to present a vernacular edition of the Missal, however, it was also the episcopal conference to make the first mistake in following the directives established by *Inter Oecumenici*. A corrected edition of that instruction had insisted that the Latin liturgical text be included with the vernacular text. Despite the bilingual title of the Catholic Book edition of the Roman Missal, no Latin text was to be found. Since the mistake was believed to have been made "in good faith," the Church within the United States was granted permission for continued use of that edition of the Missal until the supply ran out, whereupon the U.S. edition was to return to its original bilingual form. As Roman Catholics in the United States were learning to pray corporately in English, Anglican, Lutheran, and Protestant churches in the U.S. were making their own shift from Elizabethan English to a more contemporary vernacular form. Despite those inherent challenges, there is no question that Roman Catholics had the greater challenge.[125]

Other vernacular editions of the Missal continued to emerge, next in French, then in German, then in English (for England and Wales). Since the Italian liturgical commission had made no initiative in the direction of a bilingual Missal, Pope Paul VI appointed a special commission to produce the Italian edition, and it was published three months later in April 1965. There are many other items to be reported on developments in establishing criteria for translating sacramental celebrations in the vernacular and also regarding progress on vernacular translations within the eucharistic liturgy itself, but those debates would require a separate volume. Suffice it to say that the conflict about how best to translate (and how much to translate) perdured through the immediate historical period following the council. There was a strong motion, for example, to leave the preface of the eucharistic prayer permanently in Latin, both because it was part of the eucharistic prayer and also because, musically, it could be chanted more easily in Latin. Other bishops involved in those discussions quickly pointed out the weakness of such an argument, noting the success in applying vernacular liturgical texts to chant, the importance of the entire eucharistic prayer offered in the same language, and especially the intelligibility of that prayer so that the faithful would be able to comprehend and participate in that great prayer of thanksgiving being proclaimed. Once the *Consilium* had reached an impasse on the subject of the preface and left it to the Pope for a satisfactory resolution, Paul VI eventually left the decision to each episcopal conference.[126]

Debates continued for greater use of the vernacular within the liturgy—even including the entire eucharistic prayer—and some bishops suggested that the ultimate solution would be to allow for the entire Mass to be celebrated in the vernacular. This request came largely from the Dutch episcopate but was quickly shared by others. After much discussion both with bishops and major religious superiors, Paul VI decided that those episcopal conferences that had requested the entire eucharistic prayer to be prayed in the vernacular should be granted permission to proceed accordingly. The same permission applied for ordination rites in the vernacular and the adoption of weekday lectionaries. The request for the composition of new eucharistic prayers was also received positively by the Holy See.[127]

Understandably, there was reluctance on the part of some *Consilium* members to undertake the translation of the eucharistic prayer which was tantamount to tampering with the holy of holies. And even after *Consilium* membership conceded to attempting vernacular translations of the Roman Canon, initial drafts were almost immediately rejected by the Congregation for the Doctrine of the Faith (CDF) since the translations were seen as being "overly free and oversimplified."[128] Surprisingly, the CDF's solution to the problem was to allow use of the provisional translations of the eucharistic prayer found in missalettes until an official translation could be produced. Not comfortable with the idea of leaving the eucharistic prayer and its translation essentially "in limbo," the *Consilium* issued a communication on the tenth of August 1967 that was sent to the presidents of all episcopal conferences offering clear directives about how to proceed with a proper translation of the eucharistic prayer.[129] Episcopal conferences, for their part, were less than pleased with the directives and interpreted them as representing a certain lack of trust on the part of the Holy See and were more than a bit perplexed as to how provisional translations found in missalettes—generally quite inferior by comparison—could be received with less difficulty by Vatican officials than the carefully crafted texts being commissioned by different bishops' conferences.

In his classic work, *The Reform of the Liturgy*, Annibale Bugnini reflects on the rather rapid shift from Latin to the vernacular in those years immediately following the council. Was the Church misguided, he wonders? After all, the call was for a gradual shift—*piano piano* as they say in Italian—and not an abrupt and immediate transformation almost overnight. He acknowledges that the conciliar principle for translating liturgical texts was broadly interpreted, but he also admits: "This interpretation did not spring from a desire to take risks or from an itch for novelty; it was adopted after deliberation, with the approval of competent authority, and in line with the spirit of conciliar decrees."[130]

There were, of course, some bishops and advisors who wished to continue a linguistic *mélange* of Latin and vernacular within the liturgy even after the council, e.g., continuing to pray the eucharistic prayer in Latin while the rest of the Mass would be celebrated in the vernacular, but Bugnini found such a proposal to be contradictory:

"It would have been like opening all the doors of the house to a guest and then excluding him from his heart. It is in the heart that the life is to be found; it is in the Canon that the mystery resides. The Canon is a vital part of a living liturgy. It did remain in Latin for over two years from the beginning of the reform, but pastoral experience showed that a situation in which the celebration was half in the vernacular and half in Latin was intolerable. This then, is a classic example of a legitimate post-conciliar development. It was a logical consequence of premises set down by the Council itself."[131]

His reflections continue as he considers article 54 of *Sacrosanctum Concilium* which suggests that a "suitable place may be allowed" for the vernacular in Masses celebrated with the people. Bugnini asks: "what is a suitable place?" In other words, he wondered what limits the council really intended to set. He concluded by recalling the conciliar intervention made on article 54 by Mallorcan Bishop Jesús Enciso Viana who was a member of the council's Liturgical Commission:

"We have formulated the article in this manner so that those who wish to celebrate the entire Mass in Latin may not be able to force their viewpoint on others, while those who wish to use the vernacular in some parts of the Mass may not be able to compel others to do the same. . . . The door is not closed to anyone. In regard to the various parts of the Mass in which the vernacular may be used . . . we have expressly not decided to exclude any part, even though persons entirely deserving of respect wanted to exclude the Canon. . . ."[132]

5.10 CONCLUSION

The rest is history. As we assess the legacy of the Vernacular Society and its own unique contribution to the council's decision on the vernacular, the task is not easy. There is no question that pro-vernacular bishops at the council succeeded in convincing their episcopal colleagues of the importance of the vernacular, and at least some of those pro-vernacular bishops had been educated on the vernacular issue and influenced by members of the Vernacular Society. Colonel Ross-Duggan was the self-appointed permanent vernacular lobbyist at the council obtaining a press pass, and was hardly the best-suited for that position. From what we know of the actual president of the Vernacular Society during the council, Dr. Joseph Evans, he would have been a far better ambassador for the cause, as his opinions and statements were consistently balanced and respectful. A cautious response would be to suggest that the Vernacular Society's influence on the council was more indirect than direct. Some were more optimistic than others in their assessment. At the end of the council, Ross-Duggan wrote his reflections in a note to Pat and Patty Crowley, founders of the Christian Family Movement (CFM):

"I have attended all three of the sessions, and I know that a great deal of the success of the Liturgy Constitution, particularly the use of the vernacular is due in great part to tens of thousands of laity who promoted this great reform through membership in many vernacular societies throughout the world and who dispatched hundreds of thousands of petitions to the Council Fathers. To accomplish this, many of us had to take great chances in order to follow our conscientious opinion."[133]

Given all that we have seen, however, Annibale Bugnini sums it up best:

"The Council's intention was to open up the treasures of the table of the Word and of the Eucharistic table to the people. Is there anything that is not part of the liturgical action of God's people? No! Everything belongs to them. Nothing is excluded from their attention and their participation. They are to take part in the singing with minds and voices; in the readings through hearing and understanding, for the first thing a speaker wants is to be understood; in the presidential prayers and the Eucharistic Prayer through understanding, since they are to ratify with their 'Amen' what the priest has done and asked of God in the assembly's name. If, then, the purpose of using the vernacular in the liturgy is to enable the assembly to participate consciously, actively, and fruitfully, there is no justification for using in any part of the sacred action a language that the people do not understand."[134]

Bugnini, of course, was hardly radical in his "common sense" approach to postconciliar liturgical implementation. Rather, he was merely echoing the same pastoral principle employed by Roman bishops in the late third and early fourth centuries when they acknowledged the futility of celebrating the Roman Rite in koiné Greek when those in the liturgical assembly no longer understood that language. In their wisdom, those bishops opted for intelligible liturgical celebrations in the language spoken by the majority of worshipers, i.e., Latin. History is always instructive.

NOTES FOR CHAPTER 5

[1] Letter of John Agathen to Joseph P. Evans, M.D., 7 April 1962. CVER 1/11.

[2] Letter of Joseph P. Evans, M.D., to Members of the Board of the Vernacular Society, 3 April 1962. CVER 1/11.

[3] Letter of John K. Ross-Duggan (Long Beach, Calif.) to Dr. Jack Willke, 10 February 1962. CVER 2/9.

[4] Annibale Bugnini, *The Reform of the Liturgy 1948–1975* (Collegeville: The Liturgical Press, 1990) 25–26.

[5] Bugnini, 24.

[6] Kathleen Hughes, R.S.C.J., *The Monk's Tale: A Biography of Godfrey Diekmann, O.S.B.* (Collegeville: The Liturgical Press, 1991) 139–40.

[7] Gerard Sloyan, Letter to Godfrey Diekmann, 23 March 1962, as quoted in Hughes, *The Monk's Tale*, 197.

[8] Monsignor Frederick R. McManus, interview with the author. Thursday, 22 July 1999, Regina Cleri Residence, Boston, Massachusetts.

[9] Giuseppe Alberigo and Joseph A. Komonchak, *History of Vatican II*, vol. I (Maryknoll, N.Y.: Orbis, 1995) 211.

[10] Hughes, *The Monk's Tale*, 237.

[11] As quoted in Alberigo and Komonchak, *History of Vatican II*, vol. I, 218.

[12] Alberigo and Komonchak, *History of Vatican II,* vol. I, 218.

[13] Bugnini, *The Reform of the Liturgy,* 24.

[14] Alberigo and Komonchak, *History of Vatican II,* vol. I, 216.

[15] As quoted in Alberigo and Komonchak, *History of Vatican II,* vol. I, 216.

[16] Alberigo and Komonchak, *History of Vatican II,* vol. I, 216.

[17] As quoted in Alberigo and Komonchak, *History of Vatican II,* vol. I, 217.

[18] *Acta et documenta Concilio oecumenico Vaticano II apparando; Series secunda (praeparatoria).* (Typis Polyglottis Vaticanis, 1969) II/3, 370, as quoted in Alberigo and Komonchak, *History of Vatican II,* vol. I, 217.

[19] Alberigo and Komonchak, *History of Vatican II,* vol. I, 217.

[20] Monsieur le Colonel, Sur les indications de votre ami, Msgr. J. Raya, de Birmingham, Ala., vous nous avez envoyé, par votre lettre du 12 Août, quelques documents concernant les activités de votre Société dans le champ de la langue vernaculaire à employer dans la liturgie. . . .
Nous vous remercions de votre envoi, et nous prions Dieu de seconder l'action de tous ceux qui travaillent à l'extension de la participation des fidèles à la liturgie. . . .
Pour nous, la question est donc terminée favorablement, et ce fait a favorisé l'action des Pères Latins au Concile pour l'usage liturgique du vernaculaire dans le rite romain.
Recevez, Monsieur le Colonel, notre salut et notre bénédiction apostolique.
+Maximos IV
Patriarche d'Antioche et de tout l'Orient d'Alexandrie et de Jerusalem
3 September 1963. CVER 6/"Mailing Addresses and Labels."

[21] Both of these texts are treated in chapter 3.

[22] Alberigo and Komonchak, *History of Vatican II,* vol. I, 222–23.

[23] Alberigo and Komonchak, *History of Vatican II,* vol. I, 225.

[24] Thomas J. Shelley, *Paul J. Hallinan: First Archbishop of Atlanta* (Wilmington, Del.: Michael Glazier, 1989) 168–69.

[25] *Acta et documenta Concilio oecumenico Vaticano II apparando; Series secunda (praeparatoria).* II/3 (Typis Polyglottis Vaticanis, 1969) 350–51, as quoted in Alberigo and Komonchak, *History of Vatican II,* vol. I, 226, n. 242.

[26] Msgr. Frederick R. McManus, Interview with author, 22 July 1999, Regina Cleri Residence, Boston, Massachusetts.

[27] Komonchak in Alberigo and Komonchak, *History of Vatican II,* vol. I, 226.

[28] See the excellent work by John R. Quinn, *The Reform of the Papacy: The Costly Call to Christian Unity* (New York: Herder/Crossroad, 1999). Quinn is the retired archbishop of San Francisco. See also Robert J. Schreiter, *Constructing Local Theologies* (Maryknoll, N.Y.: Orbis, 1997); Walter Kasper, "On the Church" in *America* 184/14 (23–30 April 2001) 8–14.

[29] *Schemata Constitutionum et Decretorum, de quibus disceptabitur in Concill II sessionibus,* Series prima (Typis Polyglottis Vaticanis, 1962).

[30] Bugnini, *The Reform of the Liturgy,* 26–27.

[31] Letter of Joseph P. Evans, M.D., to Most Reverend Clarence G. I. Issenmann, bishop of Columbus, 4 September 1962. CJPE 62/14.

[32] Monsignor Frederick R. McManus, Interview with the author.

[33] Vincent A. Yzermans, ed., *American Participation in the Second Vatican Council* (New York: Sheed and Ward, 1967) 135.

[34] Letter of Joseph Evans, M.D., to Godfrey Diekmann, O.S.B., 27 November 1962. CVER 62/15. Vincent Yzermans was a priest of St. Cloud, Minnesota, and was director of the Bureau of Information of the United States Bishops' Conference during the council. Peter W. Bartholome was bishop of St. Cloud, Minnesota.

[35] Letter of H. A. Reinhold to Joseph Evans, M.D., 19 September 1962. CJPE 62/15.

[36] Letter of Joseph Evans, M.D., to H. A. Reinhold (The Oratory, Pittsburgh, Pa.), 27 November 1962. CJPE 62/15.

[37] Ross-Duggan received one such letter from Wall Street lawyer James V. Hayes of Donovan, Leisure, Newton, and Irvine:

"It has occurred to me that if it might be feasible, it might be wise to send each of the Fathers of the Council a letter which would set forth succinctly the reasons for the use of the vernacular in the Mass and in the administration of the sacraments. It is part of my notion that the letter would not be in the nature of a petition with many signatures but rather would be signed by selected laymen around the county within not more than one or two from any city or region.

"It is not because I have any concern that the arguments for the use of the vernacular will not be fully and ably advanced in the Council itself. . . . Rather it is that the increased appreciation of the role of the laity would lend to such a communication a dignity and a value in the minds of many of the Fathers over and beyond the value of a petition containing solicited signatures.

"It is further part of my idea . . . that the letter . . . should favor the celebration of the Mass with the priest facing the congregation. The whole Mass, including the canon, should be said aloud and should be entirely in the vernacular. Further the administration of the sacraments should be entirely in the vernacular." Letter of James V. Hayes to Ross-Duggan, 18 September 1963. CVER 2/17.

[38] Antonelli had met Ross-Duggan on numerous occasions as indicated by correspondence in the Vernacular Society archives. He was well-acquainted with the workings of the Society and always expressed gratitude for regularly receiving his copy of *Amen*.

[39] Xavier Rynne, *Vatican II* (New York: Orbis Books, 1968, 1996) 56.

[40] Mathijs Lamberigts, "The Liturgy Debate," in Alberigo and Komonchak, *History of Vatican II*, vol. II, 112, n. 23.

[41] Rynne, 56–57.

[42] "The Latin language, which is the Catholic language, is unchangeable, is not vulgar, and has been for many centuries the guardian of the unity of the Western Church. Thus now it can form a very strong bond between Christian peoples, especially when it is retained in the celebration of the Holy Sacrifice, which is the center of the whole liturgy, and it is essentially that action which requires active participation. Those who do not understand Latin may have at hand missals with a version in the vernacular; in this way they can easily follow the action of the Holy Sacrifice . . .

"As to the sacraments, it must be kept in mind that they are ordered for the sanctification of man and, by means of words and actions, to instruct and nurture his faith. Therefore, in their administration a wider place can be given to the vernacular . . ." Quoted in Vincent A. Yzermans, *American Participation in the Second Vatican Council* (New York: Sheed and Ward, 1967) 150–51.

⁴³ Yzermans, 149–50. Of course, even a cursory reading of liturgical history reveals that "the unchangeable Church" was, in fact, quite changeable, as the evolution of liturgical rites over the centuries bears testimony.

⁴⁴ Rynne, 58.

⁴⁵ Yzermans, 152. He continued with an impassioned plea: "Venerable Brothers, it seems to me that the schema on the sacred liturgy is admirable for its aptitude, rectitude and prudence. It acknowledges the need for accommodation; it offers the end and direction to this accommodation. Certain things remain to the prudence of ordinaries who, in conjunction with the Apostolic See, would accommodate the liturgical decrees, at least in part, to the pastoral needs of their dioceses. This being so, to reject this schema, in my opinion and I believe, in the opinion of many of the bishops of the United States—again I say, to reject this schema is to reject an accommodation so great that it would, in fact, negate the very great changes which, through all the ages, obtain a place in the life of both the world and the Church. This we must not, we cannot, even contemplate." Yzermans, 153.

⁴⁶ Rynne, 58–59.

⁴⁷ Rynne, 59.

⁴⁸ Thomas J. Shelley, *Paul J. Hallinan: First Archbishop of Atlanta* (Wilmington, Del.: Michael Glazier, Inc., 1989) 166.

⁴⁹ Rynne, 59.

⁵⁰ Indeed, it was only when discussions would be translated into Spanish, German, English, or French that many bishops would react either positively or negatively to what had been said. Thus, it was eventually decided to employ simultaneous translation facilities in order to assure that council participants would know what they were voting on. Rynne, 60.

⁵¹ Mathijs Lamberigts, "The Liturgy Debate," in Alberigo and Komonchak, *History of Vatican II*, vol. II, 123.

⁵² Quoted in Rynne, 61.

⁵³ Mathijs Lamberigts, "The Liturgy Debate," in Alberigo and Komonchak, *History of Vatican II*, vol. II, 120, 122.

⁵⁴ Rynne, 63.

⁵⁵ Meyer continued: "Certainly, indeed, many of the faithful expect *something* on this matter from the Council. The minimum that would satisfy the wishes of many, it seems to me, would be wider use of the popular speech or vernacular in the administration of the sacraments and sacramentals. Many, in addition, express ardent desires with respect to certain parts of the Mass, those especially that concern the readings, the common prayer and some hymns, hoping that these parts may in some way be available in the vernacular." Meyer concluded his intervention: "Let it *always* be the bishop in his diocese who is the moderator of liturgical, pastoral action under the rule of the Holy See, and not under the rule of some national commission." Quoted in Yzermans, 154–55.

⁵⁶ Rynne, 63–64.

⁵⁷ Quoted in Rynne, 64.

⁵⁸ Rynne, 64–65.

⁵⁹ Rynne, 64–65.

⁶⁰ Quoted in Rynne, 65.

⁶¹ Quoted in Rynne, 66.

[62] Quoted in Rynne, 66.

[63] Rynne, 66.

[64] Yzermans, 138, and Shelley, 168.

[65] Shelley, 167. Following his talk, Hallinan received strong praise from a number of U.S. bishops, including Cardinal Ritter, Archbishop John Krol, and Bishops Griffiths, Reed, and McDevitt, as well as from some of the Australian bishops present. Shelley, 168.

[66] Msgr. Frederick R. McManus, interview with the author, 22 July 1999, Regina Cleri Residence, Boston, Massachusetts.

[67] Yzermans, 140.

[68] Shelley, 168–69.

[69] Quoted in Rynne, 71.

[70] Quoted in Yzermans, 158. McIntyre continued: "Latin was always the vehicle of dogma because it was an apt means of thinking and establishing principles accurately, definitively and in a determined fashion. It served faithfully not only ecclesiastical disciplines, but also civil law and philosophy. If this instrument, so fit for restraining and fixing, is removed from the sacred liturgy, the stability of dogma is jeopardized. Protestant sects turned to the vernacular and dissolved into numerous factions. . . .

"Recalling both the history of early centuries and contemporary necessities, where is the justification of the opinion which wants to change the venerable language of the sacred liturgy at will? An attack on Latin in the liturgy is indirectly but truly an attack upon the stability of sacred doctrines because the liturgy necessarily involves dogma.

"In recent times, even in materialistic North America, the growth of the Church was magnificent with the Liturgy being kept in Latin. The attempts of Protestants have failed, and Protestantism uses the vernacular. We ask again: Why the change, especially since changes in this matter involve many difficulties and great dangers? All of us here at the Council can recall the fundamental changes in the meaning of words in common use. Thus it follows that if the sacred liturgy were in the vernacular, the immutability of doctrine would be endangered . . .

"If the vernacular is introduced, we foresee many interpretations of sacred dogmas. To express the eternal truth of doctrine, let sacred dogmas immutably retain their pristine meaning and form!" Yzermans, 159.

[71] Shelley, 169.

[72] Shelley, 169.

[73] Shelley, 170.

[74] "The bishops want to vote as well as to listen; they prefer the voting closely connected with the pertinent discussion . . .

"The Holy Father has made possible this *aggiornamento* by convoking the Council. We are all sensitive to his appeal to us to work with him that our beloved Church may meet this crisis of our times. . . . We will continue doing what we can to carry out this responsible role, but I do not feel that the efforts in our commission over the past three weeks have matched the spirit of profound concern and the yearning for this renewal that are so evident in the words expressed daily in the Council by the Fathers." Quoted in Shelley, 170.

[75] Shelley, 170–71.

[76] Catholic News Service, "Vernacular Impact is 'Unbelievable': Bishop Reports" (journal unknown, undated). CVER 4/14.

[77] Opponents of the vernacular were not at all pleased with Hallinan's initiative. At one point when apostolic delegate Vagnozzi met Hallinan at one of the coffee bars provided, he quipped: "You are a politician," to which the feisty Hallinan replied: "It takes one to know one." And Hallinan reported that several days earlier, Vagnozzi and Griffiths almost came to blows in the same coffee bar. Vagnozzi yelled angrily to Bishop Griffiths: "You are only an auxiliary," to which Griffiths responded: "Tell your friend Ottaviani." Hallinan's Diary, 19 November 1962, as quoted in Shelley, 173, 321, n. 34.

[78] Archives, The Catholic University of America, Hallinan Papers, Box 146, Bishops of the United States to the Presidency of the Second Vatican Council, 22 November 1962 (the Latin text is dated 26 November 1962) as quoted in Shelley, 173.

[79] Shelley, 173.

[80] Shelley, 173–74.

[81] Shelley, 175–76.

[82] Shelley, 176.

[83] Gerald Ellard, S.J. (St. Regis College, Willowdale, Ontario, Canada) to Joseph Evans, M.D., 15 January 1963. CJPE 62/16.

[84] Letter of Joseph Evans, M.D., to John K. Ross-Duggan, 22 January 1963. CJPE 62/16.

[85] Letter of Joseph Evans, M.D., to the Most Rev. Mark K. Carroll, 22 January 1963. CJPE 62/16.

[86] "The Mass: Is an ancient Latin rite to be heard in modern English?" *Look*, 23 April 1963. CVER 4/13.

[87] Professor A. H. Armstrong, "An Open Letter Addressed to the Most Reverend Archbishops and the Right Reverend Bishops of the Hierarchy of England and Wales and the Hierarchy of Scotland," 15 September 1963. CVER 4.

[88] "In view of the fact that *L'Osservatore Romano* carried an official account by Father Vagaggini on that particular decree of the Council, and that it was published in the *Catholic World*, means that to all intents and purposes there has been an official notification to every one of what the Council has decided on the Liturgy up to the present time. Also the fact that many of the bishops, after returning from the Council have made many generous statements in the press, indicates to my mind that the climate for the vernacular is now rapidly improving. Bishop John Wright was conspicuous in his opposition to vernacular formerly; now he says publicly that the consideration of pastoral care should take precedence over the general question of cultural unity. So I think, until the Council has resumed its work and gone farther into this topic in greater detail, we can presume that many more bishops are taking a wider view than they had done formerly. Hence, at the present time your second alternative of lying fallow for the immediate period ahead is far better than any move that could possibly handicap the good prospects of today and tomorrow.

"Every time I read the information I have on this Roman Decree I see more possibilities in it, and I understand why Father Jungmann says that practically everything asked for was granted." (Letter of Gerald Ellard, S.J., Regis College, Willowdale, Ontario, Canada, to Joseph Evans, M.D., 15 January 1963.) CVER 62/16.

[89] Dr. William Storey, interview with the author, 31 July 1997, South Bend, Indiana.

[90] Joseph Evans, M.D., "To the Officers of the Vernacular Society," 8 January 1963. CVER 3.

[91] Joseph Evans, M.D., "To the Officers of the Vernacular Society," 8 January 1963. CVER 3.

[92] Circular Letter of Joseph Evans, M.D., President, to the Officers of the Vernacular Society, 15 February 1963. CVER 2/7.

[93] Circular Letter of Joseph Evans, M.D., President, to the Officers of the Vernacular Society, 15 February 1963. CVER 2/7.

[94] Letter of Godfrey Diekmann, O.S.B., to Joseph Evans, M.D., 8 February 1963. CJPE 62/17.

[95] Letter of John O'Brien to John K. Ross-Duggan, 29 December 1962. CVER 2/19. A similar opinion of Ross-Duggan was held by Henry Ellis of Wallace, Idaho, who observed the Colonel during the council in Rome:
"Often Ross-Duggan spoke to me of his friendship and regard for Ottaviani, despite the deep cleavage between their thinking on such matters as Vernacular and Church policy in the contemporary world. It was suggestive to me that at one time Cardinal Ottavani had been very helpful to Ross-Duggan in some way, and that our friend remained grateful despite their differences. . . . Younger blood is probably necessary if the Society is to survive and maintain continuity. But if the Colonel's health maintains, I would think his job of 'lobbyist' and lecturer—publicity man—would be an excellent way for him to implement his title of President Emeritus of the Society. Owing to long experience and entire devotion, he is very practised in these matters, has garnered a vast knowledge and insight into the related aims and problems. He knows many bishops and priests, and whatever his personal failings as a typical example of 'John Bull'—and don't we all have so many failings?—the prestige of his name can only lend much weight to the apostolate of the Society." Letter of Henry Wallace to Joseph P. Evans, M.D., 5 February 1963. CJPE 62/17.

[96] Letter of Henry Wallace to Joseph P. Evans, M.D., 5 February 1963. CJPE 62/17.

[97] Letter of Henry Wallace to Joseph P. Evans, M.D., 5 February 1963. CJPE 62/17.

[98] Letter of Joseph P. Evans, M.D., "To the Officers of the Vernacular Society," 15 February 1963. CVER 2/29.

[99] Evans continued: "You as a soldier and I as a physician would resent lay intrusion in our own professional fields. I would hope and pray that our clergy have learned a lesson, that they have overcome their timidity and will assume the responsibility that is truly theirs." Letter of Joseph Evans, M.D., to John K. Ross-Duggan, 12 December 1962. CVER 62/15.

[100] Letter of Ross-Duggan to Joseph P. Evans, M.D., 28 March 1963. CVER 2/29. Evans responded with his usual tact, correcting the Colonel's misconceptions, reminding him: "In fact, were I a conservative as you believe me to be, I would have listened to the demands of several individuals who felt that your association with the Society was harmful and that you should be separated from all connection other than membership." Letter of Joseph P. Evans, M.D., to Ross-Duggan, 2 April 1963. CVER 2/29.

[101] Berrigan was referring to his address, "The Eternal Youth of the Church," given at the Twenty-Third North American Liturgical Week held at Seattle, Wash.,

20–23 August 1962. Cf. *Thy Kingdom Come: Christian Hope for the Modern World* (Washington, D.C.: The Liturgical Conference, 1963) 1–15. In forwarding Berrigan's letter to Joseph Evans, John Agathen wrote a postscript: "Dr: This was addressed to me. Perhaps you know the writer as he was at the [Liturgical] Week. I do not. No address is given. You know my thoughts about a lay-officered organization, but perhaps you might wish to reply . . ." CVER 62/15.

[102] CVER 4/8.

[103] The United States Bishops' Commission on the Liturgical Apostolate issued a press release on the day of promulgation:

"The Constitution on the Sacred Liturgy, promulgated on December 4, is the first achievement of Vatican Council II. It will affect the spiritual life of prayer and worship of all Catholics . . .

"One important change, however, has become the immediate concern of the bodies of bishops in different countries or regions. This is a concession of the vernacular languages in the liturgy for the sake of the people's understanding, piety, and easier participation.

"Such concessions are possible without waiting for the revision of rites, but depend upon the action of the bodies of bishops for the respective regions. For the Mass, the Council has allowed the vernacular for the lessons and for the parts of the people; in effect, for most of the parts said aloud or sung up to the Canon, and for such parts as the Sanctus, Our Father, etc. For the sacraments and sacramentals, the vernacular is allowed throughout. For the divine office, the clergy must receive permission from the individual bishops or ordinaries.

"The Bishops of the United States assembled in Rome have formally agreed to make full use of the vernacular concessions made by the Council. They have directed the Bishop's Commission on the Liturgical Apostolate to propose English translations for the consideration of all the Bishops. At a meeting of the Bishops, now proposed for the Spring of 1964, formal decrees will be drawn up and sent to the Apostolic See in Rome for confirmation. At the same time, official translations will be approved by the Bishops for publication. Only then can a date be determined by the Bishops for the actual use of English in the liturgy.

"This prompt action ensures the introduction of English into public worship during the interim period while the revision of the missal, ritual, breviary, etc., is awaited. In addition, the Bishops of the United States authorized their representatives to work with an international committee; this committee will ultimately propose translations based upon the reformed rites for the consideration of the respective hierarchies of the English-speaking world." CVER 4/9.

[104] John K. Ross-Duggan, Estelle Kissner, and Reinhold Kissner, 7 February 1963. CVER 2/7.

[105] Yzermans, 147–48.

[106] "Roman Catholics: Praying it in English," in *Time*, 29 May 1964, 45.

[107] "Roman Catholics: Praying it in English," in *Time*, 29 May 1964, 45.

[108] This is evidenced by a response of apostolic nuncio Archbishop Romolo Carboni to Ross-Duggan: "I am grateful for your kind and welcome letter of September 26, 1964, and am anxious to see you at our mutual convenience. I shall phone you in these days." Postcard to Ross-Duggan (Pensione Alto Adige, Via Crocifero, 44, Roma), from +Romolo Carboni, 7 October 1964.

[109] The Vernacular Society Archives contain an impressive list of visits made by the Colonel in 1964 alone. In Austria, he met with Josef Jungmann, s.j., at Innsbruck; the secretary to Cardinal Koenig in Vienna; and Frs. Petrus Tschieskel and Ferdinand Bakovsky at the Augustinian monastery of Klosterneuburg. In Paris, he met with Yves Congar, o.p.; Abbé Marbourac at the Church of St. Severin; Emil Gabel, secretary of the International Catholic Press; and Claude Julien, asst. editor of *Le Monde*. In Germany, Ross-Duggan visited Cardinal Döpfner in Munich; Johannes Wagner and Balthasar Fischer at Trier; both the abbot and Theodor Bolger, o.s.b., at Maria Laach; and the secretary to Cardinal Frings in Cologne. An equally impressive list continues from his visits to Holland and the United Kingdom, Spain and Italy. John K. Ross-Duggan, "Newsletter," (July 1965). CVER 5/ "Vernacular Society Newsletter 1963–65."

[110] Congar wrote from the Séminaire Français in Rome:
"Bravo for your action. My best wishes for the Liturgical Conference: it was evident that the Vernacular Society must now become one thing with the liturgical movement . . .

"I am attacked every week in some French or Italian papers. I know not a single case where these attacks don't have a political background: not from my part, who have never written or said a word in any political sense, but form *their* part. They are conservatives, against any movement in any domain."
Letter of Yves Congar to Colonel Ross-Duggan, 15 October 1965. CVER 6/ "Mailing Labels and Addresses."

[111] Cardinal Joseph Ritter to John K. Ross-Duggan (Delray Beach, Fla.), 8 December 1965. CVER 6/ "Mailing Labels and Addresses."

[112] Letter of Frederick R. McManus to John K. Ross-Duggan, 5 February 1965. CVER 6/ "Mailing Addresses and Labels."

[113] *The Register* (8 January 1965), 8, as reported in William Wiethoff, "Popular Rhetorical Strategy . . . ," 96.

[114] Letter of Frederick R. McManus to John K. Ross-Duggan, 5 February 1965. CVER 6/ "Mailing Addresses and Labels," 58.

[115] As quoted in Bugnini, 59.

[116] Bugnini, 49–50.

[117] Bugnini, 50–51.

[118] Bugnini, 51–52. In 1969, the *Consilium* moved to the fourth floor of the *Palazzo delle Congregazioni*, 10 Piazza Pio XII.

[119] Bugnini, 100.

[120] Bugnini, 100, n. 3.

[121] Bugnini, 100.

[122] Bugnini, 101–02.

[123] Bishops' Committee on the Liturgical Apostolate, Secretariat, "For Immediate Release." CVER 4/4. The press release continues:
"For the new Mass prayers, the text approved by the American Bishops is adapted from the *Daily Missal of the Mystical Body*, known as the *Maryknoll Missal*. There will be no change in the provisional translations of other parts already in use, except that the dismissal, 'Go, the Mass is ended,' will be replaced by 'The Mass is ended. Go in peace.'

"Besides the greater use of the vernacular at Mass, the new edition of *The Roman Ritual* in English, translated by Father Philip Weller of Loyola University, Chicago, was officially approved.

"Commenting on these developments, Archbishop John F. Dearden of Detroit, Chairman of the Bishop's Commission on the Liturgical Apostolate, said: 'All the translations approved are provisional. The policy thus far has been to choose the best available English translations from those already in existence. The long-range project of translation has been turned over to the International Commission on English in the Liturgy, headed by Archbishop Gordon Gray of Edinburgh.'

"As soon as the date for publication of the official missal supplement can be set, general permission will be given to publishers to use all the approved translations in books, booklets, and leaflets. In order to protect the public and the publishers against too frequent changes, the release of some texts was withheld until the additional vernacular concessions were ready.

"It is not known how long the present translations will remain in effect. This depends upon the next stages of the revision of the Roman liturgy, now being prepared by bishops and specialists from all parts of the world.

"The gradual development in the use of English at Mass represents the second step taken by the American Bishops. At their meeting in Rome in November, 1963, just before the issuance of the Council's Constitution on the Liturgy, the Bishops agreed upon the most extensive possible use of English in the Liturgy.

"The first formal step, voted almost unanimously by the Conference of Bishops in April, 1964, became effective on November 29 of that year. It permitted English for the biblical readings and for the prayers of Mass recited by the people, as well as for the sacraments, sacramentals, and funeral services.

"The second step, when it goes into effect, will mean that the United States has the complete use of the vernacular language in the liturgy, to the extent permitted by Pope Paul at the present time."

[124] Bishops' Committee on the Liturgical Apostolate, Secretariat, "For Immediate Release," (Rome, 4 December 1965). CVER 4/5.

[125] Timothy Quill, *The Impact of the Liturgical Movement on American Lutheranism*, 20.

[126] Bugnini, 103–05.

[127] Bugnini, 105–07.

[128] Bugnini, 108.

[129] See Bugnini, p. 108, for a listing of those directives.

[130] Bugnini, 110.

[131] Bugnini, 110.

[132] As quoted in Bugnini, 111.

[133] Handwritten letter of John K. Ross-Duggan to Pat and Patty Crowley, 18 February 1965. CVER 6/ "Mailing Labels and Addresses."

[134] Bugnini, 112.

General Conclusion

As the Church embarks on a new millennium, the vernacular issue
has again returned to the fore. The question is not so much about
whether or not we should employ vernacular in our worship—even
despite a faithful minority who continue to advocate a return to
Latin[1]—but rather about what type of vernacular should be employed.
In other words, how are liturgical texts best translated and what
translation principles should be used in the process? The process is
anything but easy! But lest we be discouraged by such a daunting
task, Philippine liturgical leader Anscar Chupungco, o.s.b., puts the
problem of translation in proper historical perspective, quoting the
great translator himself, Saint Jerome (+420): "If I translate word by
word, it sounds absurd; if I am forced to change something in the
word order or style, I seem to have stopped being a translator."[2]

Centuries later, at the end of the Second Vatican Council, Italian
Benedictine liturgist Salvator Marsili wrote of similar tensions:

"Everyone knows that the polemics which continually arise concerning translations stem precisely from the question as to whether it is
necessary or suitable to lose or retain this 'genius' of the ancient language which has become for the most part also the 'genius' of the
Latin liturgy. To lose it—the assertion is made—would be to disfigure
the face of the liturgy because it would be divested of something traditional to it. To retain it—is the reply—would mean to prevent the
liturgy from ever becoming a real part of *our* life."[3]

Lest there be any confusion about where Marsili stood on the issue,
however, the Benedictine liturgical pioneer made a strong call for "a
new liturgical language," as the contrary would be devastating for the
credibility of the Church's own worship in the modern age. Marsili
continued:

"If a *new* liturgical language is not created, the liturgy will remain always and uniquely a 'festive garment' which, as we know, can have
exotic forms and colors that glitter but fail to express what lies within
them. Above all, this would be the sign that our theology has not
rethought revelation as something new, as the announcement of presence *(kerygma)*, and that the 'eternal' reality of the 'history of salvation'

has not been 'temporalized' in a language which 'incarnates' it in our time, and that therefore it has ceased to be a 'history' and remained only the 'account' of a history made in terms and accents of other times.

"But today, precisely because of the summons of Vatican Council II, there is ever increasing lively awareness that not only did God speak 'in diverse manners . . . in times past *(olim)'* but also 'at the end of these days *(novissime)"* — [that is, today] he has spoken to us by his Son (Heb 1, 1-2); therefore it is just and proper that we respond to this modern Word with a *new liturgy* that is equally modern and not merely with translations. Only in this way will the liturgy cease to be a 'monument of the past' and become an expression of the mystery of Christ and of the Church in the 'present moment.'"[4]

Failure to adapt to changing sociocultural circumstances would leave liturgical language entrapped in a sort of gnosticism where liturgy remained a closed system that failed to intersect with human society. Such an approach, of course, would be the antithesis of the Incarnation, of God's breaking into history with the Word of salvation and healing: Jesus Christ. Jesus adapted his ministry according to particular needs and circumstances, even at times going beyond the accepted interpretation of the Law by healing on the Sabbath. Two thousand years later the Church continues that ministry through its dialogue with the world and its service of humankind, praising God in a living language at once "ever ancient and ever new."

We now understand translation as an art form and liturgy as metaphor in a way which we never did before Vatican II. We recognize the need to involve poets and linguists, anthropologists and composers in the translation process. Thanks to the social sciences, we also better understand the significant differences between language that is meant to be spoken and heard, sung and prayed aloud, and language intended for private reading or scholarly precision. Gilbert Ostdiek, o.f.m., professor of liturgy and theology at the Catholic Theological Union in Chicago and a consultant to the International Commission on English in the Liturgy (ICEL), writes:

"The cultures of the British Isles, in contrast to the dominant culture in this country (United States), still show the influence of orality. In particular, the Irish love of the graphic, vivid language of poetry, ballad and song and the British love of the elegant flow of language have

much to offer to balance our North American sense of blunt direct-
ness. The great poetic and dramatic works of the Elizabethan period
were written in an age when 90 percent of the people or more are said
to have been functionally illiterate. The works of Shakespeare, Milton,
and Dryden, the King James Bible, and Cranmer's *Book of Common
Prayer* were all crafted to be heard. They are still effective benchmarks
for spoken language today, not in their now dated vocabulary and archaic idioms, but in their patterns of speech stresses, assonance, allit-
eration, and rhythmic flow. Would this not be a worthwhile area to
explore in the future if liturgical translations are to bring the riches of
the English cultural heritage to the implanting of God's reign in our
midst?"[5]

If we take Ostdiek's observation seriously, as we should, then we are
speaking about something much more complex and nuanced than a
mere literal translation from Latin to English.

In the English-speaking world, restorationists and those interested
in "reforming the reform" of Vatican II have been quick to blame the
International Commission on English in the Liturgy (ICEL) for "con-
fusing the faithful" with improperly translated texts that do not faithfully render the Latin original in the vernacular. It is important to
note, however, that by and large, even those who criticize ICEL translations generally admit that we are now in a far better place than we
were before. In his book *Recovery of the Sacred: Reforming the Reformed
Liturgy*, James Hitchcock writes: "The vernacular has on the whole
been a positive change, the best evidence of which is the fact that
most lay people probably now prefer it to the Latin."[6] Eamon Duffy,
speaking at a 1996 conference organized by the Centre for Faith and
Culture at Westminster College, Oxford, made a similar point in commenting on the new liturgy: "For all that I have said, therefore, the
situation now is very much healthier than it was before the Council."[7]

That said, however, the polemics continue. Whereas earlier criticisms of ICEL were with regard to poetic style, more recent criticisms
focus on concerns over orthodoxy and desires for a literal translation
from the Latin *editio typica* into modern languages.[8] Restorationists
who are unhappy with the *Novus ordo* and vernacular liturgical translations produced and especially proposed by ICEL for the revised
Sacramentary[9] criticize Pope Paul VI and the Vatican II liturgy for
having led us down that "slippery slope" toward the Protestantization of Catholic worship.

Let us be clear. Adhering to the fundamental principle of *lex orandi, lex credendi* our liturgical language is sacred in that it expresses the heart of what we believe about God and ourselves, and transforms us and our communities. Writing on the "power and promise of liturgical language," Robert Bennett states: "the words we speak are . . . powerful shapers of who we are and of the world in which we live."[10] Thus, there can be no room for bland or pedestrian language that does no justice at all to the mystery of God and God's creation. At the same time, however, language as a living entity opposes stagnancy in all its forms. In the first of his *Four Quartets* T. S. Eliot writes:

". . . Words strain,
Crack and sometimes break, under the burden,
Under the tension, slip, slide, perish,
Decay with imprecision, will not stay in place,
Will not stay still. . . ."[11]

Words change and liturgical language evolves as contexts change and new situations emerge, necessitating a response that credibly addresses the problems within people's lives, offering a word of hope.

Change is a constitutive part of life and failure to change means death. It is that simple. This, of course, does not mean that we reinvent the liturgy every day or every week, nor that we make up our own eucharistic prayers from scratch, write our own lectionaries, or change the words of Presidential Prayers for the Liturgy to be "relevant." That is not what Vatican II had in mind. What the Second Vatican Council *was* concerned about, however, was that we listen to what the Spirit is saying to the churches and that our liturgy be a credible and prophetic voice as we take our feeble steps along the path toward God's reign of which the Eucharist is both foretaste and promise. That means liturgical language that is holy and inclusive, poetic and noble, strong, loving, and wise. But the task is not so easily accomplished, particularly as conflicting agendas are at work in the process.

Several years ago the United States Conference of Catholic Bishops sponsored a "Forum on the Principles of Translation" at its Washington, D.C., headquarters. Gilbert Ostdiek, o.f.m., was one of three major speakers at the two-day event. In his address to the bishops and other participants, he urged patience with the translation process:

"Three decades are only a brief moment in our tradition. It ought not surprise us that our efforts at crafting English words that truly 'pray and sing' have not always been as successful as one might have hoped. After all, it has been a millennium and a half since we last undertook vernacularization in the late fourth century, when Latin came to be adopted in Rome through the efforts of North Africa. The art of shaping prayer texts in the vernacular has to be learned anew and constantly honed, even as our newly minted English texts are quickly brought into our Sunday assemblies to become our prayer. And so it is appropriate now, after these few years, to pause and ask how we might do it better."[12]

As for the fears of restorationists about the Protestantization of Catholic Worship, one of the greatest gifts of Vatican II was a recovery of our common baptism in Jesus Christ that all the Churches share with the dignity of a common priesthood, even as our sad divisions remain at the eucharistic table. The fact of the matter is this: there is infinitely more that the Churches hold in common than that which divides us, and this has tremendous implications for liturgy and the language we employ in our liturgical prayer. Commenting on ICEL's proposed revised Sacramentary as an instrument of "ecumenical affirmation and admonition," Lutheran liturgical scholar Gordon Lathrop had this to say:

"This book, published and freely circulating, would be an enrichment of our *koinonia*. Then let the conversation which belongs to *koinonia* between the churches take up this book. Let the churches which have no formal relationship to the book nonetheless consider it, seeing what encouragement and critique it may offer to their practice. And then, gently, and with humility, let the conversation flow back toward the book and the communion of churches it represents, in affirmation and admonition. May such a reception and conversation soon be possible. And in the future, may *all* of our liturgical books come to be received in such a wider circle of affirmation and admonition."[13]

Such "ecumenical affirmation and admonition," however, naturally implies a conversation where both partners in the dialogue are learners and no one has *all* the answers. Lathrop continues by advocating greater use of common liturgical texts like those produced by the English Language Liturgical Commission (ELLC) and the furthering of our common interest "in finding a beautiful, biblical, and inclusive language which continues to express "trinitarian orthodoxy" as seen in the recently published Presbyterian *Book of Common Worship* and the revised liturgical books of other Reformation churches.[14]

This is hardly a task that will be accomplished in the near future. Lathrop is succinct:

"But the language task—given the challenges of linguistic change, the insights of feminism, the new awareness of the necessity of using biblical images, and the burgeoning reflection on the Trinity which marks today's finest Christian theology—is probably a hundred-year undertaking that will continue to require our best attention."[15]

So we sing our hymns of praise and proclaim God's justice and we search for that language which reveals something to us of the wideness of God's mercy: a mercy that is for all people, in every time and place.

NOTES FOR GENERAL CONCLUSION

[1] See Thomas Day, *Where Have You Gone Michelangelo: The Loss of Soul in Catholic Culture* (New York: Crossroad, 1993) 39–91.

[2] Anscar J. Chupungco, O.S.B., "The Translation of Liturgical Texts" in *Handbook for Liturgical Studies: Introduction to the Liturgy*, Anscar J. Chupungco, ed., vol. 1 (Collegeville: The Liturgical Press, 1997) 388.

[3] Salvatore Marsili, O.S.B., "Liturgical Texts for Modern Man," in *The Crisis of Liturgical Reform*, Concilium 42 (New York: Paulist Press, 1969) 51.

[4] Marsili, "Liturgical Texts for Modern Man," 63.

[5] Gilbert Ostdiek, O.F.M., "Principles of Translation in the Revised Sacramentary," *Liturgy for the New Millennium: A Commentary on the Revised Sacramentary*, ed. Mark R. Francis and Keith F. Pecklers (Collegeville: The Liturgical Press, 2000) 32.

[6] James Hitchcock, *Recovery of the Sacred: Reforming the Reformed Liturgy* (San Francisco: Ignatius Press, 1995) 146.

[7] Eamon Duffy, "Rewriting the Liturgy: The Theological Implications of Translation" in *Beyond the Prosaic: Renewing the Liturgical Movement*, ed. Stratford Caldecott (Edinburgh: T & T Clark, 1998) 123.

[8] See Rembert Weakland, "What Do 'Restorationists' Want?" in *Commonweal*, vol. 129/1 (11 January 2002) 10.

[9] See Francis, Pecklers (eds.) passim.

[10] Robert A. Bennett, "The Power and the Promise of Language in Worship: Inclusive Language Guidelines for the Church," in *The Occasional Papers of the Standing Liturgical Commission*, ed. Charles Mortimer Guilbert (New York: The Church Hymnal Corporation, 1987) 39.

[11] T. S. Eliot, "Burnt Norton" (fifth movement), *Four Quartets*.

[12] Gilbert Ostdiek, O.F.M., "Liturgical Translation: Some Reflections" in *The Voice of the Church: A Forum on Liturgical Translation*, ed. National Conference of Catholic Bishops (Washington, D.C.: United States Catholic Conference, 2001) 19–20.

[13] Gordon Lathrop, "The Revised Sacramentary in Ecumenical Affirmation and Admonition," *Liturgy for the New Millennium: A Commentary on the Revised Sacramentary,* ed. Mark R. Francis and Keith F. Pecklers (Collegeville: The Liturgical Press, 2000) 129–30.

[14] Lathrop, "The Revised Sacramentary in Ecumenical Affirmation and Admonition," 134.

[15] Lathrop, "The Revised Sacramentary in Ecumenical Affirmation and Admonition," 134.

Select Bibliography

Barnstone, Willis. *The Poetics of Translation: History, Theory, Practice.* New Haven, Conn.: Yale University Press, 1993.

Bolton, Charles A. *Church Reform in 18th Century Italy (The Synod of Pistoia).* The Hague: Martinus Nijhoff, 1969.

Bugnini, Annibale. *The Reform of the Liturgy: 1948–1975.* Collegeville: The Liturgical Press, 1982.

Cattaneo, Enrico. *Il Culto Cristiano in Occidente: note storiche.* Rome: C.L.V. Edizione Liturgiche, 1992.

Chupungco, Anscar. "The Translation of Liturgical Texts." *Handbook for Liturgical Studies Vol. 1: Introduction to the Liturgy.* Ed. Anscar J. Chupungco, 381–97. Collegeville: The Liturgical Press, 1997.

Crichton, James D. *Lights in the Darkness: Fore-Runners of the Liturgical Movement.* Blackrock, Co. Dublin: The Columba Press, 1996.

De Zan, Renato. "Criticism and Interpretation of Liturgical Texts." *Handbook for Liturgical Studies Vol. 1: Introduction to the Liturgy.* Ed. Anscar J. Chupungco, 331–65. Collegeville: The Liturgical Press, 1997.

____. "Liturgical Textual Criticism." *Handbook for Liturgical Studies Vol. 1: Introduction to the Liturgy.* Ed. Anscar J. Chupungco, 367–79. Collegeville: The Liturgical Press, 1997.

Devereux, James A. "Reformed Doctrine in the Collects of the First Book of Common Prayer." *Harvard Theological Review* LVIII (1965) 49–68.

Duffy, Eamon. *The Stripping of the Altars: Traditional Religion in England.* New Haven: Yale University Press, 1992.

____. *The Voices of Morebath: Reformation and Rebellion in an English Village.* New Haven, Conn.: Yale University Press, 2001.

Dunne, George H. "What Happened to the Chinese Liturgy?" *Catholic Historical Review* XLVII (1961) 1–14.

Ellis, John Tracy. "Archbishop Carroll and the Liturgy in the Vernacular." *Worship* 26 (1952) 545–52.

____. "Archbishop Carroll and the Liturgy in the Vernacular." *Perspectives in American Catholicism.* Baltimore: Helicon Press, 1963, 127–33.

England, John, ed. *The Roman Missal Translated into the English Language for the Use of the Laity.* New York: William H. Creagh, 1822.

English Language Liturgical Commission. *Praying Together: A Revision of "Prayers We Have In Common" (ICET 1975). Agreed Liturgical Texts Prepared by the English Language Liturgical Commission*. Norwich, England: The Canterbury Press, 1988.

Finn, Peter C. and James M. Schellman. *Shaping English Liturgy: Studies in Honor of Archbishop Denis Hurley*. Washington, D.C.: The Pastoral Press, 1990.

Foley, John. "An Aural Basis for Oral Liturgical Prayer." *Worship* 56 (1982) 132–52.

Francis, Mark R. and Keith F. Pecklers, eds. *Liturgy for the New Millennium: A Commentary on the Revised Sacramentary*. Collegeville: The Liturgical Press, 2000.

Gray, Donald. "Ecumenical Liturgical Cooperation—Past, Present, and Future." *Studia Liturgica* 28/2 (1998) 232–43.

Hoffinger, Johannes, ed. *Liturgy and the Missions: The Nijmegen Papers*. New York: P. J. Kennedy & Sons, 1960.

Hughes, Kathleen. *A Monk's Tale: A Biography of Godfrey Diekmann*. Collegeville: The Liturgical Press, 1991.

Hughes, Kathleen, ed. *Finding Voice to Give God Praise: Essays in the Many Languages of the Liturgy*. Collegeville: The Liturgical Press, 1998.

Jasper, David, and R.C.D. Jasper, eds. *Language and the Worship of the Church*. London: The Macmillan Press Ltd, 1990.

Korolevsky, Cyril. *Living Languages in Catholic Worship: An Historical Inquiry*. Westminster, Md.: Newman Press, 1957.

Ladd, William Palmer. *Prayer Book Interleaves: Some Reflections on How the Book of Common Prayer Might Be Made More Influential in Our English-Speaking World*. New York: Oxford University Press, 1942. 2nd ed., Greenwich, Conn.: Seabury, 1957.

Massey, Irving. "Words and Images: Harmony and Dissonance," *Georgia Review* 34 (1980) 375ff.

McManus, Frederick R. "Ecumenical Liturgical Convergence: Sunday Lectionary." *Studia Liturgica* 26/2 (1996) 168–77.

Menache, Sophia. *The Vox Dei: Communication in the Middle Ages*. Oxford: Oxford University Press, 1990.

Minamiki, George. *The Chinese Rites Controversy: from its Beginning to Modern Times*. Chicago: Loyola University Press, 1985.

Mohrmann, Christine. *Liturgical Latin Its Origins and Character: Three Lectures*. London: Burns and Oates, 1959.

National Conference of Catholic Bishops. *The Voice of the Church: A Forum on Liturgical Translation*. Washington, D.C.: United States Catholic Conference, 2001.

Ong, Walter. *Orality and Literacy: The Technologizing of the Word*. New York: Methuen, 1982.

Ostdiek, Gilbert. "Crafting English Prayer Texts: The ICEL Revision of the Sacramentary." *Studia Liturgica* 26/1 (1996) 128–39.

Paivio, Allan. *Imagery and Verbal Processes*. New York: Holt, Rinehart and Winston, 1971.

Porter, H. Boone. "Hispanic Influences on Worship in the English Tongue." *Time and Community*. Ed. Neil Alexander. Washington, D.C.: The Pastoral Press, 1990.

Ramshaw, Gail. *Christ in Sacred Speech: The Meaning of Liturgical Language*. Philadelphia: Fortress Press, 1986.

_____. *Worship: Searching for Language*. Washington: The Pastoral Press, 1988.

Sanneh, Lamin. *Translating the Message: The Missionary Impact on Culture*. Maryknoll, N.Y.: Orbis, 1989.

Searle, Mark. "Liturgy as Metaphor." *Worship* 55 (1981) 98–120.

Schmidt, Herman A. *Liturgie et Langue Vulgaire: Le problème de la langue liturgique chez les premiers Réformateurs et au Concile de Trente*. Rome: Analecta Gregoriana, 1950.

_____. "Language and Its Function in Christian Worship." *Studia Liturgica* 8 (1971) 1–25.

Shelley, Thomas J. *Paul J. Hallinan: First Archbishop of Atlanta*. Wilmington, Del.: Michael Glazier, 1989.

Swanson, R. N. *Continuity and Change in Christian Worship*. Studies in Church History 35. Suffolk, England: The Boydell Press, 1999.

Thiselton, A. C. *Language, Liturgy and Meaning*. Bramcote, England: Grove Books, 1975.

Trudgill, P. *Sociolinguistics: An Introduction*. 2nd ed. Harmondsworth, 1983.

Tseng-Tsiang, Pierre-Celestine Lou. "The Case for a Chinese Liturgy." *Orate Fratres* 20 (1946) 227–29.

Wardhaugh, R. *An Introduction to Sociolinguistics*. Oxford: Oxford University Press, 1986.

Wechsler, Robert. *Performing Without a Stage: The Art of Literary Translation*. North Haven, Conn.: Catbird Press, 1998.

Weil, Louis. *Gathered to Pray: Understanding Liturgical Prayer*. Cambridge, Mass.: Cowley Publications, 1986.

Wiethoff, William E. "Popular Rhetorical Strategy in the American Catholic Debate Over Vernacular Reform, 1953–1968." Unpublished Ph.D. dissertation. University of Michigan, 1974.

Wren, Brian. *What Language Shall I Borrow? God-Talk in Worship: A Male Response to Feminist Theology.* New York: Crossroad, 1990.

Yzermans, Vincent A., ed. *American Participation in the Second Vatican Council.* New York: Sheed and Ward, 1967.

Index